Praise for *The Disney*

"A complex, captivating account of the collision between hard-fought labor rights and the flights of fancy that would charm millions and make millions."

—**David Alpern**, veteran *Newsweek* senior editor

"*The Disney Revolt* is a lasting work of historiography and storytelling. With the skill and verve of a master artisan from the era he illuminates, Jake S. Friedman recounts an epic tale."

—**Michael Dolan**, editor, *American History* magazine

"Friedman provides enlightening context, offers a balanced account of the traumatic events, and brings all the actors of this colorful drama to life. It feels like taking a time machine and actually being there in person."

—**Didier Ghez**, author of *They Drew as They Pleased*

"The fact that one can come away from this book with a newfound awe and respect for Disney and Babbitt, as well as a knowledge of their all-too-human foibles, is a testament to the love and passion the author has for his two illustrious subjects."

—**Eric Goldberg**, director and animator

"In *The Disney Revolt*, Jake S. Friedman has written a detailed, no-holds-barred account of one of the most traumatic episodes in American animation. . . . Exhaustively researched, with lots of anecdotes heretofore never revealed."

—**Tom Sito**, Disney animator, Animation Guild
president emeritus, author of *Drawing the Line*

"Friedman brings to life not only Babbitt but a colorful cast of characters ranging from serious artists to government lawyers to tough union organizers to Hollywood gangsters. The story Friedman tells about these people will be familiar in its general outlines to serious Disney aficionados, of which I am one, but there is much here that will be new to them, as it was to me."

—**Michael Barrier**, author of *Hollywood Cartoons* and
The Animated Man: A Life of Walt Disney

"In his new book, Jake S. Friedman shares a very important yet often neglected part of animation history. And it, too, is a story worth telling. Of course, I'm not taking sides. These events took place long before I arrived at 500 Buena Vista Street. If you love Disney animation and animation history as much as I do, this is a book you'll want to read."

—**Floyd Norman**, classic Disney animator

"I couldn't put this book down, not even after I finished reading it."

—**Eric Daniel Weiner**, cocreator of *Dora the Explorer*,
executive producer of Disney's *Little Einsteins*

"Friedman confronts the subject head-on with a detailed, carefully researched history that considers all the threads of this complex story. Beginning in the relatively benign 1930s, when the small, unified Disney team was transforming the art of animation, Friedman tracks the inexorable changes wrought by success and expansion, leading to friction, distrust, and finally outright conflict between artists and management."

—**J. B. Kaufman**, historian and author

"For anyone who labors at the crossroads of art and commerce, or any animation fan, this is essential reading."

—**Stephen P. Neary**, supervising producer of *Clarence*,
creator/executive producer of *The Fungies*

"This well-researched, engaging study is a page-turner, relating new information about a studio that has been the subject of many publications. Highly recommended for anyone interested in animation history, American culture, or just a good read."

—**Maureen Furniss**, author of *A New History of Animation*

"This book is SO GOOD. A first-class piece of research and writing. Jake S. Friedman presents the complete story of the strike that established the Hollywood cartoon industry. . . . His writing brings clarity to a most misunderstood chapter in animation history, and is an essential read for those interested in the personalities and politics of its main players."

—**Jerry Beck**, historian and author of *The 50 Greatest
Cartoons* and *The Animated Movie Guide*

"For the first time the events that occurred in 1941 surrounding Disney and strike leaders like animator Art Babbitt are presented in a thoroughly researched and balanced manner. The fact that Friedman is an animation artist with an interest in history makes him a unique candidate to pen this important book. Artistic passion, business acumen, and social justice challenge each other in this riveting time capsule."

—**Andreas Deja**, veteran Disney animator

THE
DISNEY REVOLT

THE *GREAT LABOR WAR* OF *ANIMATION'S GOLDEN AGE*

JAKE S. FRIEDMAN

CHICAGO
REVIEW
PRESS

This is an unofficial publication. This book is in no way affiliated with, licensed by, or endorsed by The Walt Disney Company or any associated entities.

Portions of this book have previously appeared in articles published by the author at *BabbittBlog* (https://babbittblog.com/), in the *Animation World Network* (https://awn.com), and in *American History* magazine.

The Library of Congress has cataloged the hardcover edition under the following Control Number: 2022935347

Cover design: John Yates at Stealworks
Front cover photo: Courtesy of the Barbara Perry Babbitt Trust
Typesetting: Nord Compo

Printed in the United States of America

For Anya

If a person leads a very quiet sedate life with no accents,
his animation will be as flat as a pancake
and as dull and uninteresting as can be.
If a person is vicious, cruel, or mean,
no matter what he does, it will look that way.

Animation is a reflection of the animator's life—
physical and mental.

—Art Babbitt, animator, ca. 1936

CONTENTS

Part II: Turmoil

AUTHOR'S NOTE

WE TEND TO COLOR FACTS through the lens of memory. Therefore, this book is based as closely as possible on original source material. For the most part, I stuck to resources from the years during or close to the events described: press publications, legal records, studio documents, strike materials, journals, and letters. I largely stayed away from recollections conveyed after 1948, although occasionally I included retrospective anecdotes to add color and character, always being careful to place them in their proper context.

This book aims not to vilify or lionize either Art Babbitt or Walt Disney. Rather, I wanted to explore who the two figures were—what made them larger than life, and what made them relatable. I hope that the reader may identify, however slightly, with both of them and conclude that their stories are all the more remarkable for their humanity.

A final note about wages: At the time of the Disney strike, salary was commonly calculated on a per-week basis. A helpful tip to account for inflation is to keep in mind that a $50-per-week salary in 1937 is roughly equivalent to a $50,000 annual salary today.

Walt Disney in 1935.

PROLOGUE

WE ALL KNOW WALT DISNEY was a movie producer who specialized in the happily ever after. Merely the name Disney invokes childlike wonder. Walt had linked his work very closely to his public image, which also meant he took pains to keep his troubles private. Naturally, life wasn't all fairy tales for Walt Disney. His daughter, Diane, would always remember, "Two periods in my father's life were very, very tragic, and one was the death of his mother, and then the other was the strike . . . which, I think—it was incomprehensible to him, the virulence of it."

Though not commonly known, the Disney strike was a crucial event in the studio's history. It ended Disney animation's golden age, a period of unprecedented creative growth and innovation. Its aftershocks would forever change the spirit of the company and Walt's relationship to his staff. It was also a milestone in Hollywood's fight for labor rights. However, Walt himself would almost never mention it.

On the rare occasions when Walt did discuss the strike, he would speak in a pained tone that years of hindsight could not quell. And still, he could not bring himself to utter the name of the strike's key agitator, his most influential and ambitious artist during that key decade, Art Babbitt.

Babbitt had not only been one of the top animators at the studio. He also—and uniquely—shared with Walt a feverish hunger to elevate the medium. Studio documents reveal the extent of his involvement—from writing the first treatise on cartoon-character acting to first using live action as a reference source, to the very inception of the studio's art education program. After Walt himself, Babbitt did more to raise the standards of Disney animation, and thereby animation as an art form, than anyone else of his time. Walt recognized this. Within two years, Babbitt advanced from the lowest ranks to Walt's inner circle.

However, the strike was a fierce blow for both men, each shocked at the behavior of the other. Following the strike and for the rest of his Walt's life, books and articles about Disney history glaringly omitted the name Art Babbitt. Babbitt himself would grumble the rest of his life, saying things about Walt after the strike that he had never opined before.

The strike erupted during an already tumultuous time. It was the summer of 1941, when World War II was ravaging Europe and America's involvement looked imminent. The Disney studio had been at odds with an independent animators' union for several months, with Babbitt representing that union. The singular moment that ripped them apart can be pinpointed to the early evening of Friday, June 13, 1941.

It was a warm afternoon in Burbank, California. Inside the Disney studio on South Buena Vista Street, animators, inkers, and painters sat at their desks making renderings of Dumbo and Bambi. There were many empty desks around them.

The missing Disney artists had been on strike for nearly three weeks. The strikers and non-strikers saw each other every morning and evening as the "scabs" drove through the picket line and the unionists yelled epithets. The strikers brandished Disney characters on their signs and leaflets. It was a media circus.

When the mass pickets gathered outside the studio at quitting time, they learned too late that they had been hoodwinked: the non-strikers had left the lot shortly before to reconvene for a staff meeting at a high school auditorium a few blocks away. In haste the strikers relocated to the high school, led by Babbitt—five foot ten, blond, and steely-eyed. When the strikers finally arrived, most of the non-strikers had already gone home. Except for a handful of studio allies, only Walt Disney himself remained, sitting in his blue Packard convertible, tipping his hat at the many strikers in the confident style of President Roosevelt.

Out of the rabble rushed Art Babbitt to the strikers' amplified microphone. Babbitt looked directly at his employer. "Walt Disney," he yelled, "you ought to be ashamed!" He yelled it again, more emphatically, the amplified words echoing.

Walt stopped the car. His expression had changed. After months of agitation from Babbitt, something primal and uncharacteristic took over. Walt Disney leapt from the vehicle and stormed toward Babbitt. Stunned onlookers watched as the space between Walt and Babbitt rapidly closed. Cheering and booing filled the air. Babbitt had shattered Walt's last nerve, and the two were headed to a final showdown.

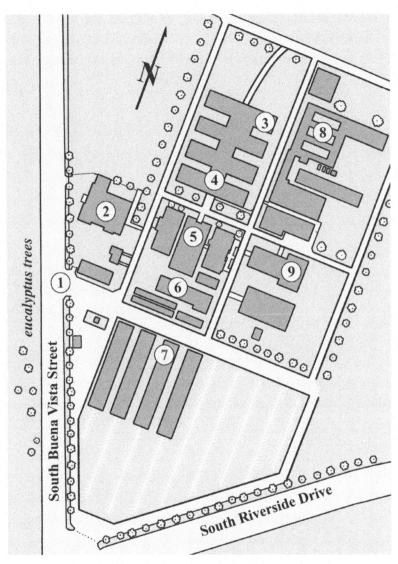

A map of the 1940 Walt Disney Productions studio in Burbank,
the location of the Disney strike, based on images published in 1942's
The Art of Walt Disney by Robert D. Feild.

1. Front entrance
2. Restaurant
3. Walt's office
4. Animation building
5. Theater
6. School
7. Parking
8. Ink & Paint
9. Shorts

PART I

INNOVATION

The *Snow White and the Seven Dwarfs* float in Pasadena's Tournament of Roses Parade, 1938. Marge Babbitt (née Belcher) sits atop the float dressed as the character she modeled for the film.

1 | MY FATHER WAS A SOCIALIST

IN JULY 1896 THE DEMOCRATIC National Convention was held in the grand Chicago Coliseum. Forty thousand citizens filled the Coliseum's seven-acre interior from the floor to the wings as William Jennings Bryan took the stage. A member of both the Democratic Party and the Populist Party, Bryan was the progressive candidate of the common man.

"Upon which side will the Democratic Party fight," he asked, "upon the side of 'the idle holders of idle capital' or upon the side of the struggling masses?"

When Bryan finished his speech, men hooted and threw their hats. Women waved handkerchiefs. The cheering lasted for thirty minutes, while delegates hoisted Bryan on their shoulders and carried him around the floor.

As Bryan was departing on his buggy, a man chased after him. This man was a laborer—lean, gaunt, and thirty-seven years old. Just a few years before, he had failed as an orange grower in Florida and had come to Chicago to work as a carpenter.

The man made it to Bryan's buggy. He extended his hand in admiration, and Bryan shook it. For the rest of his life, Elias Disney would tell his children how he got to shake the hand of William Jennings Bryan.

Bryan became the presidential nominee for both the Democratic and Populist Parties. But after he lost the 1896 election to Republican William McKinley, the Populist Party started to disintegrate, polarizing liberal voters. Many of Bryan's supporters followed him into the slightly more moderate Democratic Party. The more radical contingents eventually gravitated toward

3

the newly formed Socialist Party and its front man, Eugene Victor Debs. Faced with the choice, Elias Disney went with Debs and became a member of the Socialist Party.

"My father was a Socialist," Walt Disney would say at the comfortable age of fifty-eight. Walt and his interviewer, journalist Pete Martin, had something in common: each could say his father was "a Debs man." Walt would recall it with dissociated wonder from his perch of commercial fame and fortune. But during the years growing up in his father's home, the Socialist Party was the predominant influence—not only politically but as a way of life. Elias Disney allowed his politics to dictate how he managed his money and his family as well.

In January 1905 Debs led a Chicago convention for a larger Social-ist movement. As it became more radicalized that summer, Debs stepped away and a new, more militant leader stepped up. His name was William D. Haywood, and the group, the Industrial Workers of the World (IWW), was later suspected of being behind a terrorist bombing that almost killed Walt Disney.

Crowded, smoky—that was Chicago in 1906. It was the second most populous city in the United States, with around 1.9 million people. Horse-drawn buggies clip-clopped through the streets, and gas-powered streetlamps burned every night. The Industrial Revolution was still in full swing, and factories along the skyline billowed exhaust into the sky. For a four-year-old child named Walter Elias Disney, that was life.

Walter, born December 5, 1901, was the youngest of four sons of Elias and Flora. Elias had been born in Ontario, Canada, the son of Irish immi-grants; Flora was from Ohio and was of German and English descent. Their sons Herbert, Ray, and Roy predated Walter by several years. Two years after Walter came his baby sister Ruth.

Crime was rampant in the Disneys' Chicago neighborhood, and Elias's brother Robert beckoned him to the Missouri farmland. Fearing for the safety of his two eldest sons, now teenagers, and with hopes of farming a fortune, Elias moved his family to a farm in Marceline, Missouri.

The town was the home to fewer than four thousand citizens and was unlike anything Walter had ever known. His family moved into a white farmhouse with green trim on forty-five acres of land. There were fruit trees, berries, wild animals, creeks and brooks, and a main street that led into the quaint small town. Past the farmhouse was a tall and twisted cottonwood tree that Walter dubbed his Dreaming Tree, and he and Ruth would climb its branches or just sit in its shade in contemplation. Walt Disney would later credit Marceline as his primary creative inspiration, saying, "Those were the happiest days of my life."

Because it was easier for Elias and Flora to manage, Walter began school at the same time as his little sister Ruth. Thus, while he had two extra years of childhood freedom, he would remain old for his grade throughout his schooling.

He could remember things from his childhood with a clarity that astounded even his own family. There was the bliss of receiving his first drawing tablet and crayons from his Aunt Maggie and her endless compliments on Walter's artistry. There was the wisdom of his elderly neighbor, Doc Sherwood, who warned him, "Don't be afraid to admit your ignorance."

This was advice that Walt would cleave to throughout his life. As an adult, he would put almost blind trust in his appointed advisors. This, he figured, would free his creativity, like the unhindered child in Marceline.

That's not to say that that child couldn't get into big trouble. Out of a rain barrel he scooped wet tar and smeared a mural on the side of the white farmhouse. Flora gave him a "bawling out," but Elias spanked Walter with his leather razor strop.

Elias was strict in his ethos and in his authoritarianism. "Churchy," a neighbor called him. Yet Elias, at least in those days, was able to express his own creativity as an amateur musician. Some nights, the family gathered at Doc Sherwood's, and Elias played his fiddle while Mrs. Sherwood accompanied on the piano.

Elias hosted his own gatherings at the Disney farmhouse, but their purpose was to spread the doctrine of agricultural socialism. He was a member of the American Society of Equity, a socialist cooperative of midwestern farmers. It pressured lay leaders like Elias to run meetings and enlist other members. "Dad was always meeting up with strange characters to talk socialism," remembered Walt. "They were tramps, you know? They weren't even clean." Flora tried to support her husband but fed the strangers on the doorstep to keep them out of the house.

Nonetheless, the Equity had many harsh critics, even among the progressives in the farming community. For one thing, the Equity never committed to concrete goals for crop-withholding, price-fixing, or striking; its tactics remained strictly theoretical. For another, the Equity's founder was neither a laborer nor a farmer but an Indianapolis businessman and the editor-in-chief of an agricultural newspaper. Most important, the Equity pocketed the money paid in membership dues, whereas a bona fide union uses dues to pay its leaders. Instead of receiving a steady paycheck, Equity organizers like Elias were paid on a commission basis. He was explicitly instructed to grow membership through the Equity's aggressive methods of word of mouth and chain letters—which, by 1940, were remembered as "myriad schemes." The Equity required a $1.50 membership fee, $1 annual dues, and a subscription to the Equity newsletter. At the time of Elias's involvement, the Equity had already been publicly condemned as the "Society of Inequity."

Even Walt remembered his dad as victim of his own credulity. "He believed people," Walt said later. "He thought everybody was as honest as he was. He got taken many times because of that."

This was Walt Disney's first encounter with the organized labor movement.

Elias must have been awfully unsuccessful as a Socialist organizer; he couldn't even convince his own family of the movement's merits. By 1910 the Disney farm was failing, and Elias demanded everyone pool their earnings together for the family farm. The eldest Disney brothers, Herb and Ray, resented this passionately. Little Walter was witness to many a scorching argument between his big brothers and his father. One evening, Herb and Ray returned to the Disney farmhouse having spent half their earnings on new pocket watches. Elias was livid. The fury that erupted was the final straw for Herb and Ray. The next day they emptied their bank accounts and ran away from the Disney home, leaving the rest to manage on their own. Elias's stubbornness had broken the family.

Without the eldest brothers' help, the family sank more quickly into debt, and soon they had to sell the farm. That November of 1910, eight-year-old Walter and sixteen-year-old Roy had to post bills around town for the family's estate sale. For Walter, it was heartbreaking.

In May 1911 the family moved to Kansas City, Missouri, a city with a population of a quarter-million people. The Disneys lived in one of the small houses on a densely occupied street, a far cry from the paradise of a forty-five-acre farm. Their "orchard" was now a single tree; their vast fields were now a single small vegetable garden.

Hungry for an income, Elias bought a *Kansas City Star* paper route. He assigned the newspaper deliveries to himself, Roy, and Walter. Now Roy and Walter had to wake between 3:30 and 4:30 in the morning, go to the printing plant to pick up their papers, deliver them to each house with a pushcart, be at school when the first bell rang, and then leave school a half hour early in the afternoon to pick up and deliver the evening editions. On Sundays the paper was so thick and heavy that Walter needed to double back to the headquarters to fit a second load in his pushcart. This was in addition to his regular household chores.

Meanwhile, Elias, at fifty-two, had stopped playing the fiddle and started investing every penny his family earned into a struggling jelly and juice company called O-Zell. To earn his own pocket money, Walter covertly hired himself out to local shops as a handbill distributor, and clocked in at a drugstore during his midday recess. Only in secret could he keep a penny for himself.

Unsurprisingly, Walter became an eager escapist, particularly when it came to the movies. When Charlie Chaplin debuted, his Little Tramp character in 1914, Walter was an instant fan. Like the Tramp, Walter had a coy disrespect for authority. He would sneak out to his friend's house at night and smuggle a field mouse to school in his pocket.

Walter continued drawing, sometimes making doodles in the margins of his books so that when he flipped the pages the images seemed to move. He also copied the comic strip from his father's Socialist newspaper, the *Appeal to Reason*. As he remembered, "The *Appeal to Reason* would come to our house every week. I got so I could draw 'Capital' and 'Labor' pretty good—the big, fat capitalist with the money, maybe with his foot on the neck of the laboring man with the little cap on his head." This comic strip was called *The New Adventures of Henry Dubb* by cartoonist Ryan Walker. The anti-union laborer's clownish expressions and stubbornness made him the hapless butt of ridicule.

The New Adventures of Henry Dubb, by Ryan Walker, from *Appeal to Reason,* April 25, 1914. Young Walt Disney copied this comic strip to practice his drawing.

After one year of delivering newspapers, Roy found work as a bank teller, while Walter continued as a paperboy into his teens. In January 1917 the Kansas City Convention Center hosted a Newsboy Appreciation Day sponsored by the *Kansas City Star,* offering free movie screenings for newsboys. Thousands flocked to the building. Walter had just turned fifteen and was among the oldest in attendance.

He landed a seat in the gallery. Four screens were placed in the center of the round, each with its own projector, intending to synchronize on each side to all the surrounding children. The lights dimmed. The room hushed. The organist began the film's overture, and the projectors began to roll the silent live-action film, 1916's *Snow White*. Walter Disney sunk deep into his chair, quietly drifting into a world of silver-screen fantasy.

———————

Because the Chicago-based O-Zell company was close to bankruptcy, Elias thought it wise to help revive it. In March 1917 he sold Walter's paper route and moved the family—himself, Flora, Walter, and Ruth—back to Chicago.

At this time, Eugene Debs, leader of the Socialist Party, was touring the country, protesting the Great War that the United States entered on April 6. The Socialist Party adamantly argued that war was waged by the rich but fought by the poor. President Woodrow Wilson was not pleased. On June 15, Congress passed the Espionage Act, declaring it treasonous to protest the war.

That same month, Roy defied his father's politics and volunteered for the US Navy. The family saw Roy off to war, and his brother's enlistment struck Walter as the most noble thing he had ever witnessed.

———————

Chicago had changed in the eleven years since Elias and Flora had lived there. Most significant was the presence of the Industrial Workers of the World. Eugene Debs's once modest Socialist convention had swelled to tens of thousands, largely due to the Russian immigrants who had come after the Communist Revolution led by the Workers' and Peasants' Red Army. The IWW had a reputation for intimidation, sabotage, violence, and vandalism, planting bedbugs in hotels, burning down wheat fields along with their threshers, razing lumberyards, and destroying granary machines.

The IWW protested the Great War in swarms that outnumbered law enforcement. Members of the IWW sneaked aboard military trains and taught US soldiers how to poison fellow enlisted men. (Uncooperative enlistees were reportedly thrown from the trains.) At night, machines at artillery plants were jammed. The culprits left behind stickers bearing the insignia of the IWW: a snarling black cat ready to pounce—presumably on an unsuspecting mouse.

The icon of the Industrial Workers of the World (IWW), under the leadership of William Haywood.

During the 1917–18 school year, Walter Disney was known as the class cartoonist and amateur magician. Elias, however, thought his son was wasting his time. "He never understood me," remembered Walt. "He said, 'Walter, you're not going to make a career of that, are you? I have a good job for you in the jelly factory.'" Every day after school, Elias had Walter contribute to the family collective by doing odd jobs at the O-Zell plant. By the time the school year was over, Walter wanted to have nothing more to do with O-Zell. In June 1918, Eugene Debs was arrested and charged with ten counts of sedition for protesting the Great War.

That summer, as Debs waited for a verdict, Roy visited Chicago on military leave. Walt was tremendously impressed seeing his brother in uniform. By the time Roy returned to duty, Walter had made up his mind to join the war effort too. He was two years shy of the age minimum of eighteen, so he set out to find work instead. He landed a job in Chicago's downtown Federal Building as a substitute mail carrier.

Elsewhere in downtown Chicago, one hundred IWW members were tried and convicted of conspiracy. Fifteen of them, including leader William "Big Bill" Haywood, were sentenced to twenty years at Leavenworth Penitentiary, the country's largest maximum-security federal prison. The office of the presiding judge, Kenesaw Mountain Landis, was located in the Federal Building, several floors above where Walter Disney worked.

On the evening of Wednesday, September 4, 1918, Walter was in the lobby of the Federal Building ready to leave. Suddenly at the main door was a flash and a deafening explosion. Brick and stone were blasted in the air. Walter was a breath away from the blast. "I missed that darn thing by about three minutes," he remembered.

Witnesses reported seeing an occupant of a passing car hurl an object at the Federal Building's entryway. The police would call it a "death bomb." Four people were killed; seventy-five were injured. The police rounded up nearly a hundred members of the IWW. No charges were filed, but in the court of public opinion, the IWW was guilty. Unfortunately for the Socialist Party, papers linked the IWW to Eugene Debs.

It was then, with unprecedented resolve, that Walter defied his father's politics and joined the war effort. He learned that the Red Cross Ambulance Corps allowed seventeen-year-olds to enlist, so he got Flora to sign for him, and he doctored his birth date by a year.

On September 12, Eugene Debs was found guilty of undermining the American war effort. On September 16, Walter Disney officially joined it.

———————

By the time Walter arrived in Europe, the war was over. Armistice was declared on November 11, and Walter was assigned to help with the reconstruction of France. He would forever recall his days in France with an air of nostalgia. For the first time his artwork found a wide adult audience. He illustrated the side of his ambulance, and during his adventure Walter gave away drawings he made of the men in his unit.

He returned to the United States on October 9, 1919, measuring five feet, ten inches tall. A war veteran, he was now in stark contrast to his father.

Whereas Elias never drank whiskey, smoked, or cussed, his son now did. As if distancing himself further, he now went by "Walt."

With little left in Chicago that piqued Walt's interest, he left the city—and Elias—behind.

A drawing by Walt Disney, age seventeen, for one of his fellow soldiers, as printed in the *Colton Daily Courier*, July 23, 1941.

2 | POOR AND STARVING

WHEN HE RETURNED TO KANSAS CITY in late 1919, Walt moved back into the Disney family home, now occupied by Roy, Herb, and Herb's wife and daughter. At first, Walt dreamed of becoming a newspaper cartoonist at the *Kansas City Star*. As movie studios now started opening, newspaper cartoons became a wellspring of source material for moving pictures. Walt had been fourteen years old when many popular comic strips made the leap to film: *Mutt and Jeff*, *Krazy Kat*, and *The Katzenjammer Kids* had all premiered on-screen by 1916. Cartoonist Winsor McCay had already broken ground with his original, personality-driven film *Gertie the Dinosaur* in 1914.

Like the newspaper comic strips that begat them, too many animated cartoons starred simple characters with basic designs. Each scene resembled a square panel from a comic strip: characters were seen head to toe, moving between left and right. Emotion was shown with exaggerated stock expressions interchangeable for all characters. Sometimes symbols appeared over the characters' heads, a reminder that these were moving comic-strip cartoons and not screen actors.

Animated cartoons had already become mainstream during Walt's adolescence. In 1914 John R. Bray's New York–based studio (the first studio built for animation) released its *Colonel Heeza Liar* cartoons followed by the *Bobby Bumps* series. Then Bray's production manager, Max Fleischer, began a series of his own called *Out of the Inkwell* starring his cartoon character Koko the Clown. Koko was *rotoscoped*—drawn by tracing live-action footage—and thus had human movement and proportions. The series wowed audiences.

Walt did not get a job at the *Star*. However, he secured an illustration job at a small commercial art studio drawing advertisements for farm magazines. Besides pictures of happy cows and enthusiastic chickens, he also illustrated programs for the town's grand new cinema, the Newman Theater.

Soon a new employee showed up—like Walt, he was tall, lean, and eighteen years old. His name was Ubbe Iwwerks, and he could out-draw just about anyone. Iwwerks noticed that during breaks from work, when the other young guys were playing cards, Walt sat alone at his drawing board, practicing his signature.

After the Christmas rush, Walt and his colleagues were laid off, and Walt spent his free time drawing. As January 1920 dawned, Walt drew a political cartoon of Baby New Year oblivious to the travails ahead. Bursting through the doorjambs and windows of a house labeled THE WORLD were the words TURMOIL, STRIKES, REDS, COAL STRIKE, RAIL STRIKE, ANARCHY, and I.W.W., along with a man wielding a bomb.

It was then that Walt dreamed up his first capitalist venture. He fought Elias for his own savings to use as capital (Elias eventually sent him half) and, with Iwwerks, opened a commercial arts house named after the two of them.

Their business never got off the ground, and by March both quit the endeavor to work as commercial artists for a businessman named A. Vern Cauger. Cauger's operation, the Kansas City Film Ad Company, made motion picture advertisements for theaters. Walt's job was to draw figures on paper, cut them out, and move them under a downward-facing camera, one frame at a time. Twenty-four frames made one second of screen time. (Though uncommon now, cutout animation was prevalent across the globe in the early 1900s.) Walt began experimenting with Cauger's camera equipment in his spare time and developed aspirations to make his own films.

In the spring of 1920, Elias, Flora, and Ruth returned to Kansas City. O-Zell was bankrupt. Elias used his carpentry skills to build a garage adjacent to the family house to rent out. When the garage was complete, Walt convinced his father to rent it to him for five dollars a month as a studio, and Elias agreed. According to Roy, Elias never collected.

Only a few months later, Roy collapsed in the middle of the street. He was diagnosed with tuberculosis, contracted while in the navy, and he was transferred to Tucson, Arizona, to recuperate.

Roy had been Walt's emotional rock and strongest ally. With Roy at death's door, Walt tackled his next goal with unfounded brazenness. Using his new, ad-hoc studio space, Cauger's borrowed camera, and the experience he gained at Film Ad, Walt conceived of some shorts to play in a local cinema. In addition to animating paper cutouts, he glued cutouts onto transparent sheets of celluloid that he could shoot over a painted background. In the garage, day after day, he drew, inked, and photographed well into the night. After a month's time, he had completed some short animated clips he called Laugh-O-Grams, depicting commentary on Kansas City life and intended to play before a feature film.

Several movie theaters had sprung up in Kansas City, but the biggest and most palatial was the Newman Theater. If Walt was going to strike a deal with a theater, it was Newman's or nothing. Filled with moxie, he filmed the name of his little production, "Newman's Laugh-O-Grams," and spliced it in at the head and tail of his reel.

Walt made a date to meet with the theater manager, screened his reel, and landed a contract. Walt's audacity genuinely impressed Elias, and he would later say of his son, "He has the courage of his convictions."

Walt didn't quit his day job at Film Ad, though the local notoriety may have gone to his head. One day at work, the company bookkeeper arranged a meeting with him. Walt had not been punching in and out on the company time clock. He argued that the punch card ritual was inane. A truly inspiring workplace, he felt, wouldn't need to monitor its employees with time clocks. The bookkeeper warned that ignoring company regulations had a bad moral effect on the other employees. "I told him that if I punched it, it would have a bad moral effect on *me*," remembered Walt. Finally Walt acquiesced, but the bookkeeper's satisfaction was short-lived. The next day, Walt started punching all the spaces of his card at the same time.

Working for the product, and not for the paycheck, was Walt's ethos, and it would stay with him for the rest of his life.

––––––––––

That summer, Herb, his nuclear family, Elias, Flora, and Ruth all moved to Portland, Oregon. In November 1921 Elias and Flora sold the family home in

Kansas City. Walt, however, stayed behind. He would have to figure out his next move on his own.

In the chill of December 1921, from a cheap apartment, Walt reflected upon the animation art form. Over just a couple years, he had watched the global popularity of animated cartoons skyrocket. Felix the Cat had become the first recurring star of animation. Paul Terry directed animal-themed cartoons, called *Aesop's Film Fables*, for a company he formed with Amadee Van Beuren called Fables Pictures. Walt watched these films with admiration.

A 1926 exhibitor's magazine ad for the cartoons
directed by Paul Terry that inspired Walt Disney.

Though ambitious, Walt's desire to penetrate the animated cartoon industry was not that bizarre. What was unique was his youth as a studio head. It made an impression on other local young men who worked in animation, including young animator Isadore Freleng and young cinema organist Carl Stalling. Walt would eventually hire them both (though they would eventually make their mark at Warner Bros. animation).

In the spring Walt quit his job at Kansas City Film Ad, and on May 18, 1922, he incorporated Laugh-O-Gram Films. Walt enthusiastically hired a handful of peers from Kansas City Film Ad, including Iwwerks and his friends Rudy Ising and Hugh Harman. The company moved to an office building and began a series of fairy-tale-themed cartoons.

The Laugh-O-Gram team operated not hierarchically but collaboratively. Story premises were discussed as a group. They also drew in ink directly on the sheets of clear celluloid, or *cels*. The interiors of the inked lines were *opaqued* with white, gray, and black paint. Then they were photographed under an animation camera, over the painted background, cranking one frame at a time.

They were a guerrilla animation crew, underdogs in the industry, and they delighted in it. They drove around town promoting the Laugh-O-Gram company or rode in the Main Street parade with big Laugh-O-Gram signs. Come success or failure, they were in it together.

Over the course of the year, the little studio produced seven fairy tale films. These cartoons were made for screening at local schools, clubs, and church benefits.

Over time there were stops and starts with hopes for broader distribution, but the crew had enough work to keep Laugh-O-Gram afloat. Inspired by the *Out of the Inkwell* shorts, Walt decided to make a new film—a live-action little girl in a cartoon world, calling it *Alice's Wonderland*. This film, Walt hoped, could be their ticket to commercial success.

Laugh-O-Gram Films spent several months producing *Alice's Wonderland*, filming the child actress Virginia Davis and animating her cartoon backdrop, while Walt borrowed money against the company. In May 1922 he sought out a distributor, and he found one in Margaret Winkler.

Winkler was only twenty-eight years old but was already a name in the industry. In New York she had become the distributor of *Out of the Inkwell* and various Felix the Cat shorts. Eager for another hit series, Winkler wrote back with interest in seeing the *Alice* reel.

Walt, however, couldn't send it; it was an asset that belonged to one of his creditors. He stalled and kept up a written correspondence with Winkler, apologizing for setbacks. Winkler grew increasingly impatient.

By that summer of 1923 Walt was slipping ever deeper in debt and had to lay off his staff. He began skipping meals and soon noticed that his clothes were fitting a lot more loosely. Roy forwarded Walt some of his government checks, but these weren't enough. Walt's rent was overdue, his assets were repossessed, he started scavenging for his food, and he was evicted from his apartment. Eventually he was sleeping on rolls of canvas in the Laugh-O-Gram office.

He received mail from Roy and Uncle Robert, both of whom were now living in Los Angeles, California, urging him to join them. Los Angeles was quickly becoming the center of the country's motion picture industry. Universal Pictures (formerly Universal Film Manufacturing Company), Fox Film Corporation, and Paramount Pictures had established studios there by 1915. United Artists (co-owned by Walt's comedy hero Charlie Chaplin) was built in 1919.

If it was good enough for Chaplin, it was good enough for Walt. He headed for Los Angeles that August with $40 in his pocket and $300 of debt behind him.

Once in California, Walt finally sent Margaret Winkler a print of *Alice's Wonderland,* and she offered him a generous contract for $1,500 per film. That was all Walt needed to incorporate the Disney Brothers Cartoon Studio. By June 1924 the studio was a small but well-oiled company on Kingswell Avenue. Walt was producer, and Roy was business manager. All his Kansas City colleagues had moved to Los Angeles to join. The future looked bright.

3 | THE VALUE OF LOYALTY

IN 1924, MOVIE-STAR CULTURE was in full swing. Motion picture magazines glamorized young Hollywood to fans across the country. Movie startups dotted the Los Angeles landscape, and the Disney Brothers Cartoon Studio was only one of many. These small, B-movie companies released independent films for the open market without a distributor and were so numerous that they shared a collective nickname: "Poverty Row." Fame seemed to spring up overnight only to the chosen few, and many of these studios would go bankrupt within a year or two.

Fortunately for Walt and Roy Disney, their contract with Margaret Winkler kept them busy. Walt began growing a mustache and pomading his hair, though he kept it long in the front so that a single bohemian lock flopped haphazardly over his right eye. He now drove a stylish used Moon Cabriolet roadster. After the sixth *Alice* film was released on August 1, 1924, Walt was ready to negotiate a fatter contract. But there was a change at the distribution office: Margaret Winkler had given control of her company to her new husband, Charles Mintz.

Mintz, age thirty-four, was skinny, bespectacled, and had as much a yen for making deals as for asserting his weight. He informed Walt that the quality of his films was "lacking," so he sent his brother-in-law, George Winkler, to the studio as an in-house film editor.

The subsequent contract Mintz offered to the Disney brothers was worse than the previous one. Walt wrote to Mintz, "I am perfectly willing to sacrifice a profit on this series in order to put out something good, but I expect you to show your appreciation by helping us out." Mintz advised Walt to have patience.

Months of negotiations with Mintz left Walt exhausted. By December Walt had settled on a contract that would provide him the funds to make the films he wanted but at a cost of time. Rather than delivering one film per month, he now had a deadline every three weeks.

———————————

In early 1925 George Winkler returned to New York. In July Walt wed his secretary, Lillian Bounds, and they rented a home close to the studio. That same month, Walt and Roy placed a $400 deposit on a small, sixty-by-forty-foot lot on Hyperion Avenue, two miles from downtown Los Angeles. The property contained a one-story stucco building that used to be an organ factory, along with an adjacent vacant lot. This repurposed building would be the new site of their studio.

From January to early autumn 1925, twelve new *Alice* shorts had premiered in New York City and Los Angeles. Charles Mintz began talks of contract renewal, but Walt's hopes for easy negotiations were soon dashed. Still, Walt stood his ground, and he eventually was able to sign with Mintz for a modest increase.

———————————

In February 1926 Walt and his staff used a borrowed truck to move their equipment into the new facility. Walt and Roy had agreed on a name change: Walt Disney Studios.

In their new headquarters, Walt and Roy occupied desks in a back room. The animators, all young men, sat in rows side by side at their drawing tables. Walt led informal sessions for stories and gags for each cartoon.

Walt was already in the habit of staying at the studio after hours to scrutinize his artists' work, but with the increased pressure from Mintz, that became excessive. His ever-critical eye was infringing on their drawing, and the staff started to consider it "snooping."

Soon the stress of dealing with Mintz's constant criticisms was beyond what Walt could handle, and the young producer started to lash out at his staff. Even those who had been friends in Kansas City found him increasingly hostile. Walt began to yell and accuse people of double-crossing him, and one of his animators called the place a "den of strife and vexation." By August, some were already plotting, unprompted, to walk out and open their own studio.

At the start of 1927, when the first animator Walt had hired decided to quit (he "couldn't bear the abuse that Walt heaped upon him," remembered a colleague), Walt wooed an old acquaintance, animator Isadore Freleng, to come over from Kansas City. However, in a few months he would quit as well.

In mid-January 1927 Mintz broke some big news to Walt. "A national organization" was hungering for a new star character to headline a series of animated cartoons. "They seem to think there are too many cats on the market," wrote Mintz. "As long as they are doing the buying, naturally, we must try to sell them what they want." Mintz asked Walt to pitch him a rabbit.

Walt knew an opportunity when he saw it. He gave the assignment to his top man, Ub Iwerks (as he now spelled his name). Iwerks designed a stout, middle-aged character named Oswald the Lucky Rabbit, and Walt submitted the design to Mintz.

Mintz responded with very good news. His "national organization" was Universal Pictures, one of the biggest studios in Hollywood, and after spending a year searching, they settled on Oswald as their cartoon star.

The Oswald contract stretched from April 1927 to April 1928, and it was Walt's fattest contract yet. To help meet production demands, Walt hired a teenage artist, Leslie "Les" Clark, who was working at a local lunch counter. With all hands working on this cartoon, the studio took about five weeks to complete it. The opening title card read:

> *Universal Presents*
> *OSWALD the Lucky Rabbit*
> *in*
> *"Poor Papa"*
> *a Winkler Production*
> *by Walt Disney*

Walt wanted a glimmer of personality in the characters. "I want characters to *be* somebody," Walt said then. "I don't want them just to be a drawing." It took a couple cartoons to get his personality right, but very soon Oswald emerged as a youthful, feisty hero who succeeded in spite of himself.

Meanwhile, on May 20, 1927, Charles Lindbergh, age twenty-five, piloted a solo flight across the Atlantic Ocean in thirty-three-and-a-half straight hours. He instantly became a global hero and a symbol of American courage and ingenuity, ushering in the age of air travel.

The event had a particular resonance with twenty-five-year-old Walt Disney. Lindbergh gave all young men permission to dream big, and validated the tenacity of "the little guy." This was Oswald in the face of adversity, or Walt in the face of Hollywood.

That June, Walt and Roy bought a large property on a side street near the studio on which to build their new homes. The reviews for the Oswald cartoons started coming in later that summer, and Universal's new rabbit was a hit.

Out in New York, Charles Mintz was reading the papers too. He also knew that Walt didn't draw any of his cartoons, and he had grown tired of negotiating with him. It was evident that poor morale hung in the air; Walt's studio appeared to have a high turnover. In July Mintz sent George Winkler back to the Disney studio. Secretly, he began asking the remaining animators about making Oswald cartoons without Walt. The Kansas City cohort was interested in the offer and, as an added insult, agreed to hide it from Walt.

In the fall of 1927 Warner Bros. released the first Vitaphone feature with a vocal soundtrack, *The Jazz Singer*. The motion picture soundtrack had been invented, and audiences were wowed. However, musicians who played in the orchestra pits for silent films began to fear for their careers and started to seek support from local musicians' unions.

A different sort of conflict was rapidly brewing at the Walt Disney Studio. The animators kept working diligently, but in two separate parties: those who were planning to stay at the studio and those who were not. In late January 1928, after more secret negotiations, Iwerks pulled Walt aside and told him about the insurgency.

Walt was beside himself in shock. After February 2, when Mintz signed a new three-year contract with Universal Pictures to deliver Oswald cartoons, Walt decided to negotiate his new contract with Mintz in person. He was prepared to ask for an increase from $2,250 per film to $2,500. He invited

Lillian on a trip to New York City—a second honeymoon, he said. Privately Walt thought that if things didn't work out with Mintz, he would approach the animation studios in New York. It was a chance to hedge his bets.

Walt arrived with Lillian in New York during the bitter cold of late February, carrying two Oswald film reels and a book of press clippings. When Walt proposed $2,500 per film, Mintz counteroffered: $1,400 per film, plus a weekly salary as Mintz's contracted employee. It dawned on Walt that Mintz would only keep Walt on his own terms.

Walt sent a telegram to Roy, ordering him to draft "iron-clad" two-year contracts and have his animators sign them immediately. But it was too late; the animators had already signed contracts to produce Oswald cartoons for Mintz. In a couple months, Walt Disney Studios would be empty and out of work.

During his next two weeks in New York, Walt continued negotiating with Mintz while desperately trying to hire animators from the city. There were no takers. On March 7, Walt wired to Roy, "We are still hanging around this Hell Hole waiting for something to happen." In their final meeting, Mintz offered Walt $1,800 per film, 50 percent of the profits, plus a weekly salary. Walt refused to sign. He was furious, but powerless to keep his character or his animators.

Mintz was under no obligation to cater to Walt's whims. This was business. Mintz already had the new contract with Universal to produce more Oswald cartoons—a character that Universal commissioned and that Mintz delivered. There was nothing in any of Universal's contracts about who would produce the Oswald series, only that Mintz would distribute it. The little studio on Hyperion Avenue run by a twenty-six-year-old novice had the privilege to work on the Oswald series for its first run. His animators could choose to work where they wanted, and their experience with Walt had pushed them into Mintz's arms.

When he boarded a westbound train with Lillian, Walt was fuming. Their "honeymoon" was over. However, by the end of the four-day train ride, he had decided to produce a new cartoon, this one based on the plucky exploits of "Lucky Lindy." Like Lindbergh, Walt deemed himself a risk-taker, about to gamble it all and fly into the unknown.

When Walt returned to his studio in mid-March, just a month before the animators' contracts expired, he immediately met with Iwerks. They would put another cartoon character on the market, one that belonged to the Disney studio. They still had a couple young assistants with them that Mintz hadn't

A 1929 advertisement in the Universal exhibitor's magazine for Oswald, soon after the Disney contract expired.

bothered with (like Les Clark). Walt would hire new artists, and Iwerks would train them.

Walt and Iwerks kept to the back room, separated by a curtain lest the Mintz-bound animators share the information with their new boss. Iwerks worked furiously, averaging seven hundred drawings a day, as Lillian, her sister Hazel, and Roy's wife, Edna, inked and opaqued the cels. After photography and film developing, they had a completed cartoon, *Plane Crazy*, starring an

Oswald-like mouse named Mickey who aspires to be Charles Lindbergh. It cost $3,528.50.

Walt wrote the premise of the second cartoon, and Iwerks drew the layout sketches that went along with the typed script. Called *Gallopin' Gaucho*, it spoofed action star Douglas Fairbanks's film *The Gaucho* and cost $4,249.73. When they were done, Walt peddled *Plane Crazy* and *Gallopin' Gaucho* around Hollywood. The studio had resorted to releasing films to the open market. It had joined the forsaken ranks of "Poverty Row."

Weeks became months, and no distributor picked up Walt's new cartoons. *The Jazz Singer* was changing everything. There was tremendous appetite for new talking pictures—distributors weren't about to buy a couple silent cartoons from a no-name.

Walt went back to his studio. They would make a third Mouse cartoon, this time with the intention of adding synchronized sound. It would be a spoof on comedian Buster Keaton's film *Steamboat Bill, Jr.* It would be called *Steamboat Willie*, and music would be prevalent throughout. Walt hired a few young artists, including wild-haired Johnny Cannon and redheaded Wilfred Jackson, who had an ear for music.

Iwerks and the assistants created the roughly nine thousand drawings that would make up *Steamboat Willie*. Each scene was broken up into several layers of drawings—anything that was moving with different timing. In the opening shot alone, one layer was placed for Mickey's head and arms, one for his body and legs, and one for the ship's wheel. There were also two background layers: one of the moving landscape and another of the stationary wheelhouse.

In August 1928 *Steamboat Willie* was completed, albeit without sound. The Disney brothers needed a very specific apparatus to embed a soundtrack on their film. But sound in films was a new invention, and the Hollywood studios were keeping their soundtrack gear proprietary. As September dawned, Walt took his reel of *Steamboat Willie* to New York in search of a soundtrack apparatus.

Motion picture businessman Pat Powers, a middle-aged opportunist who had helped found Universal Pictures, did indeed hold a patent on a sound apparatus. It was called the Cinephone system, and he was willing to license it to Walt for a whopping $26,000 a year. That was more than half of Walt's annual budget for Oswald cartoons. However, Powers also had the connections and promised to introduce Walt to a top orchestra leader. Walt signed, and Powers took him to meet Carl Eduarde.

Eduarde was the pit conductor for the Strand Theatre in Times Square, located on 47th Street and Broadway. The maestro had composed music to accompany silent films like *The Hunchback of Notre Dame*, starring Lon Chaney. He assured Walt that he would lead the musicians who would perform the music for *Steamboat Willie*.

Shortly thereafter, Eduarde, Walt, and the musicians gathered in an informal recording booth. All the sound—music, sound effects, and vocals—was to be recorded at the same time on a single track. The musicians and their conductor had played for silent movies that were projected in front of them; Walt set up his projector to play *Steamboat Willie* the same way.

The cartoon played. Eduarde and the band followed along, but it was a failure—the music did not sync. And Walt had spent the last of his savings on this recording session.

Back at the studio, Ub Iwerks conceived of a bouncing ball on the side of the animation that showed each musical beat. He and Roy created a new print of *Steamboat Willie* with this bouncing ball. Walt ordered Roy to sell his Moon roadster to pay for a second recording session.

By the time Walt received the revised print in September, he had encountered something unexpected: All over New York, the musicians' union was at odds with cinema owners. New York, Walt was learning, was a hotbed of protest and union activity. The American Federation of Musicians was preventing its members from making prerecorded soundtracks. "Boy, the unions are sure tough on movie recording," he wrote on September 20. "They are doing all they can to discourage the 'Sound Film' craze."

Luckily for Walt, Eduarde's musicians were able to record for him. In the recording booth, Iwerks's new film print was projected just in front of Maestro Eduarde. He conducted according to the bouncing ball, and the orchestra followed him. To Walt's immense relief, this worked perfectly.

Now Walt had a finished reel of a sound cartoon. If he had learned anything from the Mintz disaster, it was to brand his *name*, not his character. From that point forward, the name "Walt Disney" would be inseparable from his work. The title card of this film read:

Disney Cartoons Presents
A Mickey Mouse Sound Cartoon
Steamboat Willie
A Walt Disney Comic
By Ub Iwerks

On October 1 the final film print was complete. Walt nearly landed a distribution deal with Universal Pictures, but Universal pulled out, telling him that its contract with Mintz imposed a conflict of interest. Walt took *Steamboat Willie* to other studios but could not land a contract.

Suddenly, the promoter for the Colony Theater in New York City made Walt an offer. For $1,000, *Steamboat Willie* would play for two weeks, accompanying the theater's feature presentation.

On November 18, 1928, *Steamboat Willie* premiered at the Colony. Walt was there in the darkened theater. This was the first synchronized sound cartoon that a public audience had ever seen, and the crowd's reaction was beyond Walt's expectations.

Almost instantly, this twenty-six-year-old cartoon producer was in the public eye. Audiences demanded Disney cartoons. His studio personnel enlarged exponentially as his distribution contracts grew more robust. Licensees began merchandising Disney characters, and fan clubs formed across the country. In less than three years, Mickey Mouse would be a household name. As one journalist summed it up in October 1931, "Almost overnight the Disney outfit became the outstanding producer of animated cartoons and took the lead as creators of short subjects."

In the summer of 1932, when Art Babbitt met Walt Disney, the press called Mickey Mouse "far and away, the most popular American star abroad" and Walt Disney "a man blessed by the gods."

4 | ARTHUR BABBITT: HELL-RAISER

MR. AND MRS. BABITZKY LIVED in a small house on the poor side of Omaha, Nebraska, in 1907. They were Jewish immigrants, having emigrated to America from Petrokov, a Polish city dominated by the Russian Empire. Solomon (sometimes written as "Shloime" or "Samuel" on public records), a lean man with thick glasses and a walrus mustache, was an ardent Jewish scholar with few profitable skills. He took a steamship alone to America in 1903. Zelda witnessed the Russian Revolution of 1905, a social and political upheaval dominated by labor strikes and successful in its goals of creating a multiparty system and a brand-new constitution. In 1906 she emigrated with their three-year-old daughter, but the child grew ill on the ship and died before arriving. According to family lore, she was the second child the couple had lost.

Arthur Harold Babitzky was born on October 8, 1907, in Omaha. He was the first Babitzky child to survive. A year later another daughter was born, but she succumbed to illness at the age of two. Arthur remembered being three years old and finding his mother in her bedroom, weeping and holding the child. He wrote years later, "This was my first encounter with the injustice that oftime befalls an innocent."

Soon two brothers were born—Irving in 1911, and William in 1913. They, too, would survive, but health problems threatened the Babitzky children. The fontanel, an opening in Irving's skull, was slow to close. Ever devout, Solomon begged God for mercy, going so far as to place his own head inside the synagogue's holy ark that the Lord may take him instead. Arthur remembered having a health condition that required Zelda to give him alcohol sponge baths before putting him to bed. His mother's love and pragmatism would forever cleave him to her. Conversely, he would scoff that his father was "ever an optimist—for he placed his trust unhesitatingly with an all-knowing ubiquitous God who would some day accept in trade suffering and misery as a down payment on happiness and justice."

While Solomon peddled rags or fish door-to-door, Zelda made embroidery for sale and handled the cooking and child-rearing at home. There were more than just her own offspring; she made her home a safe house for needy neighborhood children. She had a potent sense of justice; when Arthur behaved poorly, she invited a police officer to the house to scare some sense into him. "Zelda really *was* a firebrand," recalled her eldest grandchild, Susan Fine. "Her life was made up in defending the rights of others. My grandmother was very strong-willed; if she had it in for you, God help you."

To Solomon's credit, he fostered a taste for classical music in the family, and his own violin playing sometimes filled the small house. He also provided little Arthur the key ingredient for a future animator in that era: discarded newspaper comics.

Family portrait of the Babitzkys, 1915. Arthur is top center.

———————

Arthur was completing kindergarten when Omaha was ravaged by the worst tornado outbreak the Midwest had ever seen. It struck on the evening of Easter Sunday, March 23, 1914, which also fell on the Jewish holiday of Purim. The city had no siren warning system, and most homes had no telephone or radio; a few bystanders saw multiple oncoming tornados from a distance as the winds raced toward them at record speeds. Citizens bolted through the streets, hollering the warning to their neighbors.

Within minutes, four colossal tornadoes engulfed Omaha, tearing through the Babitzkys' neighborhood. Houses were ripped to shreds. Women screamed as babies were sucked through windows. Entire carriages and massive stone plinths soared through the sky, and chunks of homes came crashing down into the street. The ceiling of a bakery crushed a family of seven. A pool hall collapsed, killing everyone who had sought refuge inside.

When the tornados had run their course, they left a path of destruction seven miles long and a quarter mile wide. More than one hundred people were dead or missing. Hundreds more were homeless. Arthur's home was spared by a margin of four blocks. The mayor, in his hubris, refused federal aid.

The Babitzkys had had enough of Omaha. Solomon and Zelda decided to relocate ninety-six miles north to Sioux City, Iowa.

———————

Around that time, Sioux City was heralded as "the metropolis of the northwest where the farmer, the rancher and the captain of industry join hands." In February 1915, with Zelda pregnant, the Babitzkys made the trip by horse and wagon with all their household possessions. The strain of Iowa's harsh winter caused Zelda's baby to be born prematurely but healthy—a daughter that they named Frances.

The Babitzkys' house was located in a dense concentration of Jewish, immigrant, and Black families, "formerly homes of non-Jewish people who had improved their lot economically, and moved up to better houses," remembered Irving. Although Sioux City had its share of anti-Semitism, from name-calling to KKK marches, the Babitzkys lived safely, within walking distance of the local synagogue and near three kosher butcher shops. Meatpacking was one of the cornerstones of the economy, and the smell of slaughterhouses was inescapable.

Their rented house included a barn for the family's horse, and during the colder months, Solomon used horse manure to insulate the side of their house. For fun, Arthur and Irving leapt from the barn's rafters into hay piles. The end of winter brought the blossoming of Zelda's vegetable and herb garden, and each of the children was given a small bed of soil in which to grow radishes, lettuce, scallions, and dill. Jars of homemade pickles lined the walls of the storm cellar, and Zelda prepared traditional Russian cuisine on the kitchen's potbellied stove.

Zelda was the creative nucleus of Arthur's world, teaching homemade crafts to the youngsters and encouraging the boys to knit. After the Great War broke out, she and "anyone else who could knit" made socks and gloves for the soldiers overseas. In 1917 the family contributed to Sioux City's Jewish war relief fund—a sum that surpassed even New York City's—one example of the all-for-one support ingrained in Arthur. When armistice was announced, Zelda dressed up and paraded up and down the street, banging pots with wooden spoons, relishing in the spectacle. She was brazen and demonstrative in her politics, a trait Arthur would adopt himself.

After school, Arthur and Irving worked as paperboys for the *Sioux City Journal*, each netting forty cents a day for the family. Yet they managed to hide away a couple pennies at the bottoms of their pockets—"down south" as they called it—for a Sunday matinee at the cinema.

Arthur was also inspired by the books of troublemaking midwestern boys by Mark Twain and Booth Tarkington. Irving later joked that Arthur "was very much the leader in creating new adventures—and creating new risks of going to jail as kids." Art would admit, "I was this strange dichotomy of really being a good student in school, but a hell-raiser every spare moment." In the dead of night, Arthur led the boys to the wealthy houses, slit open the porch screens, and switched the contents of their ice boxes. Other times they climbed their high school's three-story fire escape, broke into the classrooms, and switched the contents of the desks. Once, they sneaked into the shed of a local sourpuss, a neighborhood butcher, ran off with his wooden buggy, and suspended it from a telephone pole. "We weren't vandals," he remembered. "There was some sort of a screwball sense of morals that I had. The idea was not to destroy anything or to steal anything, but to confuse everything."

Besides acts of rebellion, Arthur discovered a love of drawing in elementary school. For one school assignment, instead of drawing an assigned fairy-tale scene, Arthur drew a waterfall at sunset that the teacher hung on the wall. In fifth grade, Arthur refused to sing Christmas carols on religious principle. As punishment, he spent recess indoors with his teacher drawing Greek myths. By high school he was known as the class artist and cartoonist. Under his senior yearbook photo appeared three words: "A good Chresto." The term was borrowed from *Lives of the Twelve Caesars*, in which Suetonius had written in 121 CE, "[Emperor Claudius] expelled from Rome the Jews constantly making disturbances at the instigation of Chresto." Arthur had earned the reputation of class instigator.

Outside school hours, Arthur worked several jobs to help support the family, including in a meatpacking plant, as a stock boy in a department store, and as a golf caddy at a country club. When he wasn't drawing, he developed a fascination for the psychological science of hypnosis. It was the beginning of his budding interest in psychology.

He even analyzed the animals around him to the point of anthropomorphizing them. His father bought one defective horse after another, and Arthur saw that Joe the horse was "perpetually tired. Mother claimed he crossed his front legs, leaned against a convenient tree, pole or building, and promptly fell asleep the moment my father left him alone." Then came Masha the horse, whose "speed and stamina were incredible—particularly at feeding time."

In 1923 Arthur's life took a drastic turn. After school one day he discovered a crowd gathered outside his house. Inside, Solomon lay in bed, swathed in bandages and his face a bloody pulp. Beside him Zelda cut more bandages. There had been an accident. Solomon had placed one foot on the wagon's step when Masha bucked and galloped at full speed. Solomon slipped and was dragged under his own wagon for blocks, mangling his spine. From then on he would have progressive and debilitating pain.

Solomon could never again be the main breadwinner for his family, and Zelda had a house of children to care for. The role now rested on Arthur, the eldest child.

The Babitzkys decided to move to Brooklyn, New York, where Zelda had family. They also knew that the move would help Arthur foster his creative potential. Arthur rushed to earn his high school diploma one semester early. In the spring of 1924, the Babitzkys started a new life in New York City.

5 | FIGHTING FOR HIS SALARY

NEW YORK IN 1924 was the glittery epicenter of the Roaring Twenties. This was the Jazz Age, and America was finding its voice.

Dreams of a better life graced both the streets and skyline. Nouveau-gothic skyscrapers dotted southern Manhattan. New York Governor Al Smith, hero of the labor reform movement, pushed policies for social welfare and public works projects.

Solomon Babitzky arrived first, working as a live-in caretaker, or *shamas*, in a Bronx synagogue. Arthur and Irving followed, occupying an alcove under the synagogue staircase. Arthur remembered surviving on day-old bread and expired milk, and the two pilfered from the synagogue's Saturday kiddush luncheon. Once the others arrived, the entire family crowded into a little Bronx apartment. Zelda found work as a cleaning lady and Arthur as a stock boy hauling enormous burlap sacks of flour for a local grocer.

In May, Arthur's fortune took an uncanny turn. He found a business card for an advertising agency in the street, called the number, and got a job.

Arthur began an unpaid apprenticeship at the Pitts & Kitts Manufacturers & Supply Company, which designed interior labels for shirts and coats. For each six-day workweek, Arthur was tasked with running errands, delivering packages, and stalling creditors on the telephone. Soon he was able to try his hand at designing layouts and rough artwork. Following his trial period, his employers paid him forty cents an hour for any commercial art they used. When they realized that the ambitious teen was netting about sixteen dollars a week this way, they changed the terms of their agreement and gave him a straight ten-dollars-per-week salary.

Arthur began to work on an art portfolio, and he was permitted to use the facilities after hours, setting a precedent of working late. In October, when he left punctually to celebrate his seventeenth birthday, his supervisor chastised him for not staying overtime. Disgusted, Arthur quit and took his art samples with him.

Next, Arthur found work for twelve dollars a week at a more reputable commercial art agency, the Harold W. Simmonds Studio. This job also entailed running errands and the like, but Simmonds knew talent when he saw it and gave Arthur his first break on true advertising production work.

Simmonds was a strong and stocky thirty-two-year-old art-school graduate. He and his talented crew taught Arthur techniques like hand lettering, photo retouching, and airbrushing—all in the imitation-woodcut style with floral borders popular at the time. These illustrations appeared daily in newspapers and magazines advertising men's and ladies' fashions and products.

Arthur had an additional task he had not bargained for. According to him, each Friday it was his job to collect Simmonds at the local speakeasy before Simmonds spent everyone's paychecks. Once at the office, Simmonds insisted on wrestling with Arthur. Once Arthur had taken a couple falls, his boss would relinquish their earnings. After about four months, the studio struck a low period, and Arthur was laid off.

But Arthur's experience had reinforced his principles. Whether advocating for his quitting time or wrestling for his paycheck, he had an underdog's will.

———————

As Solomon's disability worsened and the Babitzkys moved closer to Zelda's relatives in Brighton Beach, Brooklyn, tension grew between Zelda and Solomon. Arthur's God-fearing father was now the family's burden.

Arthur tried in vain to freelance from home, working with a fountain pen on the surface of his parents' bureau. Aware of his own artistic shortcomings, he enrolled in classes at the Educational Alliance Art School. This not-for-profit institution, located on the Lower East Side, was run mainly by volunteers and charged tuition on a sliding scale. It had been cofounded by the Young Men's Hebrew Association and had roots as a settlement house for Jewish immigrants. Arthur must have felt right at home, especially studying under one of the school's top instructors, Raphael Soyer. Soyer exemplified social realism, an artistic movement that glorified the working class. Though only eight years older than Arthur, Soyer painted his portraits of humble subjects with prodigious skill and passion.

After many months of study, Arthur began getting freelance work. Late in 1925 he opened an office of his own in Manhattan amid the growing theater district of Times Square and adopted the professional name Babbitt. He was now an independent contractor and accepted any work that came his way, including lettering, cartoons, and advertisements. His youth caused considerable confusion, and he was derided as "the boy from Babbitt's." After about nine months, he brought in a business partner to handle the layouts, lettering, and contacts.

Ever deviating from his father, Babbitt painted butterflies on the thighs of chorus girls. He began a photo collection of his many female acquaintances, among them a picture of two cabaret girls blowing him a kiss.

By 1927 Babbitt had integrated himself into New York's artistic community. He had peers at the Association for Young Advertising Men, the Industrial Art School of the Metropolitan Museum of Art, and the Art Students League. He had learned many trade secrets from his colleagues for promoting himself. An outlandish suggestion was to win a new client with a poster-sized letter sent special delivery to the client's secretary, the boss's gatekeeper, who was more likely to open it. He designed an ornate die-cut business card that opened like a greeting card. It imitated the cover of the popular Sinclair Lewis novel *Babbitt*, and inside were examples of his own lettering and illustration.

Times Square in 1927 was bright with the lights of stage and screen. Vaudeville theaters promised stage shows of comedy, dance, and musical acts, while movie palaces ran the latest silent features, newsreels, shorts, and animated cartoons. The glitz of Manhattan reflected the showmanship of Mayor Jimmy Walker, who had been a popular songwriter years before.

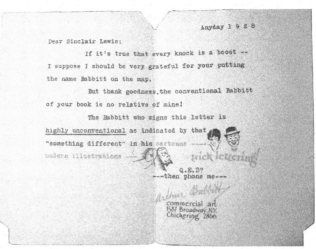

Art Babbitt's business card.

When Babbitt's commercial building was to be demolished to make room for the Ethel Barrymore Theatre, he relocated around the corner to 1587 Broadway on 49th Street. Coincidentally, this was next door to the Strand Theatre, where Carl Eduarde conducted his musicians who would play for *Steamboat Willie*. In the summer of 1928 Walt Disney and Art Babbitt likely stood within spitting distance of each other.

For fun, Babbitt fostered his love for fine music, practicing the mandolin and listening to classical radio. Being in New York City, he could find inspiration all around him, from the music clubs to his Italian barber, whose witticisms included, "Death—she's anot such a bad athing in life!"

In the summertime, he joined friends at the beach, accompanied by Rose Cohen, a brunette from Passaic, New Jersey. She came from a large, well-to-do Jewish family, but like Babbitt she was the child of Russian immigrants, and also a designer herself, specifically of hats. She was Art's first courtship, and in January 1929 the two were engaged.

Babbitt's career was expanding. In his midtown studio, he landed an illustration assignment for *Scientific American*. Soon he accepted an animation project for a local medical institution, making instructional short films for educational screenings. He acquired a camera and animation stand and started animating these moving diagrams. (Today animated visual aids are called *mechanisms of disease* and are still used in hospitals and medical schools.)

He was not enthralled by the medium of animation itself—it was little more than a novelty as far as he was concerned. Then, around September 1929, while at the cinema, he was struck by the opening cartoon. It was Walt Disney's first Silly Symphony, *The Skeleton Dance*. In those six minutes, Art Babbitt became a Disney fan.

———————

Arthur and Rose were married on September 29, 1929. From the start, she and her family dominated. The wedding was a high-profile ceremony in the Park Manor, Brooklyn's premier kosher catering hall. It was attended only by immediate family and the bridal party; all of Babbitt's groomsmen, including his best man, were Rose's brothers. Immediately following the wedding, Art and Rose honeymooned in Bermuda and returned on October 14 to their new home in the suburbs of Passaic, New Jersey.

Two weeks later, the stock market crashed; the Great Depression had begun. Babbitt's business accounts started drying up. His business partner mentioned that Paul Terry, the successful animation director of *Aesop's Fables*, was organizing his own cartoon studio in the Bronx and was looking to build its staff. Babbitt would have dismissed it if not for one thing: Terry was making cartoons *with sound*. Babbitt closed his business and got an entry-level job at Terrytoons for thirty-five dollars a week. His first task was opaquing the inked cels with paint and then, after they were photographed, washing them at night for reuse, earning an additional penny apiece.

Paul Terry had opened his studio in Thomas Edison's former production building. In 1929 the lower floor was still used for costume storage and a soundstage rental space. Upstairs, a staff worked for Paul Terry to produce a six-minute cartoon every week. Each cartoon amounted to roughly forty-three hundred drawings.

In the high-ceilinged Terrytoons studios, a room of animators sat at their animation desks in rows like garment workers. Each desk was equipped with a large hole in the center on which sat a circular pane of frosted glass called a *light disc*, through which a lightbulb underneath could illuminate several drawings stacked atop one another. The animators flipped their drawings of main poses back and forth. Babbitt learned that these drawings were called *extremes*, and the drawings that connected them were called *inbetweens*. In this well-oiled assembly line, drawings went from the animators to the inbetweeners to the cel inkers to the opaquers to the camera, and finally to the editor who viewed the film negative of the footage on a Moviola machine.

In his cardigan and glasses, Paul Terry was the image of a father figure, though he was only forty-three. He had been animating since 1915 and was one of the company's four supervising animators, along with Jerry Shields, Frank Moser, and his older brother John Terry.

Paul Terry had his own office away from the other animators, where he worked out schedules for budget and distribution. He was notoriously cheap. His studio furniture was a hodgepodge from thrift stores and estate sales. He kept daily records of each artist's productivity to ensure the studio churned out cartoons weekly. He referred to his product as "merchandise," and he refused to make a cartoon any longer than the bare minimum. Producing more than the required six minutes was, he later said, "a waste because we never got a nickel more for it."

There was no story department. Instead, Terry pulled from a gag file, from which he would proudly "take elements that already existed and put different combinations together. And then you create something seemingly new." He had *A* gags for big laughs, *B* gags for medium laughs, and *C* gags for chuckles. "I've got the finest collection of jokes in the world," he said. "I save jokes, because they never change. They're good from one generation to another." He saw no point in having style guides or model sheets for his characters. It was a seller's market, and as long as theaters kept buying, Terry saw no reason to change.

Around late February 1930 Babbitt graduated to trainee animator under Frank Moser. Like Terry, Moser kept careful track of how much animation each worker produced, even counting each employee's bathroom time. Moser himself was responsible for roughly half the footage of each cartoon, often bragging that he was the fastest animator in the business. Babbitt thought, *That's like being the fastest violinist in the world—he can't play worth a damn but he can sure play fast.*

Nonetheless, Babbitt enjoyed working alongside John Terry. John had a side job writing and drawing his comic strip, *Scorchy Smith*. He had tuberculosis and at times would start laughing at his desk for no apparent reason.

When asked what was so funny, John Terry would smile and reply, "Every day is gravy." This memory of random, apparent carefree laughter stuck with Babbitt, worming its way into his ever-growing mental library.

Because the four supervisors were older—all born in the 1880s—and had worked as newspaper illustrators, they approached animation as comic strips in motion. However, Babbitt's generation had been influenced by vaudeville and movies. For the youngsters, it was not the image that made the humor but the way the image moved.

Babbitt tested animation by flipping his drawings at his desk. His art classes had taught him that growth comes from experimenting and trying new things. But at Terrytoons there was no experimentation; all animation was final. Animators saw their completed animation only after two months, when a final print was developed and returned. Terry required all animators to stick with actions they already knew how to do.

When the studio's twelfth cartoon, *Monkey Meat*, began production in May 1930, Babbitt was finally a character animator on his own. His first scene was a monkey playing a hippo's teeth like a xylophone, a gag used in Disney's *Steamboat Willie* two years before.

Original layout drawing by Art Babbitt of his first-ever character animation scene, from *Monkey Meat*, 1930, at Terrytoons.

Around the shop, some folks talked about Terry's "good animator" who was studying fine art in Europe. Then late in December 1930 he arrived, resembling a tall, mustachioed Cossack with a New York accent. His name was Vladimir "Bill" Tytla.

Today, Tytla is considered one of the greatest animators who has ever lived. In those early days, Babbitt couldn't ignore Tytla's energy, describing "little sparks of electricity coming off of him all the time." Babbitt and Tytla had a lot in common. Their parents were immigrants; each bubbled with ambition and industriousness. It was not long before a friendship blossomed. Babbitt teased Bill's Ukrainian heritage by calling him "Vladjo." Tytla teased Babbitt's skinniness by calling him "Bones."

Babbitt introduced Tytla to fine music, and Tytla opened Babbitt's mind in other ways. Tytla introduced Babbitt to fine art and to the socialist novel *Penguin Island*, and he brought Babbitt into his circle of commercial artists. Above all else, Babbitt credited Tytla with giving him the courage to be creatively inventive.

Soon Babbitt began to flourish at Terrytoons. He delivered scenes better and faster. Periodically, Paul Terry's wife, Irma, popped into the studio and goaded Babbitt to negotiate for a raise. "Go in and tell Paul you want fifteen dollars more a week or you're going to quit, and then you'll get five," he recalled her telling him. Babbitt did so more than once, and each time received his raise. The episodes reinforced Babbitt's notion that employees had to fight for their fair share.

Some of the top Terrytoons Crew, circa early 1931: (left to right) Jerry Shields, Bill Tytla, Frank Moser, Art Babbitt, Charles Sarka, unidentified, Paul Terry.

By early 1932 Babbitt supplemented his income contributing drawings to a humor magazine called *Merry-Go-Round*. He also kept his sights on Disney. For one magazine gag, he drew Mickey Mouse responding to the 1932 presidential race. Furthermore, a one-time Paul Terry animator from the Van Beuren studio, Norm Ferguson, had become a supervising animator at Disney.

Rose Babbitt was not enthusiastic about Hollywood. She had a life in Passaic and a job designing hats at Bergdorf Goodman in New York. According to Babbitt's cousin, Rose "didn't give him breathing space." The two separated, and Babbitt stayed with Tytla in his Bronx apartment. They eventually divorced, and Babbitt would fail to even acknowledge that they were ever married.

Using a strategy that he had picked up as a commercial artist, Babbitt made a run for Disney. He bought an enormous piece of paper—about fifteen feet by twenty feet—got down on his hands and knees, and wrote an enormous request for an interview. He addressed it to Walt Disney's secretary, Carolyn Shafer, and mailed it special delivery.

In May 1932, activism and corruption proliferated in New York. Seventeen thousand destitute war veterans marched to Washington, DC, demanding an advance on their military bonuses. On May 14 a hundred thousand New Yorkers marched for the end of Prohibition in the We Want Beer parade. On May 25, the charming and charismatic mayor Jimmy Walker was ordered by Governor Franklin D. Roosevelt to testify under suspicions of corruption. (He would retire from politics that November.)

May was also a milestone for Art Babbitt. It was the month he received a call to interview with Walt Disney.

'ROUND and 'ROUND on the MERRY-GO-ROUND

RHYME AND REASON REMOVED BY BABBITT

"Business isn't really so bad," says J. P. Morgan. "It's just the way you look at things."

While Smith—Ritchie—Roosevelt—Garner and nine others scrap amongst themselves, the Democratic Party in a final desperate move, appeals to Mickey Mouse to run as the dark horse.

"But I don't want to be president," says Mickey, "I'd rather do funny things in the movies, than in the White House."

Miss Lillie P. Jones of Saginaw, Michigan—just a wisp of a girl—with 49, 576 victims, claims the record for number of men nonplussed by a single woman in limited time. Her method of procedure is remarkable in its simplicity. Just repeating "You want me only for my body" several times works wonders, she says.

Japan, in a Christian moment, acts to prevent Manchukuo harming itself.

Shepherd D. Sheep, Dry senator from Texas, says, "We must not repeal the 18th Amendment, because by so doing we show disrespect for the Constitution.

Illustration Babbitt drew while still in New York for the humor magazine *Merry-Go-Round*, commenting on current events and parodying Mickey Mouse's popularity. From summer 1932. *Mickey Mouse © The Walt Disney Company.*

6 | YOU CAN'T DRAW YOUR ASS

OUTSIDE THE WINDOW of Art Babbitt's transcontinental train stretched the Midwest in July. The Depression had ravaged the region since Babbitt had last been there. The national Farmers Holiday Association was in the midst of an enormous strike and export embargo as farmers demanded fair prices for their goods. Soon the strike would span seven states and barricade the highway between Babbitt's two hometowns, Omaha and Sioux City.

When Babbitt arrived in Los Angeles, he saw a growing city surrounded by undeveloped brown hills and dotted with red streetcars and opulent cinemas. The city exuded the mystery of Greta Garbo, the exuberance of the Marx Brothers, the austerity of Spencer Tracy, and the seediness of Edward G. Robinson.

In a miles-wide radius from Griffith Park and its HOLLYWOODLAND sign stood the movie studios: Paramount Pictures, Columbia Pictures, MGM, Warner Bros., Fox Film Corporation, Universal Pictures, and United Artists. Far beyond them to the east, in the rolling desert near the remote Silver Lake Reservoir of Los Angeles, was Hyperion Avenue. Its streets were cracked. Gophers darted across the hill facing the tall concrete wall of number 2719.

In the middle of the wall was a small gate that led to a grass courtyard and an inviting flagstone path. The path lead to a quaint Spanish colonial–style building, two stories tall, with stucco siding and a red terra-cotta roof. On it rested the neon sign in the shape of Mickey Mouse, with the words WALT DISNEY STUDIOS. Shutters hung from every pair of picture windows. Inside, everything was dazzlingly painted in bright tints of light blue, raspberry, and gleaming white—far from the institutional tones of the New York studios. Walt Disney's office was on the second floor; Carolyn Shafer showed Babbitt in.

Walt Disney, age thirty, sat at his wide wooden desk. He normally donned slacks and a thin sweater, and when he wasn't primed for publicity photos, a shock of his straight black hair tumbled over the side of his face. He wore an expression that was all business. Those who met him were surprised by his youth. "You had a feeling that there was some part of him that was either more mature than most people his age or he had a fixation about something," one artist remembered. "From the beginning I had that feeling that this man wants things his way."

Walt corrected anyone who called him "Mr. Disney"—it was strictly "Walt." When Babbitt sat down, Walt was straightforward, saying that the studio was full and could not afford to hire him. Babbitt volunteered to work for a free three-month trial period. Babbitt recollected, "[Walt] said, well, he didn't have any room for me. I told him I only take up a space about four feet by six feet and I'm sure they could squeeze me in someplace."

It didn't come to that. Walt remembered in 1942, "Mr. Babbitt came into my office and said that there was nothing he wanted more than to work for me because he thought I was doing something for the business. It was that enthusiasm on Mr. Babbitt's part, and that sales talk, [that] was the reason I hired him."

Babbitt rented a house near the Hollywood Bowl, and started at the Disney studio on Saturday, July 23, 1932. The workweek was from 8:30 AM to 5:30 PM Monday through Friday, plus 8:30 AM to 12:30 PM on Saturday. Babbitt began as an inbetweener, earning thirty-five dollars a week.

He was placed with a group of other new men in the inbetweeners' room, known as the "bullpen"—in the basement of the main building. It was the days before air-conditioning, and sweating inbetweeners would often strip to the waist as they worked.

The assembly-line process that Babbitt was familiar with at Terrytoons was similar to Disney's, with two directors each supervising several animators and inbetweeners, though Disney animators had assistants to clean up their roughs. One artist from New York remembered, "The only difficulty in 'adjusting' to the Disney approach was that there was no acceptance for slipshod animation, and no thought of cost relative to quantity."

Unlike Terrytoons or any other cartoon studio, Disney animators didn't have to wait months to view their work. Their rough animation was shot under a test camera, and the processed film negative was returned to the animators the next day. This animation, called *pencil tests*, came back either in a strip or a loop. The animators threaded it through a Moviola machine mounted on a small table, observing their work through a lens-like aperture. Sometimes an action required multiple pencil tests to get just right, and each time the familiar sound of the Moviola running, "like eggs frying," permeated the studio. These tests cost more time and money for the studio, and as opposed to Terry's rate of one cartoon per week, Disney released one cartoon every three weeks.

Babbitt was assigned to work under Chuck Couch, an animator one year younger than Babbitt. Couch handed Babbitt a folder containing the drawings for his assignment and gave him one week to inbetween it.

The scene was for the upcoming short *King Neptune* (directed by Burt Gillett), and it was a doozy. A horde of pirates had to scurry up a galleon's mast. Babbitt placed two extreme drawings on his light disc, put a blank sheet of animation paper over them, and started to inbetween.

He came to Couch late the following day with a stack of drawings in his hands. Couch asked him if he had questions. Babbitt responded no, he had completed the assignment. Couch incredulously sent the scene to the test camera. When the pencil test came back, Couch threaded the film through the Moviola and watched it through the aperture. To his shock, the scene worked perfectly.

News of Babbitt's speed and skill spread throughout the studio, and soon word reached animation supervisor Ben Sharpsteen.

Art Babbitt animating at Disney, next to a Moviola, circa 1932.

Sharpsteen held significant sway. He had been at the studio since 1929, and now, at age thirty-six, he was among the oldest on staff. Walt had chosen Sharpsteen to manage and mentor new hires in a trainee program. Others remembered him as "a hard but fair taskmaster. He insisted on good draftsmanship, staging and action analysis. You had to learn—no shortcuts, just do it right."

Sharpsteen took his role very seriously. "They had to go through a very humble indoctrination," Sharpsteen later said of the trainees, "learning how to animate the way we did, learning how to pick your work apart, learning how to diagnose, learning to cooperate with others, learning to accept criticism without getting your feelings hurt, and all those things. We had a saying, 'Look, this is Disney Democracy: your business is everybody's business and everybody's business is your business.' If you did not have that attitude, you were not going to stay very long."

Sharpsteen would personally review Babbitt's next animation test. If Babbitt passed, he would advance from the inbetweeners' bullpen to Sharpsteen's mentorship.

A folder with Babbitt's next assignment appeared. It was for *Touchdown Mickey* (directed by Wilfred Jackson), and it was of just one character, Pluto the pup. However, this scene required Pluto to display a thought process and a change in emotion—in essence, to *act*. Pluto was to casually move to screen right, do a take, and run back to screen left in a panic. This required a four-legged walk and a four-legged run. Babbitt began animating. If Pluto's timing was off, the character would seem mechanical and fake. If it was good, Pluto would come alive.

The scene was approved. Babbitt became a trainee in Sharpsteen's unit, and he was moved to a new animation room among seven others, including Couch.

The distribution of scenes from supervising animators to trainees was called "the handout," and each trainee tackled his handout for the next Mickey Mouse cartoon, *The Klondike Kid*. Director Wilfred Jackson assigned challenging or important scenes to his top animators, and the remaining scenes would provide a training ground for Sharpsteen's unit.

As the days wore on, the other trainees began taking their summer vacations. Babbitt could not; he had not yet earned his vacation time. So, while his coworkers left their desks unattended, Babbitt tackled their scenes as well, and handed those in. In all, Babbitt completed ten of the film's sixty-six total scenes. He had out-produced every other animator on the cartoon.

Walt spent much of his creative time with the Story Department (a far cry from Paul Terry's gag file). Nonetheless, Walt had an awed admiration for his animators, the "actors" of his studio who breathed life into the characters. Walt wanted to capture what Charlie Chaplin had, and it was not only the gags. The hot-button word across the studio was *personality*. But without any formula for conveying personality, the directors grasped blindly, hoping for success with each attempt.

The Disney studio was a Hollywood anomaly. It was the largest and most critically acclaimed cartoon studio in the world, yet it was dominated by men and women in their twenties. There were baseball games on a makeshift field in the studio lot, pitting the Marrieds against the Singles. To tame the studio culture, Walt staggered the lunch hours between the male-dominated Animation Department and the female-dominated Ink & Paint Department. This didn't stop the staff from comingling, or, as they called it, "dipping your pen in company ink." Amorous couples would shack up at local hotels, the men all signing the same alias for the registry: "Ben Sharpsteen."

From the sporty to the bohemian, the coarse to the sophisticated, the studio "had a conglomeration of various types of people, all thrown in together, which made things very interesting," remembered an early animator. These artists all shared a goal: to be the best. This caused the most biting insult to be "You can't draw your ass!"

One of the animators that Babbitt gravitated toward was Les Clark, a fellow who could "draw his ass." Although Clark was more experienced and had been with the studio since the Oswald cartoons, the two had a lot in common. Clark was also born in 1907; like Babbitt, his father had a spinal injury that caused Les to become the family breadwinner, and he had worked as a commercial artist to make ends meet. Also like Babbitt, Clark strove for perfection in his work. His assistant recalled, "He would get you all the quality that was within him."

Babbitt and Clark shared meals as well as weekend camping trips. Rather than the sports lovers or the jokesters, they were among the studio's quiet intellectuals. However, Clark differed from Babbitt in one key way that would become evident in the years ahead. Clark had an unwavering loyalty to Walt.

7 | THE DISNEY ART SCHOOL

WALT SAT IN THE DARK, overheated projection room watching a work-in-progress reel of the latest cartoon, *The Mad Doctor*. When he wasn't in a story meeting, Walt spent a lot of his time here, in what the fellows termed the "sweatbox." They called it that for both climatic and psychological reasons, as Walt had a piercingly critical eye.

It was around late October 1932. His perfectionism was already paying off. In a few weeks, Walt would attend the fifth annual Academy Awards ceremony and accept an award for *Flowers and Trees*, winning in the new category of Best Short Subject: Cartoons. He would also collect a special award for the creation of Mickey Mouse. In the sweatbox, the final pencil tests had been cut together into this test reel. The director, Dave Hand, sat alongside Walt and the supervising animators. Trainees like Babbitt were not invited to sweatbox sessions. A film cutter operated the projection booth, and by request he could splice out a few frames at a moment's notice and play back the sequence almost instantly. A change might be as fine as a single drawing or as extensive as an entire sequence. "Walt seemed to know what he wanted to see before it was even on the screen," one of his animators recalled. A supervisor would then pass sweatbox notes among the team of animators for revisions.

Walt watched each scene intently as Mickey Mouse attempted to rescue Pluto from the Mad Doctor. Then one scene caught his attention. The Mad Doctor hung Pluto by his tail and bisected his shadow with scissors. It was neither cute nor funny; it was terrifying, not like a Disney cartoon at all.

Ben Sharpsteen knew which trainee had been given this scene. It was Babbitt. Sharpsteen leaned over to Walt. "We're going to have to hold this guy down," he said.

"No," Walt replied, "we'll bring the other guys up!"

———————

When notes were distributed, Sharpsteen passed the compliment along to Babbitt. Something about "bring the other guys up" activated Babbitt. He reflected on the art classes he had taken in New York. There was an ethos best expressed by Kimon Nicolaides, one of the Art Students League's top instructors when Babbitt was there: "Where no class is available, I suggest you try to organize a small group to share the expense of a model. In such a group one student should be elected monitor so that there will not be any confusion."

Babbitt decided to host figure drawing sessions in his home. One of the other trainees, Hardie Gramatky, suggested finding a model at his alma mater, the nearby Chouinard Art Institute. Babbitt arranged to hire one of the school's models for a private nude figure drawing session. He invited the seven other animators from his room.

That night, every animator from Babbitt's room showed up—as well as every animator from the adjacent room. In all, fourteen young men crammed into Babbitt's home to sketch the model from life. Babbitt acted as monitor, keeping time for poses as well as collecting the model's fee.

He invited the animators back the following week. This time, twenty animators arrived; they had to find space in Babbitt's quarters by sitting on orange crates.

Not long before hiring Babbitt, Walt himself had driven some of his animators to Chouinard for evening drawing sessions. It had never occurred to Walt to bring the sessions to his animators. Shortly thereafter Walt called Babbitt into his office.

Walt told Babbitt that it might be bad for the studio's public image if word got out that Disney artists were gathering with nude women in a private home. Instead, Walt suggested hosting the drawing sessions at the studio soundstage, under company auspices. He even volunteered to provide drawing materials and the models' fees. He asked Babbitt how much models usually charge. Knowing that the fee was usually $0.60 an hour, Babbitt responded, "$1.25 an hour, plus car fare."

Walt obliged, and drawing sessions began at the Disney soundstage. Babbitt remained class monitor, but they needed an instructor. Once again, Babbitt consulted Hardie Gramatky, who suggested a young art professor at Chouinard named Donald W. Graham. On Babbitt's invitation, Walt gladly hired Don Graham, and thus, as Graham would recall, "On November 15th 1932, the Great Disney Art School was born."

The classes were held two evenings a week, and twenty to thirty artists attended each class. Though not an animator himself, Graham demonstrated an uncannily intuitive understanding of the medium. His anatomy lessons concerned the body as consisting of moving parts, and how they are affected by physics, gravity, and motion. Graham would later write, "Only if the drawings utilized are true action drawings, drawings that convey the idea of action, can convincing action be realized." It was nothing short of groundbreaking.

At random times, the sound of marching music could be heard through the windows. One of the story men, Vance DeBar "Pinto" Colvig, had organized an ever-growing band. He was tall and gangly, a self-identified goofball, having previously worked as a clarinet-playing circus clown. At the studio, he enlisted fellow artists in his band, proudly proclaiming in the studio bulletin that the ensemble included Wilfred Jackson on "Horrible Harmonica," Chuck Couch on "Terrible Tuba," and Art Babbitt on "Mussy Mandolin." Colvig's repertoire of silly voices included that of a "corn-fed hick," and Walt liked it enough to use for a reoccurring character named Dippy Dawg (later known as Goofy).

Walt was eager to grow his cast of recognizable characters—the Disney brothers had just begun working with a merchandising executive, and it was important to brand their cartoon stars. Thus, Dippy Dawg was cast opposite Mickey and Minnie Mouse in the upcoming cartoon, Ye Olden Days. Director Burt Gillett worked with his musical composer, Frank Churchill, timing out the action note by note on an upright piano. Like all Disney cartoons, Ye Olden Days would have a continuous musical score from beginning to end. "It is the rhythm that has appealed to the public," Walt had said in 1929. "The action flows along and we have to work hard to keep the movement flowing with the music." Because a director was paired with a composer, a director's office was called the music room. A supervising animator knew to pick up scenes in the director's music room, where the action and timing were notated.

Burt Gillett teemed with nervous energy, and the cartoons he directed were particularly loud and fast. The artists noticed that the room Gillett shared with Churchill "was especially noisy, as Burt acted out all the parts, beating on the tables, chairs, or the piano top and hitting the rhythm with a heavy foot." Gillett timed every movement on screen to a musical note and was called "the first 'tink-tink-tink' director. Every time Mickey took a step, there was a metallic 'tink.'" Churchill, meanwhile, had a versatility that fit whatever the scene required and could write what the artists called "foot-tappin' and whistlin' music." As with his musical tastes, he appreciated sophistication, dressing well and enjoying expensive drinks—yet was not above an impromptu jam session.

One day around November 1932, Wilfred Jackson was startled by the "thumping and bumping" he heard coming through his ceiling from Burt Gillett's music room upstairs. He rushed up to see "Frank Churchill over at the piano with his cigarette hanging down, with his eyes closed and his foot stomping away." Across the room, Gillett was swinging his fists madly at supervising animator Fred Moore, who had his back against the wall trying to dodge the blows. Before Jackson could act, the music suddenly stopped, and the three men walked to the center table to make timing notations of their choreography. They were role-playing a fight scene for *Ye Olden Days.*

Ben Sharpsteen picked up his scenes for *Ye Olden Days* and handed Babbitt his assignment: Dippy Dawg as a dastardly prince, forcing his jowly lips on Princess Minnie Mouse's arm before she slaps him in the face.

Dippy Dawg had always been a well-meaning and comical goofball, but this role in *Ye Olden Days* was ill-fitting and out of character. He was unconvincing, either as a villain or as comic relief. He was simply a plot device, lacking an independent personality. As Walt would later say, "Without a definite personality, a character cannot be believed. And belief is what I'm after."

Babbitt pencil-tested his animation on the Moviola, and it was then sweatboxed by the supervisors. His work must have been impressive; after *Ye Olden Days*, he graduated out of the animation trainee program. He was now invited to pick up his assignments himself. In Burt Gillett's music room, Babbitt received his next assignment. It was not a Mickey Mouse cartoon but a Silly Symphony. Like all Silly Symphonies, it would be experimental, this one being the ultimate experiment in personality animation.

8 | THREE LITTLE PIGS

BY DAY THE DISNEY ANIMATION WING was abuzz with experimentation. The animators had already advanced far beyond anything that had been done before, and new tricks were being discovered every day. After hours, when an animator left for home, Babbitt and the others would pick up a stack of drawings from that animator's desk and flip the pages. Bursts of invention rippled through the whole department, mostly coming from three animators in particular: Fred Moore, Dick Lundy, and Norm Ferguson.

There was something youthful in Fred Moore (beyond being only twenty-one), and many of the fellows called him "Freddie." When he drew, he perched jauntily on the edge of his chair, his curved pencil strokes perfect each time. His ability to make appealing designs was uncanny. It was Moore who had redesigned Mickey, discarding the mouse's thin limbs and long snout for shapes that were rounded and childlike. As Mickey's design had changed, his personality morphed from that of a trickster to an all-American kid. Moore was slowly becoming the studio's specialist in animating Mickey Mouse and anything else that was round and cute. This included drawings of young nude women, and his sketches of coy nymphets with perky breasts and supple buttocks became known as "Freddie Moore girls."

Dick Lundy, age twenty-six, had been at the studio for three years. In that time, he had found his own way to give his animation personality. He had discovered that each character can have a signature movement and a distinct action for a particular emotion. He thought of it as giving a character a dance that fit the tone, one that the audience could identify. In a couple years, Lundy would become the studio's Donald Duck specialist.

Norm Ferguson, or "Fergie," was a senior animator at thirty years old. He had a nervous New York energy and as he drew he constantly jiggled his feet. He was a little dressier than the others, regularly wearing a vest and tie, but his habits were purely zen. He had a practice of zoning out while sketching, abandoning clean and crisp lines for messy, impulsive gestures. He attempted to get into the minds of his characters, and when animating he added pauses to show that the character was thinking. He was a master of pantomime, was called the Charlie Chaplin of the studio, and would soon be known as the studio's Pluto specialist.

Pinto Colvig, by Disney artist T. Hee.

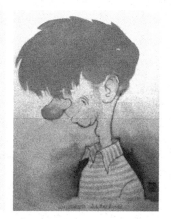

Wilfred Jackson, by Art Babbitt.

Norm Ferguson, by Disney artist T. Hee.

Dick Lundy, by an unknown Disney artist.

Fred Moore, by Fred Moore.

The Story Department took its role seriously as well. These half-dozen men tackled each story session with integrity to plot and character, critiquing and revising. They had a reputation to maintain as the best in the business.

The story team, including Walt, pitched idea after idea to each other. When Walt proposed a rough idea for a "Three Little Pigs" cartoon, his staff wasn't sold on it. It took Walt time to workshop it in his mind until the idea of the pigs dancing and playing different instruments crystallized. He pitched it again, and this time the story men accepted it. "I don't mean they threw up their hats, or that even I thought it would be a tremendous hit," said Walt at the time. "We considered it a typical *Silly Symphony.*"

Walt had learned that he could only sell ideas with clear visions. This lesson would play into everything he did from then on.

While the radio played "Brother, Can You Spare a Dime?" the first public memo for *Three Little Pigs* circulated in the studio. As expected, Walt wrote that he sought "to develop quite a bit of personality in them." By mid-December the Story Department completed a three-page outline, which was tacked on the bulletin board as an open call for gag ideas. A good gag could earn the submitter a twenty-five-dollar bonus—about a week's salary for the lower-bracketed employees.

Like all Disney cartoons, there would be music throughout, and the pigs would disclose their motivations in song. Frank Churchill sat at his piano and tickled a little trill on the keys. Story men Ted Sears and Pinto Colvig helped with the lyrics, asking, "Who's afraid of the Big Bad Wolf?" with Colvig providing the voice of Practical Pig.

Fred Moore was assigned as lead animator for the cute pigs. Dick Lundy was to animate them dancing their jig—an exercise in character choreography. Norm Ferguson would supervise the animation of the Big Bad Wolf, whose cunning had to be evident to the audience.

Following Babbitt's work animating the villainous Mad Doctor and dastardly Dippy Dawg, he was given a few scenes of the wolf. He had a short scene in which the wolf grabs the first two pigs by the tails and collides into a tree. He would also handle the climax: the wolf climbs onto the brick roof and squeezes into the chimney like it was a girdle; Practical Pig removes the heavy lid off his cauldron and pours the contents of the heavy turpentine can into it; the wolf dips himself in, registers pain, and shoots up out of the chimney howling, dragging his fanny off into the horizon.

Walt had several goals with this cartoon. The wolf had to appear cunning; the pigs had to appear organic. But most important, he wanted the identical pigs to exhibit individual characteristics. This was tricky. Actors in the movies were always distinguished by their unique looks, as were Mickey Mouse, Dippy Dawg, and the rest. However, the Three Little Pigs all shared the same basic design; it was how they *acted* in the cartoon that would differentiate them. While Burt Gillett was directing the cartoon, Walt practically lived in Gillett's music room, spending more time on it than he had on any cartoon yet.

Babbitt's scenes were assigned on Monday, February 20, 1933, and were due in seven weeks. Gillett went over the timing notations, as written on the *exposure sheet*, with the other animators. The layout man provided drawings of what the final staging would be. With his exposure sheet and layouts at his desk, Babbitt made his drawings. He flipped the pages, erasing and redrawing as needed, passing them along to an assistant to be inbetweened. When he had a stack of drawings ready to be pencil-tested, he had them delivered to the test camera. The roll of test film arrived the next day, and Babbitt ran it through the Moviola.

Babbitt was in the habit of staying at his desk after hours. He had fashioned a workspace that he found comfortable and inspiring, placing some expressionist art atop his desk. It was a print of Paul Cézanne's painting of a green jug that he had bought for eighteen dollars and had framed himself with four pieces of door molding from a hardware store.

Late in the evening, when most of the staff had left for the day, Walt walked up and down the narrow corridors of his studio, smoking his cigarette and peeking into the animators' rooms. Each room had several animation desks, and each desk had several hundred drawings stacked on its shelves. Some stacks were nice and neat, and others were a haphazard mess. Some stacks were tall; some were not quite tall enough. At this, Walt might lower one eyebrow and raise the other, a signature expression that his animators knew all too well.

Babbitt would retell one exchange that occurred when Walt found him drawing at his animation desk after hours. According to Babbitt, Walt pointed to the Cézanne print and lowered his brow.

"I don't like it," Walt said.

Babbitt stopped and asked why Walt didn't like it.

"The top of that goddamned jug is crooked!" said Walt.

Babbitt argued in favor of expressionism, relating it to animation such as how Mickey's appendages might vary their length as needed.

"Anyway, I don't like it," said Walt, and left. Babbitt bitterly packed the Cézanne print and took it home.

———————

While animating the pigs, Fred Moore made an incredible discovery.

Any animator with a pencil knew the challenge of maintaining a character's shape from drawing to drawing. Characters' dimensions were never supposed to change.

Fred Moore tossed that aside. He did not envision the pigs as circles or even as spheres but as voluminous sacks. For a few frames, he stretched them slightly taller or squashed them slightly wider. He kept their mass consistent, not their shapes. This, to everyone's amazement, created the illusion of appearing soft, lively, and organic. The studio would call this technique *squash & stretch*, and once Walt saw it, he wanted more of it.

Fergie made faces at the small mirror on his desk and translated them onto the page. His own eyes became those of the Big Bad Wolf. The wolf's eyes were the keys to observing the character's thoughts. Fergie's wolf also glanced at the audience, breaking the fourth wall with nothing more than a sly smile.

The artists were in the midst of a breakthrough in personality animation.

———————

Around April 1, when his animation on *Three Little Pigs* was nearly complete, Babbitt picked up scenes for another assignment. This cartoon, *Mickey's Gala Premiere*, centers around Mickey and his friends being honored in Hollywood. The studio hired a new artist, Joe Grant, to design celebrity caricatures for the short.

Walt analyzed each scene for *Three Little Pigs* in the sweatbox. He especially loved how the pigs' houses have different wall art: dancing girls for the first, boxing champs for the second, and family portraits for the third (including "Father" as a string of sausages and "Uncle Otto" as a football). *Three Little Pigs* was moved to the Ink & Paint Department, then to the Final Camera stage, and at last to the Technicolor laboratory for distribution prints.

© WALT DISNEY PRODUCTIONS   WALT DISNEY presents   PERMISSION IS HEREBY GRANTED TO MAGAZINES
68/7003   "THE THREE LITTLE PIGS" AND NEWSPAPERS TO REPRODUCE THIS PICTURE
                             An Animated Cartoon • Technicolor® ON CONDITION THAT IT IS ACCOMPANIED BY
                             Re-released by Buena Vista Distribution Co., Inc. THE COPYRIGHT NOTICE "© WALT DISNEY PRO-
                                                                              DUCTIONS".   PRINTED IN U.S.A.

A lobby card featuring one of the scenes animated by Art Babbitt
in the groundbreaking cartoon *Three Little Pigs*. © *Walt Disney
Productions*

Around the end of April, Walt and his artists sat in the back row of the
nearby Alexander Theatre in Glendale and studied the preview audience's reaction to *Three Little Pigs*. It was a practice they did with every cartoon the studio
released, taking notes to see which gags worked and which ones flopped. This
time, however, was different. The response was extraordinarily enthusiastic.

At the official release on May 27, 1933, *Three Little Pigs* was a breakout
success. It "hit the country like wildfire," remembered a Disney artist. The song
"Who's Afraid of the Big Bad Wolf?" played on the radio, becoming a rallying
cry against the Great Depression and what *Time* magazine called "the tune by
which 1933 will be remembered."

The competition was swept up in pig fever too. Animators at MGM
couldn't stop humming the song. Animators at Warner Bros. looked at it "with
absolute awe." With that single cartoon, the Warner animators felt that Disney
was suddenly miles out of their league.

Original artwork from the cartoon was displayed in local theater lobbies.
Below each piece were the names of the Disney artists who created it. Under
one was Art Babbitt's name.

Audiences were paying good money to see features with *Three Little Pigs* on the bill, and theaters were paying Disney good money for prints of the cartoon. *Variety* wrote, "*Three Little Pigs* is proving the most unique picture property in history. It's particularly unique because it's a cartoon running less than ten minutes, yet providing box office draft comparable to a feature, as demonstrated by the numerous repeats."

The cartoon brought Walt and his company added fame, and on July 1, the Disney company was able to negotiate an enormous new merchandising deal. Soon books, playing cards, dolls, and countless toys all featured Disney characters. When a deal was struck with Southern Dairies, Walt got all his top artists to pose for a photo holding Mickey Mouse ice cream. On the studio lawn, Walt Disney, Art Babbitt, and twenty-three others smiled for the camera. The faces reveal jubilant camaraderie, like a college club yearbook photo. Babbitt appears fully at home among the group. The only person missing in his life was his best friend, Bill Tytla.

In early September 1933, Babbitt visited his family in New York. He discovered that his brother Ike had also developed a flair for performance, practicing being a one-man band. Solomon's spinal injury had worsened, his broken body nearly entirely bedridden. Zelda Babitzky had become Solomon's caregiver. Not wanting to burden them, Babbitt stayed with Bill Tytla's parents, visiting Bill and the friends the two had shared. Babbitt unabashedly tried to coax Tytla to join Disney. After Babbitt returned to Hollywood, he wrote to Tytla that he would keep a light in the window for his arrival.

Despite the popularity of *Three Little Pigs*, the cartoon was slow to recoup its cost. It had been an expensive cartoon to make, significantly more than the average $25,000 for a Disney cartoon. Walt presented records showing that it had cost $60,000 and had made $64,000. Some eager journalists estimated the short to have netted nearly $100,000. "I've heard estimates from outsiders, of course, placing the gross from the 'Three Little Pigs' as high as $300,000 to date," said Walt around that time. "Every time I produce another *Mickey Mouse* or *Silly Symphony*, I'm accused of making another million dollars. I only wish it were true."

Even at this time, Walt's prerogative was not to enrich himself or Roy (another way he differed from Paul Terry) but to reinvest everything back into the company. Notwithstanding, his goal of making better cartoons was not economically viable. It became clear that cartoon shorts would never command the same price that theaters were paying for feature films. To continue his quest for innovation, he had to move beyond shorts. Walt would have to think bigger. No one had conceived of a feature-length cartoon before. It would require more learning, more skill—and a much larger staff.

———————

By late November 1933, while he was animating on *The China Shop*, Babbitt moved to a more luxurious, Spanish-style home on Tuxedo Terrace, surrounded by a bed of wild golden poppies atop a hill overlooking Los Angeles. It had a bar and a comfortably sized salon—perfect for hosting either a large or intimate get-together—and he still had a spare room downstairs, a yard out back, and a Japanese fellow who helped tend the house.

"I'm not going to bait you," Babbitt wrote Tytla on November 27, "but you could if you wished—share my house—my grand piano—my view, my 2 fireplaces—my grandfather clock—my tropical fish—my flowers—my 'Cezanne' and 'Daumier'—my wines—my hills and warm weather and my houseboy (the last—with reservations)."

Babbitt went on to disclose a new ambition that Walt had shared with him: "We're definitely going ahead with a feature length cartoon in color—they're planning the building for it now and the money has been appropriated. Walt has promised me a big hunk of the picture."

It was remarkable that Walt envisioned a feature film at this early stage but also likely that he would not give further details yet. Like Walt's initial pitch for *Three Little Pigs*, this feature was still rough in his mind. He needed a clear vision, and that would take some time.

As evidenced in Babbitt's letter, there was no greater pride for a Disney artist than recognition from Walt. On the flip side, Walt's scrutiny could be crushing. So it was for Babbitt's work on *The China Shop*.

Walt and Babbitt sat in the sweatbox, screening Babbitt's animation of the slow-moving old man leaving his shop.

There is a very good reason why animated cartoons didn't have many slow-moving characters. Speed is easy in animation; fast action has more freedom to vary drawings from one to another. Slowness is extremely tricky; those drawings must be nearly identical, and their slight differences have to be carefully measured. It is far easier to bungle a slow-moving action than a fast one.

Babbitt's scene was a bit of a mess. He had animated the character's slow shuffle toward the door, yet the doorknob was on the far side of the door, and so the old man had to shuffle downstage. Then the door opened inward, and he had to shuffle backward to pull the door—then shuffle back and pull the door again. Babbitt had treated the man and the door too literally, without any creative license. Walt was not thrilled.

"You know what I'd like you to get in this character here?" said Walt.

"What?" asked Babbitt.

"Some of that exaggeration, some of that sensitivity and stuff—you know," said Walt, "like Cézanne gets in his still lifes."

9 | ENTER BIOFFSKY

ON THE MORNING OF SATURDAY, March 4, 1933, as the Disney animators were putting in their half-day at the studio, Franklin Roosevelt—one-time governor of New York—was inaugurated as president of the United States. "Let me assert my firm belief," he told the nation, "that the only thing we have to fear is fear itself."

There was plenty to fear. The stock market had plummeted 85 percent. A quarter of the workforce was unemployed. More than a million people were homeless. It was the height of the Great Depression, and the day after his inauguration, Roosevelt closed all of the country's banks for a four-day "bank holiday" while he and Congress devised a plan.

On March 9 Roosevelt enacted the Emergency Banking Act, the first act of his proposed New Deal, thus beginning his renowned "first hundred days." Another of his first orders was the establishment of the National Recovery Administration—an agency that was authorized to set fair working conditions, maximum hours, and minimum wages. It required renewal in two years, at the approval of Congress.

Throughout the nation, 1933 marked a surge of labor union news. The president's National Industrial Recovery Act of June 16, in part, protected union negotiation rights between workers and employers. That July in Hollywood, the Screen Actors Guild was founded, and later that year, the Screen Writers Guild earned union status. But there was more than one union fighting to represent each craft in Hollywood. The International Alliance of Theatrical Stage Employees (IATSE) represented unions of stagehands and projectionists. However, it was at odds with the International Brotherhood of Electrical Workers (IBEW), the two undercutting each other for jobs and salaries.

At a time when powerful producers ruled Hollywood, union recognition was paramount. It enabled a large number of workers to bargain collectively as a single entity, and the management could not change contract terms without consent from the union. The union's elected representatives (who were paid out of members' dues) could bargain for terms like pay scale, safety conditions, working hours, and grievance procedures. On average, union members—especially at the bottom of the pay scale—earned more per week and had fewer accidents at work than non-union members.

Salary for sound engineers varied wildly, from $75 to $175 a week, so the IATSE audio workers demanded union recognition and a set pay scale. On Saturday afternoon, July 8, the IATSE sound engineers (of Sound Local 695) called a strike against one of the titans of Hollywood, Columbia Pictures. Movie production screeched to a halt. Frank Capra had to leave his director's chair in the middle of filming *It Happened One Night* because there was no one to record his actors' voices.

About four hundred other IATSE members walked out on July 8 in support of the striking sound engineers. On July 24 all IATSE members across Hollywood walked out. But instead of attempting negotiations, the producers brought in non-union sound engineers and members from the competing IBEW. The producers and the IBEW began approaching the IATSE strikers individually, offering attractive contracts to break the strike. Many strikers caved and took the contracts.

If the IATSE union had had more members in Hollywood, it may have succeeded. However, the producers began replacing the IATSE sound engineers with IBEW sound engineers (as well as all IATSE property and grip workers with the members of the Carpenters Local 946). When the IATSE strikers realized that they had lost not only the strike but also their jobs, they deserted the union. It was a sad reality that the sitting IATSE president was an ill-equipped leader.

Like a saving grace, the government's newly established National Labor Relations Board intervened and officially ended the strike on August 23, 1933. Producers were instructed to rehire the strikers without prejudice, but this edict was not enforced. Union rights were still unclear, and there was no single federal policy to handle labor disputes. Without such a policy, government intervention appeared to be just empty talk. Hollywood unionists were on their own, and after the failed strike, IATSE membership dropped from nine thousand to a couple hundred.

On the streets of Chicago, a short, broad-shouldered mid-thirties roughneck barreled by. Named William Bioffsky, he was known throughout the speakeasies, casinos, and local precincts as Willie Bioff. He had come to Chicago as a child from Odessa, then part of the Russian Empire, and at some point earned himself a scar on the left side of his chin. His overcoat flapped in the Windy City's foul air as he secured a cigarette between his fat fingers and entered one of the swankiest joints in the city: the 100 Club.

Willie Bioff was a two-bit wiseguy. In his youth, he drove a bootleg beer truck for Al Capone's henchman Nick Circella. In his twenties, he ran a brothel/speakeasy for mobster Jack Zuta. Bioff was caught, charged with pandering, and sentenced to six months in jail. But Bioff had connections and left jail after only seven days. In 1930, when Zuta was gunned down in his own car, Bioff moved on to greener pastures, forcing his way into the poultry handlers' union. He made good money bribing and threatening poultry distributors, but the Chicago police caught up with him, and in February 1933 they listed him as a public enemy.

Later that same year, Bioff read about motion picture unions—particularly the stagehands, projectionists, and electrical workers who were often threatening to go on strike. Then he met George Browne, head of Chicago's branch of the IATSE.

Browne, a tall Irishman, had been a member of the IATSE since 1915. In 1932, he ran in the biennial race for national president of the IATSE and lost. Browne remained in control merely of the Chicago branch.

Bioff understood that a person in charge of a union could decide when that union goes on strike. Strikes were notoriously expensive for management—the lost income, the machine maintenance, the wasted rent. An employer might pay through the nose to prevent a strike from happening.

Once Prohibition was repealed in December 1933, bootleggers were out of business, and organized crime was looking for the next big score. In early 1934

Willie Bioff in 1937 (left) and George Browne in 1941 (right).

union culture was novel, and the motion picture industry was in its infancy. Not many regulations were enforced on motion picture unions, and so Bioff and Browne had room to play.

A local chain of Chicago movie theaters, Balaban and Katz, had a contract with IATSE members that was about to expire. The chain resisted wage negotiations for its projectionists, stagehands, electrical workers, and musicians. The owner, Barney Balaban, made a quiet offer to George Browne: salaries would remain unchanged, Browne would stave off a potential strike, and Balaban would gift him $100 a week. When Browne told Bioff, Bioff asserted, "We can get a lot more money than that—and get it all the time!" Browne and Bioff made Balaban a counteroffer. They started negotiations at $50,000 and settled for $20,000, which Bioff and Browne split down the middle.

The pair had tapped into a new scheme that was bound to make them both rich. That night, Bioff met Browne amid the glitz of the 100 Club. Between platefuls and glassfuls, the two celebrated their lucrative new venture. By the end of the evening they had blown $300—and caught the eye of the club owner,

Nick Circella. Circella contacted his boss, Frank Rio. Rio was one of Capone's bodyguards. While Capone was serving time for tax evasion, Rio was among the highest-ranking active members of the gang.

A few days later, Rio pulled his car up to Bioff and invited him to go for a ride. He drove Bioff to the edge of the river where they had a little talk. The deal was simple: if Bioff was to pursue this venture with Browne, he was now an employee of Capone's syndicate, and the gang was going to get a cut for its support and protection. He and Browne would share a third of their total earnings, and the syndicate would keep the remaining two thirds.

Bioff agreed. He was determined to make this worth his while, and he had just the plan for how to do it.

At a private table in Chicago, Willie Bioff eagerly sat with partner George Browne, opposite the top men of Al Capone's gang. They included Nick Circella, Frank Rio, and Frank Nitti—all infamous in the world of organized crime.

It was the spring of 1934, and the biennial IATSE convention would be held in June. A new national IATSE president would be elected; Bioff wanted it to be Browne. Since Browne was only a regional head of IATSE in Chicago, their influence could only extend over Chicago unions. But Bioff was low on scruples and high on moxie. He suggested that the gang utilize their connections across the cities of the East Coast to influence the elections. There is much money to be made, he told them.

The mobsters liked what they heard, and they pointed out that Browne's clean background made him the perfect front man. When Browne had lost the national election two years prior, it was due to delegates in New York City, St. Louis, Cleveland, and New Jersey. Frank Nitti had contacts in all those places. Several union delegates across the country were already tied to the mob. If Browne won the election, Bioff's scheme could potentially earn them $1 million in Depression-era currency. Nitti said that the election was in the bag.

That June, at the IATSE convention in a Louisville hotel, Browne won the national IATSE presidency by a unanimous vote. All the while, large men from Capone's gang lurked in the hotel lobby. There would be no dissidents. Once his position was verified, Browne immediately installed Bioff as his personal representative.

10 | THE CULT OF PERSONALITY

IN HIS BRONX ANIMATION STUDIO, Paul Terry was furious. He did not want to spend a dime more than he had to. Christmas was coming, and Terry was already preparing his Christmas bonuses: bags of oranges from his personal grove. However, each time his star animator, Bill Tytla, came to him with the prospect of leaving him for Disney, Terry was obligated to increase his salary. Tytla's salary at Terrytoons far outstripped the $100 a week that Ben Sharpsteen was offering, even at Art Babbitt's personal recommendation. Terry didn't understand the appeal of working for less at Disney or the appeal of pencil tests. He told Tytla, "When I hire a man to animate, I want him to know *how*."

In December 1933 Babbitt laid it on the line for Tytla. "Remember this one thing," he wrote to his friend, "Disney is progressing a damn sight faster than Terry ever will and where it takes six or seven years to develop a man at Terry's—the same man can develop the same amount here in one year. . . . This doesn't mean that your ability is any the lesser but the longer you wait the more time it will take to catch up with the fellows here who are constantly progressing."

Indeed, Babbitt was progressing himself, and he was getting recognized for it. On January 29, 1934, Roy Disney called Babbitt into his office, tore up his $100-per-week contract, and handed him a new contract at $125 a week— with another raise when the option would be renewed. Babbitt was overjoyed.

"Ben [Sharpsteen] told me that Walt is hot for you," Babbitt wrote Tytla in February, "so if you're still interested I think (I'm positive) you can get $150 to start. If that sounds good and if the weather there has frozen your nuts plenty then write me—and say that 'If I could start at $150 at least then I'd make the move.' I know you'll get it."

He added that he recently saw a Terrytoons cartoon, and it "seemed to me like some disconnected rantings of a half-wit just tied together by main and end titles. I was ashamed to think that I once considered that crap pretty good."

Babbitt was not bluffing about Disney's hiring spree. New employees were coming in all the time, and additions to the studio space were being constructed every few months. Work started on the large new animation building directly behind the main building. In March 1934 Walt called his entire 110-person staff to the front lawn for a photo-op with their new Disney-licensed Post Toasties cereal. Babbitt posed behind Fred Moore, and as the shutter prepared to snap, Babbitt, straight-faced, tickled Fred's ear.

On March 16, 1934, Walt Disney sat in the Fiesta Room of Hollywood's Ambassador Hotel, dressed in his finest, surrounded by movie stars. It was the sixth annual Academy Awards ceremony, and he was there to receive the gold statuette for *Three Little Pigs*. Walt, as the producer (and the only credit on screen), graciously accepted the award. The cartoon's director, Burt Gillett, left the company later that month for the Van Beuren studio. Production manager Ben Sharpsteen would step up to fill the vacant director spot as soon as he finished supervising trainees on a new Silly Symphony called *The Wise Little Hen.*

The humor for this cartoon mainly came from the funny new voices, much like Dippy Dawg had emerged from Pinto Colvig's "hick" voice. For this new short, the studio had hired Florence Gill, an actress and opera soprano who could impersonate a singing chicken. A new voice actor named Clarence Nash voiced a swine in a sweater named Peter Pig and a waterfowl in a sailor shirt named Donald Duck (his first appearance).

Wilfred Jackson directed the short. Sharpsteen supervised the hen animation done by a trainee named Woolie Reitherman, who had graduated from art school the previous year. Babbitt animated scenes of Peter Pig and Donald Duck doing their funny dances and then faking bellyaches.

The studio staff found the Duck hilarious. Even before *The Wise Little Hen* premiered, the Duck was already cast against Mickey Mouse in *Orphan's Benefit*. Now the Duck's temper and ego were crystallized. Animator Dick Lundy invented the signature choreography for Donald when he got hopping mad, swinging his fist back and forth. (The cartoon also marked the renaming of Dippy Dawg as "Goofy.")

However, it was Norm Ferguson who shook the studio that spring. Ever since the print for *Playful Pluto* came back, the staff had been studying his sequence. He animated Pluto wrestling with a piece of flypaper, and the audience could follow not only Pluto's actions but also his thought process. Pluto, annoyed and puzzled, acted entirely in pantomime. It was brilliant. Ferguson had tapped into the wellspring of personality animation.

Babbitt had a piece of animation that was scrutinized too. Unfortunately, it was hailed as an example of what not to do.

The fellows were cracking up at Babbitt's old man in *The China Shop*. Babbitt's scene had become a "laughing lesson" in poor planning, repeatedly shown to the animators as an example of how to tackle an assignment completely the wrong way. "I think he used half the footage of the picture trying to get out through the door!" an animator remarked. Though it could be considered a layout error, Babbitt was mocked for it more than either the director or the layout man.

Babbitt was a perfectionist, so this flawed scene from *The China Shop* rankled him. No doubt he wished he could laugh at his own mistake as well.

By mid-1934, Hollywood was abuzz about a new acting technique from Russian theater artists Konstantin Stanislavski and his student, Richard Boleslawski. Known as *method acting*, it instructed actors in using their personal experiences to elicit authentic performances. Babbitt eagerly bought two books on the subject.

Hollywood was continuing to influence animation in other ways as well. Like other comedy trios (the Three Stooges, the Marx Brothers), the Disney studio would team up Mickey Mouse, Donald Duck, and Goofy. The trio would be pitted against Peg-Leg Pete, portrayed as a mobster with a Russian accent.

It was after hours at the Disney lot, and the sky was draped in sunset colors over the neon Mickey Mouse sign. Thirty-two-year-old Walt Disney waited alone in the studio soundstage.

One by one the artists returned from dinner. Animators and story men found the soundstage filled with seats, and they sat down. Walt stood alone at the front. This time he wasn't pitching story ideas for a short cartoon. He was selling the enchantment that he himself had experienced in 1917 as a boy in Kansas City.

He told them that they were going to start work on the world's first feature-length animated cartoon, a retelling of the Brothers Grimm fairy tale "Snow White." Walt began acting out the movie, entirely by himself. His artists sat spellbound for hours. When Walt finished, every artist was all in. Preproduction would start immediately.

The art classes would have to be ramped up. Don Graham would increase his teaching schedule to three days a week, critiquing rough animation in sweatbox sessions and leading day and night classes. Two more art instructors would be hired to fill out the five-day class schedule. The engine was accelerating.

––––––––––––

On August 7 an outline for the new Mouse-Duck-Goof cartoon, called *Mickey's Service Station*, appeared on the bulletin boards. Unsurprisingly, it included a memo requesting gag ideas, although exclusively centered around *personality*. "There is a chance of working in personality gags and situations around the Goof and the Duck, who help Mickey run his small, rural garage, in which every type of well-known service is performed by them in an exaggerated comedy manner," it read.

But the outline didn't actually leave room for personality. In fact, it was typical of all the cartoons up to that point, packed with slapstick, action, and puns, ending with a high-speed chase. The outline concluded, "Kindly draw up gags and have them ready by noon on Wednesday August 16, 1934."

Babbitt did not submit any gags; he had already left on vacation August 11, having gone to New York City through the extravagance of commercial air travel. He met up with his Disney friends Les Clark, Dick Lundy, and Frank Churchill (who had traveled to the Century of Progress Exposition in Chicago);

boarded a steamship with them on August 17; and sailed through the Panama Canal to dock in Los Angeles on September 3.

When he returned, Babbitt began animating on *Two-Gun Mickey*. He was assigned nearly all of the cartoon's Peg-Leg Pete scenes—he had risen to animating the studio's key villain. In a 1934 publicity shoot for another cartoon, *Peculiar Penguins*, Walt posed for several photos with different groupings of creative staff: directors, story men, and lead animators. Babbitt was included in all of them.

As a lead animator, Babbitt was now privy to story meetings. He sat among the brain trust of Walt and the directors as they dissected plot points. Pushpinned across several large corkboards like an endless comic strip were five hundred storyboard drawings illustrating *Mickey's Service Station*. A single panel showed the Goof sitting atop a hollow tube, his arm reaching down through one hole and coming up out of the hole behind him.

Babbitt saw much potential in this little bit of business. He begged Walt for this scene of the Goof, but Walt had Babbitt scheduled for Peg-Leg Pete's scenes. Walt relented under the condition that Babbitt complete his Pete scenes first.

On Babbitt's exposure sheet, director Ben Sharpsteen had timed the Goof scene to be 4.16 seconds long. Babbitt considered the scene not as simple slapstick, but as dimwitted character's attempt to solve a problem. Watching stupid behavior wasn't nearly as interesting as watching someone carefully calculate and still do the task completely wrong—just as Babbitt had on *The China Shop*.

Similar to Fergie's animation of the Big Bad Wolf and of Pluto, Babbitt attempted to indicate the Goof's thought process. Doing so would require adding drawings and run time, known disparagingly as "padding" a scene. But in a manner similar to what Stanislavski taught, Babbitt attempted to identify with his character. It wasn't a matter of imitating life but of caricature—of pushing the edges of what he knew.

By the time he finished animating the scene, the final version had swelled to a whopping thirty-six seconds. Babbitt had exceeded the scene's allotment tremendously without once checking with the director. The incident made him rather unpopular among the story staff.

The scene was cut into the final reel and sweatboxed for Walt. Not only was it funny, but it endowed the Goof with true personality, like a comic actor with a mind and soul. Babbitt may have been insubordinate to the director, but Walt liked the work, and that was that.

From *Ye Olden Days* to *Mickey's Service Station*, Babbitt saw untapped potential in the Goof. *The China Shop* incident was still fresh, and he began to recall others he had known who possessed either the optimism he admired or mental limitations he could laugh at:

- Joe, the leg-crossing narcoleptic horse.
- Bumpkins from Sioux City, like the butcher who couldn't see his buggy dangling right above him.
- His Italian barber in New York and his backward witticisms.
- John Terry at Terrytoons, who laughed off tuberculosis with, "Every day is gravy."
- His father, a religious man whose faith in the supernatural kept him going.

Taking a page out of Stanislavski's method, Babbitt began doing something that no animator had ever considered: psychoanalyzing his character. He began to write.

Babbitt described the Goof "as a composite of an everlasting optimist, a gullible Good Samaritan," and, "a hick. . . . He can move fast if he has to, but he would rather avoid any over-exertion, so he takes what seems the easiest way. He is a philosopher of the barbershop variety. No matter what happens, he accepts it finally as being for the best, or at least, amusing. . . . He is very courteous and apologetic and his faux pas embarrass him, but he tries to laugh off his errors. . . . He is in close contact with sprites, goblins, fairies and other such fantasia. . . . The improbable becomes real where the Goof is concerned."

Babbitt assembled his summary into a two-and-a-half-page typed treatise. He called it "Character Analysis of the Goof" and distributed it throughout the studio.

It was immediately hailed as the studio's latest breakthrough, and the long-sought key to personality animation.

11 | A FEATURE-LENGTH CARTOON

ADDITIONAL YOUNG ARTISTS seemed to be hired every day, many of whom with more schooling than Fred Moore, Dick Lundy, Norm Ferguson, and Babbitt. These art-school graduates, including Milt Kahl, Frank Thomas, and Ward Kimball, started their six-month rite-of-passage in the inbetweeners' bullpen. Once at the top of their art class, they now did "assembly-line work" in crowded rows of drawing desks, without air-conditioning, in the Los Angeles swelter. They each made drawing after drawing of inbetweens, "like a drawing robot," for $22.50 a week while dodging the wrath of the cantankerous department supervisor.

Bill Tytla may have been the last animator Walt hired without a six-month trial in the bullpen. In November 1934 Tytla left Terrytoons and moved into the downstairs bedroom of Babbitt's home on Tuxedo Terrace. Babbitt was thrilled. He now shared a home with his best friend.

Amid his busy schedule, Walt Disney frequented the studio soundstage where a new model, a teenage dancer, donned a fairy-tale dress. Some artists and directors sat close by with their papers and pencils, sketching her movements. Walt was very protective of her, and in a studio dominated by rambunctious young men, Walt made her and her father feel safe in his charge.

The model, Marjorie Belcher, had been dancing her entire life. Her father, Ernest Belcher, was a Hollywood "dance director" (now called choreographer)

73

who managed one of Hollywood's most prestigious dance studios. British and very proper, he raised Marge with high standards of decorum, intent on sheltering her from Hollywood's debauchery. He had a standing rule forbidding Marge from auditioning for screen roles—but having her movements drawn by Disney artists was permissible.

Marge arrived at the studio a couple days a month to model as Snow White for a very small group of Walt's top creatives. She earned ten dollars a day to pantomime the princess in full costume so that the movements of her and her ruffled clothing could be carefully studied.

———————

While the Disney men who drew Marge remained on their best behavior, others were painting the town red. Employees hosted parties and went to dance clubs. Art Babbitt had built a reputation as the swinging bachelor of the Disney studio, inviting large numbers of coworkers to soirees at the home that he shared with Tytla, though Tytla would not always partake. There were drinks from the fully stocked bar, and guests splayed across the floor on pillows like a Persian harem. Music from his extensive record collection projected from his top-of-the-line Capehart Automatic record player, able to play up to ten records in automatic rotation. Guests would recall the decadence wistfully for decades to come.

Babbitt's gatherings evolved into grand salons, attracting Hollywood's creative community. Musicians entertained on lute and his grand piano, authors recounted their adventures, and fine artists showed their handiwork. Babbitt's parties were mentioned in the local high-society column of the *Hollywood Citizen-News* on multiple occasions. He had become a man-about-town, one evening the personal guest of Alexander Pantages (who owned the Pantages theaters), the next an honored "screen celebrity" guest at a Hollywood supper club. He kept company with Hollywood screenwriters like Leonard Spiegelgass, concert pianist Richard Buhlig, and actress Jeanne Cagney (sister of Jimmy). The press made him the most famous Disney animator.

Models from the Disney art school also showed up. The head of the modeling agency, the curly-haired brunette Doris Harmon, performed a half-nude tribal dance. Another performed a reverse striptease on Babbitt's bed while he

Photo of Babbitt entertaining at his home, circa 1935. Babbitt is at left;
Les Clark is at center, in front of Jeanne Cagney.

filmed her for research (labeling the footage "dressing action"). Above Babbitt's
bed, festooned with pillows (and no headboard), was a print of Manet's sug-
gestive nude, *Olympia*, and his print of Cézanne's *The Green Jug*. He pursued
a passionate romance with one of the models, a raven-haired would-be starlet
named Sändra Stark. (In her later days she would say that he was the only
man she had ever loved.)

Babbitt was not prudish about his affections toward whichever woman
had earned his attention. Oftentimes when Bill Tytla returned late to their
darkened house, he begrudgingly had to use the back entrance lest he step
on Babbitt and a paramour necking on the living room floor. At a time when
people were holding fundraiser parties to help pay the rent, Art Babbitt, age
twenty-six, was living like a Hollywood Jay Gatsby.

The lifestyle was completely contrary to his father's values. Clearly, Babbitt took after his mother, down to her open-door policy for needy children.
One day, an animator in Babbitt's room said he knew a young single mother
who had been hit hard by the Depression and needed someone to care for her

two-and-a-half-year-old son for a couple of weeks. Babbitt volunteered. Soon a little blond boy named Dickie arrived. Tytla objected at first, but it wasn't long until Dickie was a member of the household. Their housekeeper doubled as an additional caregiver. Months later, Dickie's mother came to retrieve her boy, and Dickie and Babbitt remained close from then onward. (Dickie grew up to be Oscar-winning film editor Richard A. Harris and continued a relationship with Babbitt's children.)

––––––––––

Babbitt's private exploits never interfered with his work. In January 1935 Disney management experimented with profit-sharing, introducing a "semi-annual bonus." Babbitt received a percentage earned by the cartoons he had worked on since 1932. His work was rated "100% Plus." Babbitt's bonus check totaled $503.72, with his $125-per-week salary set to increase to $150 in February.

The incentive-based bonus thrilled the artists. Now they were not merely hired hands but also personally invested in the success of each project. The Disney management took note of the morale boost and began brainstorming ways to expand it.

––––––––––

Snow White still had huge hurdles to overcome. The most glaring one was the problem of believable human animation. Walt wondered if they could even achieve drama or suspense without it. Sure, a drawing could make you laugh. But could a drawing make you cower? Or cry? In early 1935 Walt wasn't yet sure his vision could be realized, and he stopped holding story meetings for Snow White.

However, Walt did notice one particular phenomenon within his staff: as they trained and honed their skills, each artist began to have a different specialty. Previously, each artist was expected to be moderately versatile, but now everyone was handed a specific task. The studio was already structured like a mass-production assembly line. Now Walt saw it becoming even more so.

Babbitt's success with *Mickey's Service Station* pinned him as a Goofy specialist. Around early March 1935 he began animating Goofy in the Mickey Mouse cartoon *On Ice*. Goofy attempted to ice-fish by baiting his hook with chewing tobacco and, when the fish surfaced to spit, clubbing it on the head.

The animators' rooms were equipped with a full-length mirror for studying their movements in action. Babbitt had seen the movements of his own tall, thin body. It was a simple transference to animate *Mickey's Service Station* as if the Goof were a tall, thin actor. But now that he had delved deep in the Goof's psyche, he considered delving deeper into his body mechanics as well.

The animators had newly discovered a property that they called *follow-through*, in which a moving character had parts that dragged behind, like a tail or a skirt, settling a few frames after the main mass. This, thought Babbitt, could be leveraged into a personality trait for the Goof. Babbitt treated Goofy's joints as if they were prone to drag in the air. This meant that, at moments, his legs and feet bent the wrong way. Goofy's personality was distilled in this loose, gangly walk. Babbitt called this technique *breaking the joints*.

As Babbitt was animating Goofy in *On Ice*, the character was also being animated in *Mickey's Fire Brigade*, albeit in a much smaller role. These supporting Goof scenes were assigned to Woolie Reitherman, one of the art-school graduates who had completed the trainee program. Reitherman's Goof in *Mickey's Fire Brigade* is treated like a glorified extra.

Tytla animated on *Mickey's Fire Brigade* as well, particularly a frantic sequence in which Mickey and his friends try to rescue a bathing Clarabelle Cow. It is hilarious and rich with personality; Tytla's superior skills were already rising to the surface.

The Disney studio did not have its own commissary, but the employees of the "Mouse House" often congregated at one of the neighboring lunch counters that they affectionately nicknamed the "Mouse Trap Café." Naturally, it was a good place to share studio gossip. One hot item that May was about Babbitt: he was suing the owner of a local hardware store for the sum of one dollar and twenty-nine cents.

The discrepancy concerned the new California state sales tax, which took effect at the start of the year. Babbitt was adamant about the injustice of having to pay the 3 percent sales tax. He argued that the merchant ought to pay it, not the customer. One California newspaper wrote, "If Babbitt's contention is upheld, it may bring about an entire adjustment of workings of the sales tax law in this state." Many of his peers at the studio thought the suit was ridiculous, but that hardly mattered to Babbitt. He was willing to battle for his beliefs.

Babbitt was proud of this identifier. At one point, a young production control manager named Herb Lamb approached Babbitt and animator Frank Thomas. Ribbing them both, Lamb asked sardonically why animators were even necessary when a director can point a camera at an actor. Being one of the newly hired art-school graduates, Thomas began defending the value of artists in society when Babbitt interrupted him. Animation, Babbitt explained, is about capturing the impression of something. He pointed out that when Lamb looked at him, Lamb saw something more than glasses, a nose and a mouth. He saw something that said "stubborn," "aggressive," and "I fight for the things I believe in, no matter what."

Around this time, Babbitt became better acquainted with the company's chief legal counsel, Gunther Lessing. Lessing was nearly fifty years old, stone bald, mustachioed, and impeccably dressed in a three-piece suit. He had worked for Walt since 1928 or 1929 and had a successful career as a Texas lawyer beforehand. He often recounted his days representing Pancho Villa during the Mexican Revolution. Babbitt sought Lessing out for legal and personal advice, and the two became friendly, even exchanging dinner invitations to each other's homes. Lessing may have genuinely liked Babbitt. He also may have seen Babbitt as a convenient go-between with production staff.

Animating at the Disney studio could be grueling. There was a constant striving for excellence, and drawing did not always come easily. The animators spent hours at their desks, squinting through the light behind their animation discs, struggling to get each drawing perfect. Every blank page brought with it infinite possibilities. "Occasionally," said Walt in 1935, "one [animator] will have an off day on which he can't draw anything worthwhile. Then he has to be pampered and pulled out of his slump with all the diplomacy that would be used on a [movie] star."

The animators had ways of working through their animator's block, blowing off steam during lunchtime on the studio lot. They tossed film canister lids like Frisbees, played volleyball, or rehearsed in Pinto Colvig's marching band. They threw painted animation cels onto the linoleum floor and slid across them like ice skaters, or they played darts by throwing pushpins against storyboard corkboards. Babbitt preferred to be an observer, never competing and no longer participating in the band. He would often spend his weekend hours off work trekking in his outdoorsman's jacket, camping, hiking, or canoeing in the hills of California. Sometimes he went with his friends Les Clark and Bill Tytla. Other times he took a female companion for an intimate rendezvous.

A small enclave of Disney men was fond of polo, and Walt and Roy enlisted some staff to join their team and mingle with Hollywood royalty like Will Rogers. Babbitt and Tytla were invited to Rogers' ranch to sketch him for an upcoming cartoon, *Mickey's Polo Team*.

But for Walt, the shorts were only stepping stones toward *Snow White and the Seven Dwarfs*, which was still in production limbo. He wanted to ensure its success. Forty-five percent of his cartoon distribution went to Europe. A European visit might indicate how well *Snow White* would run overseas, so that summer, Walt, Roy, and their wives took a grand tour of Europe. In Paris something unexpected caught Walt's attention. Cartoon shorts had always been used for filler in every movie theater program, but one theater played an afternoon of Disney cartoons at a single run, and audiences were paying for tickets. Walt's confidence was assured, and he sailed for home on July 24, 1935, ready to resume work on *Snow White*.

While Walt was away, director Dave Hand was the creative supervisor of the studio. Because of his height and broad chest, some of the fellows called him "Shoulders." It fit his style. He strove to inject a military-like structure into the studio—not an easy feat among the loose community of temperamental artists. Some animators considered him tough but fair. Babbitt called him "a boy scout."

Hand directed *Mickey's Polo Team* that summer. The lead animators were now given scenes according to their strengths, as actors might be cast in roles. Because of the Goof, Babbitt was now considered a specialist in bumbling characters. He also had excelled in animating caricatures of W. C. Fields and

Zasu Pitts in the short *Broken Toys*. It was a natural choice to have Babbitt animate Laurel and Hardy climbing onto their polo horses. Dave Hand planned the sequence to take up only a small portion of screen time and thus very little space on the exposure sheets.

A Disney animator was expected to complete about five seconds of footage a week. With twelve to twenty-four drawings per second, per character—not including pencil test do-overs and sweatbox notes—this was already fairly tight. For an animation director, especially one as organized as Hand, precise planning was of the utmost importance. Hand used a stopwatch to time each scene, half-second by half-second. Once the timing was settled, the animator would pick up the scenes from Hand's music room. Hand and the animator would discuss the scenes, making any changes then, until both were on the same page.

Babbitt didn't often ask for changes in a director's room. He simply sat his animation desk working on his Laurel and Hardy scenes, ballooning their length far beyond Hand's allotment. Scene 17—a moment of Laurel help-ing Hardy onto his horse—expanded to 17, 17a, and 17b, tripling in length. Scene 18 doubled. Scenes 19 and 20 tripled. By the time the animation was completed, Babbitt had contributed more animation to the cartoon than any other animator.

Babbitt had ignored the director's exposure sheet and padded his sequence yet again. But it was excellent work. The caricatures of Laurel and Hardy appear not only to move like them but also to think like them, and he'd transferred the same behavior into their horses, all with perfect pantomime.

Hand was furious. His protocols had been completely ignored. However, Walt was pleased, and his opinion was the one that mattered. Padded or not, Babbitt's animation stole the show.

In August 1935 Roy Disney asked the Bank of America for a loan to make a feature-length cartoon. He budgeted $250,000—ten times the cost of a short cartoon. The bank president, "Doc" Amadeo Giannini, granted the loan.

Roy and Walt made it known throughout the studio about the loans they took out, traveling down the line like all studio gossip. The company's financial risk was no secret, and everyone's contribution was crucial if the company was going to survive this endeavor.

Every month, as more Disney artists dedicated time to *Snow White*, the studio needed hands to complete the short subjects. Studio debt was skyrocketing as Walt demanded the hiring of three hundred more artists.

One of them was a Dr. Boris V. Morkovin, a Russian-born professor of film studies from the University of Southern California. With a wide smile and broken English, Morkovin stiffly lectured the men on the elements of humor. He analyzed the different types of jokes in a cartoon, categorizing them and charting them on graphs. Behind his back, the animators mocked him as a blowhard, and Babbitt drew a caricature of him as a big-headed dimwit. Still, the Disney studio was looking more and more like a graduate school.

But there was more to learn. Babbitt had bought a small movie camera, another expensive luxury item, as a lark. Then he hit upon a momentous notion: a movie camera could be a valuable teaching tool.

In the fall of 1935 director Ben Sharpsteen gave Babbitt another sequence with the Goof in the cartoon *Moving Day*. In his scenes, Goofy had to move a piano. Babbitt asked Pinto Colvig, with his circus clown experience, to pantomime Goofy's movements for his movie camera. Putting on his best "cornfed hick" performance, Colvig modeled Goofy's gangly-legged walk and his frustrated stomp for Babbitt's camera. When he was through, Babbitt watched the footage on his own 16mm viewer, one frame at a time, through its two-inch aperture. There were subtleties Babbitt saw in frame-by-frame analysis that he had never seen before. In fact, no animator had ever seen it before; Babbitt had filmed animation's first live-action reference. Studying Colvig's action frame by frame, he was shocked to find that real life sometimes violated the animation principles that animators had taken for granted.

He shared his discovery with the head of the Disney art school, Don Graham. Graham was captivated and overnight began integrating frame-by-frame film analysis in his evening classes at Disney. Graham called this overall study "Action Analysis," and in late October he began holding Action Analysis classes every Thursday night. The animators studied the way humans and animals moved, the way glass broke, the way fabric flowed, the way Charlie Chaplin anticipated his own action with a clearly readable gesture. (Walt noticed that the animators' favorite action was that of a beautiful female model disrobing.)

"Animation is based on caricature because it is based on good drawing, and good drawing is based on caricature," Graham lectured. It was essential to differentiate artistry from simply tracing live action, or rotoscoping. "The rotoscope is a crutch, and any way one looks at it, the reason for its existence is that the draftsmen in the Studio are weak. . . . Caricature must be the expression of an artist." Babbitt would eventually rue how right Graham actually was.

Meanwhile, in meeting after meeting, Walt and his top staff chiseled away at the visual script of *Snow White*. They sat in the music rooms with hundreds of storyboard panels on giant corkboards, figuring out the best cinematic way to present this film. Gag submissions came in throughout the studio. Dave Hand was enlisted as head director of the film.

Hand and the sequence directors, including Wilfred Jackson and Ben Sharpsteen, had narrowed down a list of dozens of possible dwarfs to seven. Character designs were discarded and replaced, then discarded again. All the while, more employees were rolling in.

When Harold "Hal" Adelquist had joined Disney as a Production Department office boy in mid-1934, Babbitt was one of the first people he met. Adelquist ran errands for six months before he was promoted to the Checking Department in 1935. There, he checked the serial numbers of all the productions on all the paperwork before it went out to the different departments. Adelquist was among the guests at Babbitt's Tuxedo Terrace soirees.

Adelquist's sweetheart (later wife) was a friend of young Marjorie Belcher, the model for Snow White. One evening, after a night out, the Adelquists were walking together with Marge down Hollywood Boulevard when they ran into Babbitt. Marge and Babbitt were introduced there, and Babbitt invited them all up to his house.

Babbitt was deeply intrigued by Marge. She possessed the kind of discipline that Babbitt himself cultivated. However, Babbitt had earned his through hardship brought on by his father's disability; Marge had earned hers through her father's love and guidance.

During Marge's next scheduled trip to the studio, Babbitt visited her on the soundstage. With his movie camera in hand, he filmed her dressed in her princess costume, pantomiming to invisible dwarfs. She responded by putting her thumbs up to her head and wiggling her fingers at him.

Image of Marge as Snow White wiggling her fingers at Babbitt.

Shortly thereafter, Babbitt and Les Clark took the movie camera to a Main Street burlesque house. In between dancing girls and stripteases, physical comedian Eddie Collins took the stage. At fifty-two years old, roly-poly, and dressed in baggy clothes, he moved like a graceful flour sack. Babbitt's camera started whirring. Collins was a perfect reference for the dwarfs. Soon a bouncer caught on to the camera's noise and threw the two animators out the door. But Babbitt had his footage of Collins and presented it to *Snow White*'s supervisors.

While the reference film of Marge would be carefully followed, the footage of Collins was interpreted and caricatured. The animators watched Collins move in slow motion, frame by frame. They could analyze the action of his round body and baggy clothes and then apply those discoveries to how the dwarfs moved. Babbitt had discovered a whole new approach to animation. A breakthrough had been made.

12 | BIOFF STAKES HIS CLAIM

IN JANUARY 1935 TOMMY MALOY was a successful Chicago union racketeer. The press called him a "film union czar." Since 1916 he had been running the IATSE Chicago Projectionists' Union, Local 110, while receiving kickbacks from theater owners to ensure that the projectionists didn't strike. When approached by George Browne for a possible collaboration, he flatly refused. He did not need Browne or his Capone cronies to take a cut.

On the morning of February 4, 1935, Maloy was driving to work when his car was showered with deadly machine-gun fire. A week later, Browne took over Local 110. Other heads of IATSE locals took notice, and IATSE allegiance continued to grow.

Clyde Osterberg, at thirty-two, was the organizer of a brand-new Independent Union of Motion Picture Operators in Chicago. He detested the IATSE and refused to have any dealings with them. In early April, Willie Bioff met him in Browne's office. "Start a new union," warned Bioff, "and we'll make an example of you." Osterberg refused to concede. Then on the night of May 13, he, his wife, and his bodyguard left a friend's home. They were standing on the street corner when a car pulled up and a gunman shot Osterberg in the elbow and chest. Osterberg fell, and the gunman fired two bullets into Osterberg's head and drove off into the night.

Louis Alterie was the head of the Theatrical Janitors' Union in Chicago. A forty-three-year-old loudmouthed gangster, he began talking about expanding his enterprise. His officials boasted that they were going to go after the moving picture unions, into the IATSE's territory. "It looks mighty good," they said.

On the morning of July 18, as Alterie walked from his apartment building to his car at the curb, an ambush of gunfire riddled his body. The shots were fired from a building across the street, with the killers abandoning their weapons at the scene. Willie Bioff was questioned, but without hard evidence, the police set him free.

———————

On the West Coast, union membership had been climbing. Labor unrest was rampant in Hollywood and showed no sign of slowing down. The federal government had a new policy on the table called the National Labor Relations Act, set to take effect in early July. Commonly known as the Wagner Act, this statute promised to empower unions and union members, protecting their jobs and their right to organize without threats of being blacklisted.

Many Americans objected to the president's "New Deal" and its new laws. Citizens challenged the extent of federal power that Roosevelt assumed. Newspaper magnate William Randolph Hearst instructed his papers to denigrate the New Deal. Wealthy Democratic industrialists had abandoned their party to form an anti–New Deal organization dubbed the American Liberty League. Journalist Westbrook Pegler, the loudest pundit in all of right-wing media, trashed the New Deal and labor unions in his syndicated newspaper column.

The dispute peaked on May 27, 1935, when the US Supreme Court ruled that the National Industrial Recovery Act and the National Recovery Administration, two pillars of the New Deal, were both unconstitutional. The court was ideologically split, with four conservative justices, three liberal justices, and two who were middle-of-the-road. The average age of the justices was seventy-one years. Millions of Americans protested this apparent gerontocracy. President Roosevelt voiced his frustration to the press, calling the stalwart Supreme Court justices "nine old men." The phrase caught on, and soon the public mocked the Supreme Court as Roosevelt's "Nine Old Men."

By the end of the summer, the Chicago-based IATSE controlled projectionist unions as far as Pittsburgh and Newark. Now Willie Bioff and George Browne tackled New York City. They ordered a projectionists' strike in all New York theaters owned by Loew's and RKO Pictures. The presidents of Loew's and RKO, Nicholas Schenck and Leslie Thompson, agreed to meet with Bioff and Browne. At the meetings, monitored by Capone henchman Nick Circella, Bioff and Browne called off the strike and signed seven-year contracts with RKO and Loew's that included a no-strike clause. In exchange, the presidents paid Bioff and Browne $150,000.

In December 1935 the IATSE forced the movie studios it influenced to agree to closed shops. In a closed shop, employers are only permitted to hire union members. Meant to strengthen a union, this gave IATSE greater control over its theaters and studios. If non–union members wished to keep their jobs, they were forced to sign with the IATSE and pay union dues. For a worker, it was more attractive to sign with the bigger union than with the smaller, so workers tended to sign with the IATSE.

Bioff and Browne gradually began increasing the fees for IATSE union dues. They added an initiation fee for new members. In December they instituted a 2 percent tax on every paycheck—called the "2% assessment"—and never disclosed to the members where these funds were channeled. The members complained, with no resolution. If the stagehands and projectionists stopped paying dues, their union memberships would be relinquished, and they would be out of work. In a Depression-era economy, anything was better than being unemployed.

On April 25, 1936, at a secluded table in Hollywood, representatives both from the smaller studios of RKO and Columbia, as well as the titans of Paramount, Fox, Warner Bros., and MGM, sat opposite Willie Bioff, George Browne, and Nick Circella. The studios desired assurance that their electricians, carpenters, lab technicians, property workers, grips, and non-first-unit cameramen would not go on strike. A strike would cost each studio hundreds of thousands of dollars.

Browne and Bioff, who now controlled some twelve thousand workers, wanted a substantial kickback. After a negotiation, the producers signed a Basic Studio Agreement. Collectively, they would pay IATSE $500,000 over two years to prevent any strikes. It was by far the fattest contract Bioff and Browne had ever received.

Browne returned to his headquarters in Chicago. Bioff, however, stayed in Hollywood. That's where most of the business was, and that's what he wanted to control.

13 | A DRUNKEN MOUSE

STARTING IN SEPTEMBER 1935 the Disney studio began constructing a building across the street from the main gates, at 2710 Hyperion Avenue. It was called the studio's annex, and it would replace the bullpen as the place for new hires to try out their inbetweening skills. It was also the newly designated place for Don Graham's art classes. When the annex was finally complete in November, it bore a facetious sign above the door: DON GRAHAM MEMORIAL INSTITUTE. (Graham was very much alive.) Beneath that was inscribed SEMPER GLUTEUS MAXIMUS, or as the animators translated, "Always Your Ass."

Besides classes in figure drawing and action analysis, the studio scheduled lectures in the elements of cartoon-making. The Disney animators were so advanced that literally no animation experts outside the studio could meet their needs. Therefore, they began to hold formal lectures for each other.

On November 27 Walt addressed a group of story artists, animators, and a stenographer. "Now that you have attended two lectures on the personality, continuity, technique, et cetera, of the animated cartoon," he said, "we got the happy idea that—before going any further—we would put these lectures to some practical use by applying this new knowledge to a story."

Beside Walt stood Dr. Morkovin and the head story man of the next cartoon (soon to be called *The Country Cousin*), Dick Rickard. Walt, director Wilfred Jackson, and the story team had been working on a new cartoon based on "The City Mouse and the Country Mouse" children's story. Several artists sat before Walt that day, including some of the art-school graduates who had sprinted up the ranks.

Dr. Morkovin lectured about comedy in the cartoon, and Rickard discussed the story. In it, the Country Mouse visits the City Mouse's opulent home, gets drunk on champagne, kicks the housecat, and flees back to the country. The artists made their comments. Babbitt scribbled down their suggestions with his pencil, noting who offered each idea.

Babbitt was silent at the meeting. His $1.29 civil court case against the hardware store had been dismissed. But the outcome hardly seemed relevant anymore. The lawsuit itself strengthened Babbitt's reputation as the studio's man of principle.

Walt continued expanding his art school with film presentations. He rented theater space in North Hollywood, and every Wednesday night he presented a movie to stimulate creative growth. As per the rule, the front two rows were reserved for supervisors and directors. The other artists would dare not sit in one of these seats, even if an entire row was vacant.

The screenings included everything from Charlie Chaplin comedies and Fred Astaire musicals to masterpieces of German expressionism like *Nosferatu*. One unfortunate night, an underwater nature documentary was shown, which displayed one large aquatic specimen with a vertical slit and pink, labia-like folds. The Disney artists began chuckling as the folds slowly opened. When the folds had fully spread apart, the room was filled with uncontrollable laughter. Walt was fuming; he immediately terminated the Wednesday night screenings.

Friday night's figure-drawing class was exclusively for supervising animators. During one such class in December 1935, Bill Tytla paid particular attention to the brunette model.

The models of Doris Harmon's Southern California Modeling Club fought for Disney modeling jobs. They had an eye for the young men at Disney. Babbitt had already had a relationship with the model Sändra Stark, and she told her fellow model, Adrienne le Clerc, of Babbitt's attractive friend and housemate. He was also a supervising animator and a "wild Russian." Adrienne requested the Friday night slot so she could see him for herself.

The two were lovestruck. A romance between the artist and the model was born.

For several weeks, Bill and Adrienne were inseparable. On Sunday afternoons, they arrived at the house on Tuxedo Terrace with foodstuffs from a Japanese produce stand. But the home was now filled with the sound of

Babbitt's amateur piano playing, banging out *Moonlight Sonata* on the living room's baby grand.

Babbitt was managing his emotions as best he could. It was not only that Babbitt was single and Tytla wasn't. He was also silently grieving the death of his father, Solomon Babitzky, who died on January 17 at age fifty-eight. Babbitt never joined Bill and Adrienne for dinner, instead opting to leave them and return on his own time.

It would have been easier to avoid them if his room had a separate entrance, as Tytla's did out back. To have his own secret door, like the speakeasies of his youth, would have been the ultimate convenience.

The first animation for the seven dwarfs had been assigned right before Christmas 1935, and the first animation of Snow White herself began in January 1936. Walt made good on his promise to Babbitt and assigned him a major section: supervising animation for the Wicked Queen, in addition to animating some Dopey scenes. Fred Moore and Bill Tytla would supervise the dwarfs' animation. Norm Ferguson would animate the villain as an old hag. Woolie Reitherman would handle the Magic Mirror, a relatively minor assignment. He and the other art-school graduates shared most of the smaller roles, with perhaps the biggest among them going to Frank Thomas, who had to animate the dwarfs mourning the recumbent princess.

Walt insisted on perfecting each sequence with the director and supervisors until it was ready. He didn't seem concerned that time was money. More than once, Roy walked in on Walt with director Dave Hand, complaining that they were overspending. Walt responded sharply, "Roy, *we'll* make the pictures, *you* get the money. Now goodbye, I'm busy."

As sequences for *Snow White* progressed through the Story Department, the animators kept busy on shorts. In early 1936 Babbitt completed much of his Goofy animation for *Moving Day*. Woolie Reitherman animated most of the Peg-Leg Pete scenes in the cartoon.

When Babbitt previewed his test animation at the studio, he was surprised by the reaction—it was how Goofy expressed his emotions that got the biggest laughs, and not the gags themselves. Personality had proven to overshadow the slapstick.

Like Goofy's physicality, Babbitt made his own physical health a public affair. He regularly promoted pop health science. For a period, he preached the benefits of eye exercises to strengthen one's vision. One week he wouldn't stop expounding on the benefits of hydration and pure drinking water. Fortunately for him, every animator's room had its own Sparkletts water cooler. One afternoon, as Babbitt confidently drank from his cooler, he suddenly saw three live fish surface from its shadowy depths. Babbitt spat and raised hell, but the prankster wisely never came forward.

Now that the studio's education initiative was underway, lead animators were scheduled to attend story meetings and sweatbox sessions for all the shorts. On February 5, 1936, Babbitt and Les Clark sat in a story meeting with writers and directors (and a stenographer) for the cartoon starring Abner, the country mouse, and Monty, the city mouse. They were talking about the climax, in which the mouse breaks a porcelain china cat, when Babbitt interjected, "In the opening of the picture, when the mouse knocks on the door, instead of Monty coming out and shushing him, why couldn't Monty have his own little door made of brick? Have it open up like a speakeasy door."

The writers hadn't intended on giving the mouse his own door. "We would like to avoid such things," said head story man Dick Rickard. "We didn't want to give the impression that Monty had his own house. . . . I don't like the idea."

That closed the topic. Discussion shifted and Babbitt spoke up again.

"I would like to see the first part of the china cat taken out," he said. "It has no value. You are trying to build up the fact that Abner imitates his city cousin but there should be some other reason for Abner disturbing the real cat. The idea is too forced."

The story men stood by their script. "I think the idea is good because Abner is drunk," Ted Sears said.

"I like the idea," said Ben Sharpsteen.

The topic changed once again, and the meeting continued for another twenty minutes.

Though unanimously spurning Babbitt's ideas outright, the story team realized that Babbitt was right and incorporated his ideas in the end. Babbitt was no longer merely an animator. He was now a member of Walt Disney's creative elite.

On the morning of March 17, 1936 (twelve days after accepting an Academy Award for *Three Orphan Kittens*, directed by Dave Hand), Walt participated in a story conference for the City Mouse–Country Mouse cartoon. The topic was Abner the Country Mouse's encounter with a glass of champagne. Babbitt attended the conference as well.

"We see him drinking," said Walt. "He is making a lot of noise. Get a quick cut to Monty—just a flash—then back to Abner and how he is right in the glass. The last thing he does is to suck the champagne right from the bottom of the empty stem. Get a big 'hic!' from him."

Babbitt spoke next. "When he tries to get out of the glass he could get to the very rim, only to slip and go down into the stem."

"I don't see the mouse that small," Walt said. Then he suggested, "Get a sound of a sink emptying when Abner is sucking up the champagne!"

The two were on a roll now, and for the next several minutes, Walt and Babbitt riffed, building on ideas for drunken Abner and the wineglass.

Every day Walt gauged the progress of *Snow White*, and there were not enough hands to finish it by its deadline on Christmas 1937. The studio needed hundreds of new artists, and each of them required several weeks of training. Ads for Disney jobs started appearing in newspapers in February, and soon young people across the country began applying. Art instructor Don Graham and inbetweening supervisor George Drake left Hollywood on March 19, 1936, for a two-month hiring spree at Disney's Manhattan recruitment office.

Near the end of March, Babbitt walked to director Wilfred Jackson's music room and picked up his animation assignment for the City Mouse–Country Mouse cartoon. Babbitt and his friend Les Clark were assigned the two largest sequences: Clark would handle most of Monty the City Mouse, and Babbitt would animate drunken Abner. This was a chance to show real comedy and pantomime through a character's personality and thought process.

Walt found Babbitt in Jackson's room picking up the assignment. Walt told him that he hoped Babbitt would do as good a job as he did on *Moving*

Day. With a straight face, Babbitt replied that he'd try, but he was going to need a research fund for this assignment.

Walt's face hardened. He demanded what Babbitt meant by a "research fund." The front office was already complaining about expenses!

"If I'm going to do a drunken mouse," said Babbitt, "I ought to know what it feels like to have alcohol in my system."

Walt stood there, raising one eyebrow and lowering the other—then left the room without another word. Babbitt wasn't sure if Walt got the joke.

As Babbitt began animating, he struggled with himself. He was among the top animators of the studio—and therefore, of the entire industry—yet he felt his work on Abner was falling short in many ways.

Like his character analysis of Goofy, Babbitt inserted himself into the psyche of the cartoon mouse. "The important thing in analyzing a scene when you pick it up," he told others then, "is first of all to know your character. The drawing should mean something to you—a certain definite personality. You try to make yourself feel the way that character would feel under the same circumstances, and you try to think as he would think. Your animated figures must think. If they don't, they will go static."

He put his pencil to his paper and began to draw.

Drawing of drunken Abner in the wineglass from
The Country Cousin. © *The Walt Disney Company*

14 | DISNEY'S FOLLY

IN THE LOCAL RESTAURANT during lunch, Marjorie Belcher sat with Babbitt and the other animators. As a parlor trick, Babbitt would sometimes hypnotize on command. Marge dared him to try it on her. As much as he tried, his powers of hypnosis were useless on her. She merely laughed.

A generous new policy went into effect on April 1, 1936. It was known around the front office as "Adjusted Compensation," but the animators called it the "Bonus Plan." According to this new incentivizing system, all animation would be rated. Work that was merely excellent earned an A-minus. Work that was excellent *and* innovative earned an A. Directors would award all the grades, and Walt would sign off on them. The grade, plus an amount of profit from the short, would merit a cash reward.

The staff may have been skeptical at first, but within the first week, the bonuses were distributed. On April 7 Babbitt received a lump sum beyond any previous bonus. His grade A work for *On Ice, Broken Toys*, and *Mickey's Polo Team* earned him $958.00.

It hardly mattered that the metrics for determining the amount remained confidential, that only management knew the criteria. It was unlikely this idea came from Roy, who tried to conserve costs at every turn. Rather, it had all the trappings of someone who wanted to control others without claiming accountability, a strategy used by the chief legal counsel and now senior vice president, Gunther Lessing.

A new Mickey Mouse cartoon called *Mickey's Amateurs* was in the story phase. Mickey would host a radio program for amateur performers. The plot was a string of clownish musical gags—perfect for the musical clown in the writer's room, Pinto Colvig, to codirect. The finale would be Goofy as a one-man band, just like Art Babbitt's brother Ike. Colvig would voice the character, Babbitt would animate him, and Goofy would play a clarinet (and many other instruments) in full bandleader regalia. Goofy had to march on stage and twirl his baton. For reference, Babbitt filmed an attractive majorette marching and twirling a baton in the studio parking lot.

While Babbitt conducted his own action analysis with his camera, the studio pushed on with its Thursday night Action Analysis class. Topics now ranged from "Anticipation" to "Color Composition" to "How to Maintain Interest in a Spectator." Speakers included Dave Hand, Don Graham, and Dr. Morkovin. But this art school wasn't cheap to maintain, and neither were the constant pencil tests and reworking of scenes. Roy and Walt openly bemoaned the studio's mounting expenses. In May 1936 Roy negotiated with the Bank of America to increase their loan from $250,000 to $630,000.

The bank was reluctant. Hollywood was skeptical about whether audiences would sit still for a feature-length cartoon. *Snow White and the Seven Dwarfs* was being called "Disney's folly" around town. Many of the bank's contacts in Hollywood discouraged them from sinking any more money into *Snow White*. Walt's employees knew the risk and took their chances.

However, one did not. That spring, Babbitt's friend Hardie Gramatky left Disney to pursue his dream as an independent artist in New York. Around that time, Tytla moved out to cohabitate with Adrienne. Babbitt's relationship with his friend Hal Adelquist had changed too. The one-time errand boy who had introduced Babbitt to Marge was promoted to assistant director of *Snow White* around June. He was now the eyes and ears of director Dave Hand.

Babbitt's animation on the shorts had become among the most praised in the field. When *Moving Day* premiered on June 20, 1936, it was a hit with audiences and animators alike. Babbitt imbued Goofy with a kind of new animation that excited the whole industry; Warner Bros. cartoon directors got hold of a copy and ran it frame by frame in their Moviola just to study it. As Babbitt completed his animation on the City Mouse–Country Mouse cartoon, now called *The Country Cousin*, he received his *Moving Day* bonus—a whopping $1,204.

On September 23, after returning from a New York vacation, Babbitt partici-pated in the studio's new Training Course Lecture Series, addressing the new inbetweeners and assistants.

"The animator must have innate fine taste and sensitivity," said Babbitt, encouraging them to use the whole of their experiences as creative influence. He then began discussing timing—how a director's notations were to be followed closely and scene-padding was absolutely prohibited. He held up an exposure sheet as an example—and it unfurled like a scroll, tumbling past his knees and onto the floor. The artists laughed—they knew Babbitt's reputation for padding.

"The animator must have a feeling for direction and not just follow orders," he said. As animators, you will have to be your own director too." He showed Goofy's walk from *Moving Day*, frame by frame, saying, "Later on when you know the basics, experiment once in a while, and try to break some rules. It's lots of fun and you will be surprised at some of the results you will get. It's fun breaking rules, anyway." Only Babbitt could weave into his lecture a treatise about insubordination.

He concluded with this message of integrity and hope, revealing the stu-dio's one-for-all mentality: "This business has been treated as a racket, by some people, to squeeze nickels out of it. But you can—with the aid of God, a fast infield, and the squelching of Hearst—create an art that will pay you handsomely in nice great big dollars—unless we go broke in the meantime." Like a ship of explorers, they would either share in *Snow White*'s rewards or sink together.

That October, Walt and the filmmakers watched the preview of *The Country Cousin* from the back of the Alexander Theatre. It was another hit. The two mice, without any dialogue, achieved perfect acting, rich in personality.

Walt and the creative team gathered outside to debrief. Nearly everything about the cartoon was flawless, and Babbitt was able to pull off a drunken mouse, even without his proposed "research fund."

There was a twinkle in Walt's eye. He hadn't forgotten. "Hey Art," he said as the group dispersed, "how 'bout a cocktail?"

Babbitt paused, meeting Walt's smile with his own. "No thanks," he retorted, "I've got a date with a blonde."

Production Schedule for *The Country Cousin*

	1935					1936									
	Aug	Sept	Oct	Nov	Dec	Jan	Feb	Mar	Apr	May	Jun	Jul	Aug	Sept	Oct
Conceptualization	■	■	■	■											
Story					■	■	■	■	■						
Animation									■	■	■				
Cleanup											■	■	■		
Ink & Paint, Camera													■	■	
Technicolor															■
Premiere															■

Conceptualization: August 8–November 31, 1935
Story: December 2, 1935–circa April 2, 1936
Animation: April 3–circa June 30, 1936
Cleanup: May 29–circa August 14, 1936

Ink & Paint, Camera: circa August 14–circa September 30, 1936
Technicolor: October 2, 1936
Premiere: October 31, 1936

The information on this chart is derived from existing records from the Walt Disney company. It has been checked for accuracy by J. B. Kaufman.

Babbitt was kidding—she wasn't blonde. But he wasn't about to tell his boss he was dating Marjorie Belcher.

––––––––––

After *The Country Cousin* officially premiered on October 31, 1936, Babbitt received a memo. His work on it was graded "A1, 100%." And just like with *Moving Day*, animators across Hollywood studied it frame by frame. Soon, *The Country Cousin* was called "the Studio's tour de force. For mastery of animation, apart from technical ingenuity, a point was reached that has never been surpassed." For Walt, the cartoon indicated to him that his animators could now tackle the seven dwarfs.

For *The Country Cousin* alone, Babbitt received a bonus check for $1,201.00. He also put in his first request for a raise, from his $150 per week to $200 starting December 7. An additional clause in this new contract about the adjusted compensation for exemplary work suggested the bonus plan would complement his salary. But even in print, the criteria for these bonuses remained a mystery.

Still, that was a minor detail in a friendly, family-owned company like Disney. If there was any doubt to Walt's affections, they were put to rest when he rented out the Barney Oldfield country club and hosted a staff-wide Christmas party.

Drinks flowed, and a live band played. Babbitt brought his movie camera with him and filmed his friends, including Marge. Walt sat at a table with his top men, laughing, smoking, and drinking. Babbitt put down his camera and found a cop who would go along with a prank. In a few minutes, an officer entered the country club and told Walt to keep it down, there were noise complaints. Walt laughed, pointed at the cop's chest, and told him he would "have his badge."

It was a last hurrah before the *Snow White* crunch, and what followed was harrowing. Walt scrapped two complicated sequences that were already in production: an argument between the dwarfs, and a bed-building sequence. Precious time and money were spent on them, but the studio could not afford to finish the film unless these sequences were abandoned. Babbitt's scenes remained intact.

On January 4, 1937, the first completed animation was delivered to Ink & Paint. Each inker was expected to trace thirty cels per day and each painter to complete seventeen cels a day. The first completed cels were scheduled for Final Camera by March 13. In all, *Snow White and the Seven Dwarfs* required 250,000 drawings to be animated, inked on cels, painted, and photographed—all by December.

While the Animation Department was crunching to accomplish this, the Story Department was in the clear. Obliviously, Pinto Colvig pushed his marching-band club. By February, Colvig had amassed an entire twenty-five-piece circus-style band of Disney employees, complete with uniforms. Colvig was eager for Walt's endorsement and informed his boss that he was "trying to find an hour each week for practice when some of the members weren't working or attending art classes." Walt couldn't believe that Colvig prioritized something so trivial when the fate of the studio hung in the balance.

Babbitt had been spending his off-hours with Marge. She observed the rules of propriety that governed her upbringing, including saving sex until marriage. Babbitt was patient and protective. He was prepared to settle down with her.

His evenings were often spent at home, where he had his own animation desk and worked on his craft in his spare time. It was getting competitive at the studio. Now Babbitt was one of 32 Disney animators, along with 102 assistants and 107 inbetweeners. To fit all the artists needed to finish the film, the studio was constructing yet another animation building on the lot.

Woolie Reitherman, Frank Thomas, and the other art-school graduates had become full-fledged animators too. When Reitherman completed animating the Magic Mirror, he naturally picked up assignments for short cartoons. Around late February director Ben Sharpsteen assigned him to supervise the Goofy animation in the cartoon *Hawaiian Holiday*. For the first time, a major Goofy segment was assigned to someone other than Babbitt, who had already established Goofy as a slow hick. Reitherman, an active sportsman with a love of airplanes, contemplated how he would surf a wave if he were inside Goofy looking out. With his pencil to his animation paper, he began to draw.

Meanwhile, Babbitt's working style had come back to bite him. He had once again padded his scenes, this time a Dopey sequence in *Snow White*. On March 3, with less than ten months before the premiere, director Dave Hand was not about to tolerate Babbitt's insubordination. He called a formal meeting to address it.

"Here is what I think—I am quite open with you," Hand said to Babbitt. They sat in screening room Sweatbox 4, flanked by two sequence directors (likely with assistant director Hal Adelquist) and a secretary taking stenographic notes. "I think you are going off in your corner and taking it upon yourself to present something in the sweatbox which is entirely out of the line, or away, from what we as directors have tried to follow through—from the story conferences into the sweatbox . . . as if, say, you were superior to the three of us working together and agreeing on one way of handling it. . . . We spent a lot of time with you, which we should do. It is our duty to do it in order to get the scene right. We spared nothing. We acted it out, timed it with a stopwatch, [and] had you agree to what we were talking about before you left the room or we wouldn't have let you leave. When you present it in the sweatbox, you have added footage without permission. You have not done the scene the way we say it."

Babbitt retorted: "Do you want to see the scene the way we laid it out? I did it just that way."

"Then it's your duty to come up and tell us we're not doing it right," said Hand. "You have got to work with us, to give us the kind of stuff we want—and the kind of stuff we are trying to follow through from Walt's angle. There is nothing personal in this. You have got to work with us or work by yourself. I can't work with you this way!"

"In the first place," said Babbitt, "you're wrong in assuming anybody is trying to get off in a corner by himself. That is the way I've always worked. When I see a thing and I know it's wrong, I take a stab at making it right. But in this instance, I tried to explain to you—I'm not making excuses—that these things weren't satisfactory to me, but I had to get them in. . . ."

"If you needed more time," said Hand, "you should have come up and gotten it, not misinterpreted the scene. It occurs in other scenes, too."

"I'll go up and get the exposure sheets and the test we did!" said Babbitt.

"We want to do that," said Hand, "but that has nothing to do with the point we're making. I've worked with a group of animators and directors and I see a condition that needs to be remedied. It's a bad condition, with one animator. Whose fault it is, we'll find out. But we must correct that condition.

That's my point. I bring it up directly to the animator in order to work out the differences and clear it up so you can be productive."

Babbitt responded, "Don't get the misunderstanding that anybody is working against you. The blame lies right with myself. I would like to say it wasn't my work, but it so happens that is the result gotten. I have done a lousy job and wanted to fix it."

Hand pointed out another of Babbitt's scenes in which he extended footage—when Snow White first terrifies Dopey. "I remember saying to you that the directness and shortness of speed of the scene were what made the comedy," said Hand. "I heard the same words repeated by Walt this morning—exactly what I told you. When I hear Walt speaking the words that we have spoken, well, a mistake is being made and I don't like it for the sake of the picture."

"I have the test and I will show it to you," Babbitt rebutted. "I animated it exactly in the time allotted."

"We went over it eight or ten times with a stopwatch and put it on the sheets!" said Hand. "I say directly that you didn't animate it properly. And that's my argument here. You are wasting time that we need badly to finish the picture."

Babbitt tried to interrupt with what he thought about it, but Hand jumped in.

"I don't care what you think," continued Hand. "I could go to Walt and say, 'That's just no good, get him off the picture!' My object is to line you up so you can move the stuff through—to help you so you can move it through properly. I like to allow an animator freedom on a scene, but now we find you're making mistakes in your direction. You mustn't go off into a corner. You mustn't use some of your ideas without talking them over with us. We'll drop it now," Hand concluded. "Anything we can do from our end of it—to help you or change our ways of working with you—we want to do it. And we'll be glad to do it. Think it over and come back and tell us what we can do to help you."

"Well," said Babbitt, "you might animate it for me!"

———

That evening, Babbitt donned his finest eveningwear as Walt's guest to the Academy Awards ceremony in the Biltmore Hotel banquet hall. Walt accepted the award for *The Country Cousin*. Babbitt, meanwhile, filmed the Hollywood glamour with his movie camera, pointing it at stars like Frank Capra, Jack Warner, W. C. Fields, and Cecil B. DeMille.

That night, he drove his car back to his new house, a home on Hill Oak Drive overlooking Hollywood. This house had a large dining room, a sizeable kitchen, and a living room with a fireplace and a baby grand piano. It was not the house of a playboy but of a committed sophisticate ready for the next step with Marge.

As their courtship blossomed, Babbitt shared his world with Marge. They went camping and skiing. They and the Adelquists went to the beaches of Santa Barbara. He took her to Red Rock Canyon to shoot skeet. He and Marge hosted brunch with their friends. It was a life and a love that excited them both.

In June, Walt Disney cut out another finished scene from *Snow White*, one with the dwarfs eating soup. For the sequence's animator, Ward Kimball, it was a punch in the gut.

But Walt's bank loans were drying up. The studio could not afford to produce the film with this sequence. From the initial proposed running time to this final cut, the animation in *Snow White* dropped from ninety-one minutes to seventy-eight.

As the film neared completion, sections were screened in-house. Because of his perfectionism, Babbitt felt his animation of the Queen was riddled with flaws. Others saw it as exemplary, recognizing the "depths of passion" that he bestowed on her.

His own passion came to fruition on August 8. With a princely $886 bonus check for *Mickey's Amateurs* cushioning his bank account, Art Babbitt and Marjorie Belcher were wed in Santa Barbara. Hal Adelquist was one of the groomsmen. (Two days later when Marge performed a ballet at the Redlands Bowl, rice and not flowers was thrown at her feet—to the bafflement of the general audience.)

Babbitt's Goofy animation was the highlight of *Mickey's Amateurs*, and it holds up as an exceptional one-man comic ballet. Nonetheless, Walt was unhappy with the story that Pinto Colvig assembled. It did not give the characters' personalities room to shine—and it made Donald Duck a

A frame of a home movie with Art and Marge Babbitt with the Adelquists on vacation. Hal Adelquist sits nearest to camera.

tommy-gun-wielding psychopath. In mid-August, Colvig wrote Walt a letter asking for a raise.

In Walt's words to Roy, "This crying attitude expressed in Pinto's letter is typical of him. He is very unreliable, and I do not need his voice for the Goof badly enough to tolerate him any longer. I am not going to renew his contract."

Soon, Pinto Colvig was gone from the Disney studio lot.

15 | DEFENSE AGAINST THE ENEMY

NEW YEAR'S DAY 1937 was approaching in Flint, Michigan, home to the largest automobile plant in the world. The city manufactured more than two million cars a year for General Motors, using enormous machine rooms that ran day and night. On the evening of December 30, 1936, thousands of workers walked into three Flint auto factories, carrying bags of food and clothing. They locked the doors from the inside, pulled the main switch, and stopped production. They held a sit-down indoors and refused to budge.

Auto plant workers were tired of suffering arduous work in concrete rooms that were either freezing or sweltering, depending on the weather, surrounded by thunderous machines. There was no paid overtime or job security. Trying to negotiate for better terms was a losing battle: a member of lower management would bargain on behalf of the workers to upper management. This "union leader" might claim he had the workers' best interests at heart when actually looking after the interests of the company. The General Motors workers demanded the right to be represented by the union of their choice—not by an in-house company union but by an independent, industry-wide union. They wanted the right to join the United Auto Workers.

From the windows of all three Flint factories, workers hooted and hollered. They waved protest signs and dangled effigies. Outside they were monitored by factory police, cheering supporters, and the press. Workers at General Motors plants in five other cities went on strike in sympathy. Supporters drove in to picket around the buildings and to shield them from factory police. By January 4, the sit-down had become a national headline.

General Motors refused to negotiate. They filed seeking a court injunction to force the strikers to leave, but the United Auto Workers discovered that the ruling judge owned shares of General Motors stock. The union sent its list of demands: union recognition, rates per day instead of per unit (called a "piece-work system"), grievance procedures, reinstatement of all those who had been fired for union activity, and a thirty-hour workweek. GM retaliated by shutting off the heat in the building. The sit-downers bundled up with the added layers their supporters and families pushed through the first-floor windows.

On the night of January 11, the factory policemen arrived wearing riot gear, bearing guns and tear gas. Those inside retaliated by making slingshots from inner tubes, flinging 1½-pound car door hinges. The fight lasted until dawn. Fourteen workers were injured by gunfire, and some were carried out in stretchers, but the sit-down continued.

As GM enlisted more militia, newsreels projected images of gas bombs and gun-wielding police. Never before had such a large corporation been shut down by its employees. The governor of Michigan requested a peaceful solution. President Roosevelt urged GM to accept the workers' terms.

Finally, on February 11, General Motors signed a one-page contract with the United Auto Workers union, affiliated under the Committee for Industrial Organization (CIO), granting employees the right to choose their union representation. The contract permitted union talk on employee downtime, and there would be no discrimination against union members. The victorious sit-downers marched outside to cheering crowds waving enormous American flags.

On the evening of March 9, 1937, President Roosevelt addressed the nation in one of his fireside chat radio broadcasts. After years of combating the unmoving Nine Old Men of the Supreme Court, the president described his plan to retire every judge over the age of seventy, as was customary in the military and civil service. Those who refused would receive a younger assistant with equal voting power. Detractors criticized Roosevelt for trying to "pack the court" with his own appointees, but by April the proposal was moot. The two swing-vote justices joined the three liberal judges. When the National Labor Relations Act was challenged, the Supreme Court ruled on April 12 to uphold it. American unions would be strengthened again.

Immediately after the ruling, some Hollywood labor leaders revived a dormant group of unions called the Federation of Motion Picture Crafts (FMPC). The FMPC had about sixteen thousand members. Most of them came from two large unions: the International Brotherhood of Painters, Decorators & Paperhangers Local 644, known colloquially as the Painters Union (which included set painters, scenic artists, makeup artists, and hairstylists), and the Studio Utility Employees Union (which covered roles such as carpenters, plumbers, boilermakers, and machinists).

However, if the FMPC was to thrive, it would have to simultaneously battle both the studio producers and its rival, the Bioff-held IATSE.

Hollywood producers were still participating in Bioff's schemes. In 1937 RKO and Loew's saved $3 million in labor costs by paying the IATSE $100,000—their share of the $500,000 kickback that all the studios had agreed to cough up. On top of that, Bioff and Browne were totaling $1.5 million on the "2% assessment" garnished from members' wages.

On April 30, 1937, the Painters Union and the Studio Utilities Employees Union went on strike, demanding union recognition and higher wages. One picket captain and Painters Union member was a tall, forty-year-old ex-boxer named Herbert K. Sorrell. He refused to be intimidated by the IATSE. First the IATSE bribed the strikers with free membership if they returned to work. Then the IATSE carpenters walked through their picket line. Within days, goons from Chicago arrived and began pushing nonstriking cinematographers across the picket lines. The IATSE enrolled the Teamsters Union to drive trucks of actors and technicians past the strikers, who retaliated by shoving the vehicles and shouting epithets. The Teamsters brought more goons from Los Angeles, so Sorrell brought in local longshoremen and industrial laborers. Physical altercations turned bloody, and violence spread from the picket line to the local IATSE office, where ex-strikers were pummeled.

On May 21, the FMPC's Studio Utilities Employees caved. The IATSE arranged to get them an 11 percent pay raise to break the strike. The FMPC Painters now stood alone on the picket line. As they held their ground, painter unions around the country picketed in sympathy and spread boycotts. In early June, IATSE offered the Painters Union a 10 percent raise and closed-shop status if members returned to work and signed with them. The strikers voted unanimously against.

Finally, on June 14, the studios surrendered and signed with the FMPC Painters. Its members earned a contract and a 15 percent salary increase and became the first local union to be granted closed-shop status. There were resounding cheers of victory. It had been Hollywood's largest labor strike up to that time, and this monumental win left a lasting impression on filmmakers and animators alike.

Bioff, however, considered it a missed opportunity. Perhaps the few crafts under IATSE jurisdiction—the stagehands and projectionists—were too limited. He began formulating a plan to expand his enterprise.

During that same time in New York City, nearly a hundred animation artists at the Fleischer Studios went on strike. The men and women who drew Popeye and Betty Boop filled Broadway with illustrated signs demanding higher pay and union recognition. It was the first strike at an animation studio and lasted from May 7 through October 12. In the end, the seventy-five strikers won a union contract. They returned to work with wage increases, a forty-hour workweek, paid vacation, sick leave, overtime pay, and a bargaining agent to represent them.

The ripples of the successful Fleischer strike reached Hollywood, where the Warner Bros. animators drew Porky Pig and a daffy, darn-fool duck. They signed up with a new independent union in Hollywood that had formed that fall. Called the Screen Cartoon Guild, it was run by animators and attested to be "the only bona fide organization representing all of the studios in the Animated Cartoon Industry."

By September Roy Disney was at the end of his rope. Even with the additional loans, the studio had gone way over budget on Snow White. Roy lamented to Walt that there was no choice but to ask the Bank of America for an additional $327,000. They'd both meet a representative at the studio, he said, and together make their request as they presented a scrappy, work-in-progress reel of Snow White.

Walt would recount the event years later with a storyteller's flair: at the designated time, Roy wasn't there. Walt sat in the studio projection room with young banker Joe Rosenberg and screened the unfinished reel. When it was over, Walt walked Rosenberg to his car, unsure if the loan was secured. Once in his car, Rosenberg turned to Walt one final time, told him the film was going to make a heck of a lot of money, and drove off.

Walt stood there alone, sighing with relief.

Walt had big plans if *Snow White* turned out to be a success. The Story Department had already started preproduction work on two more animated features: *Bambi* and *Pinocchio*. There was also talk of animating a Mickey Mouse cartoon to Paul Dukas's music of "The Sorcerer's Apprentice." But these ideas meant nothing if *Snow White* failed. To hundreds of the artists, their jobs rested on this gamble. "There would be all kinds of opportunity if *Snow White* was a success," remembered one artist, who added, "I'm sure those voices of doom haunted the people working with a frenzy to complete *Snow White* in time for the grand première before Christmas."

Snow White was still far from complete. On October 15 the staff learned that their 8:30 AM–5:30 PM weekday work hours now extended from 7:30 AM to 6 PM, with no paid overtime. It was no secret that Walt promised his workers reimbursement bonuses after the film recouped its cost. Soon the artists were extending their Saturday hours for no pay, and many worked Sundays as well.

In the weeks before its premiere, the Disney artists were working "night and day." One frazzled artist painted a watercolor sketch transforming the dwarfs' bedroom into a torture chamber, with an exhausted animator sprawled in a corner and Walt, in his pajamas, praying on his knees with his hands clasped, "Please God, send me an animator who can work twenty-four hours a day." In the studio hung the air of a collective nervous breakdown. A sign outside the writers' room said, IT WAS FUNNY WHEN IT LEFT HERE. For a week, stressed animators swapped doodles of the characters in a full-blown orgy.

Finally, on November 11, the animation for the film was complete. The inkers, painters, and camera operators raced against the December 1 deadline. It would then take more than two weeks to process and distribute the film before its December 21 premiere.

It happened one morning in early December 1937. Art Babbitt was walking through the studio when suddenly he was buttonholed by Dave Hilberman, Bill Tytla's assistant. Hilberman had started at the studio in July during the influx of new talent. Knowing Babbitt's reputation for being staunchly principled, Hilberman showed him a page from *Time* magazine.

The article concerned mobster Willie Bioff and the IATSE. Apparently, Bioff—described as a South Side gunman and bodyguard for George Browne— was seeking to enroll all Hollywood crafts. Bioff blamed industry corruption on Communist interference, calling his detractors Communists too. The representative from the Carpenters Union (which succumbed to the IATSE during the FMPC strike) warned the public: "You've no more chance of doing any good in this situation than a snowball in hell."

Babbitt took the magazine and headed toward management. He found the production control manager and head of the camera department, Bill Garity, who told Babbitt that an IATSE group had already visited the studio. He suggested Babbitt "cook up something" to enroll Disney employees before the IATSE did.

With that, Babbitt went to Roy Disney, who pointed Babbitt next door to the office of Gunther Lessing, the company's chief legal counsel and the senior vice president. Lessing read the article, listened to Babbitt, and suggested a nonofficial, social organization. He offered Babbitt his professional services, as well as the studio's space and resources. Lessing also handed Babbitt a book about unions, designating a couple of chapters for him to read.

"I knew nothing about unions and really stepped into this," Babbitt said in 1942. He read the book cover to cover.

Later that week Babbitt sat at his desk and listed thirty-five artists across the studio to invite to his first committee meeting. He took the list to a music room secretary to be typed, and she handed it off to the Copy Department that day. When the Copy Department returned it to her through interoffice mail, she called the Traffic Department, and an errand boy delivered a copy to each name in the memo. It read, "A very important meeting affecting everyone listed is to be held in Sweatbox #4 at 4:30 today, Friday. Please be present and don't worry."

By phone, Babbitt also invited Gunther Lessing.

That afternoon, thirty-five employees from every department sat in the projection room, including Hal Adelquist and supervising animators like Norm Ferguson, Fred Moore, Woolie Reitherman, and Frank Thomas. Babbitt stood up front, elucidating the *Time* article and the impending threat of Bioff and Browne.

Then Lessing took the floor. He warned that a "solid, compact group" would make them prey to an outside union; rather, if they remained loosely knit "along social lines," they could act quickly against any IATSE attempts. The majority of attendees voted in favor of starting this social organization, and they unanimously appointed Babbitt as its chairman.

There were other reasons to keep this merely a loosely knit social organization. Unions had a bad rap among conservatives. One was national columnist Westbrook Pegler, who called President Roosevelt's government corrupt, saying unions were linked to either Communism or organized crime. In a country that voted for a Democratic president by a landslide, Pegler's right-wing diatribes were read by nearly six million Americans, six days a week.

The next morning, Babbitt drafted another memo on an interoffice slip and distributed it to all studio personnel that afternoon. It heralded the new social organization at the studio comprising representatives from every creative branch. The memo concluded, "It was decided that a 100% membership in this organization was imperative to enable it to most fully benefit everyone in this studio. You'll probably be pleased with the plan." Babbitt signed it "Chairman."

Within the next ten days, Babbitt led five more meetings across all departments throughout the studio. Up to fifty people attended each group meeting, and Gunther Lessing accompanied Babbitt to nearly every one. Each of the five groups elected two or three representatives, which formed an executive board.

The organization needed a name, but that would come later. First, there were other pressing matters. The very first feature-length animated cartoon was about to premiere.

On the evening of Tuesday, December 21, one car after another pulled up to the Carthay Circle Theatre in Hollywood. A frenzied mob of thirty thousand people crowded to bear witness. Flashbulbs burst, and newsreel cameras whirred. Costumed Disney characters greeted the public. Stars like Ginger Rogers, Cary Grant, Charlie Chaplin, and Shirley Temple walked the red carpet. Finally, Walt and Lillian Disney stepped out of their car, dressed like Hollywood royalty, greeted by a roar from the crowd.

Art Babbitt, Marge, the Clarks, and Gunther Lessing.

One of Babbitt's house staff drove him and Marge up to the red carpet. Walt had given everyone who worked on the film a ticket to the event. The public craned their necks to catch a glimpse of a star. When the animators arrived, there were audible grumbles of disappointment. "Aaaah, that's nobody!"

Ushers handed out programs. The Disney employees found their seats in the back of the theater. Then the lights slowly dimmed, and the crowd grew silent. The theater's enormous red curtain rose to the rafters, uncovering the huge dark screen. A beam of projected light pierced the darkness. The words A WALT DISNEY FEATURE PRODUCTION lit up the screen with the swelling of the soundtrack's orchestration.

After long hours, mounting debt, and cries of "Disney's folly," the loyalty of his employees was Walt's most precious resource. Following the title card, a message from Walt appeared on screen: MY SINCERE APPRECIATION TO THE MEMBERS OF MY STAFF WHOSE LOYALTY AND CREATIVE ENDEAVOR MADE POSSIBLE THIS PRODUCTION.

And there, in front of Hollywood's elite, were the first Disney screen credits the public had ever seen following a title card. Listed were Walt Disney's creative supervisors, story adapters, designers, background artists, and finally, animators. For the first moment in his life, Babbitt saw his own name emblazoned on a film. This was finally proof of his contribution to the art form that meant so much to him. There it would remain, for all time, across nations and generations—evidence that Arthur Babbitt had animated on *Snow White and the Seven Dwarfs*.

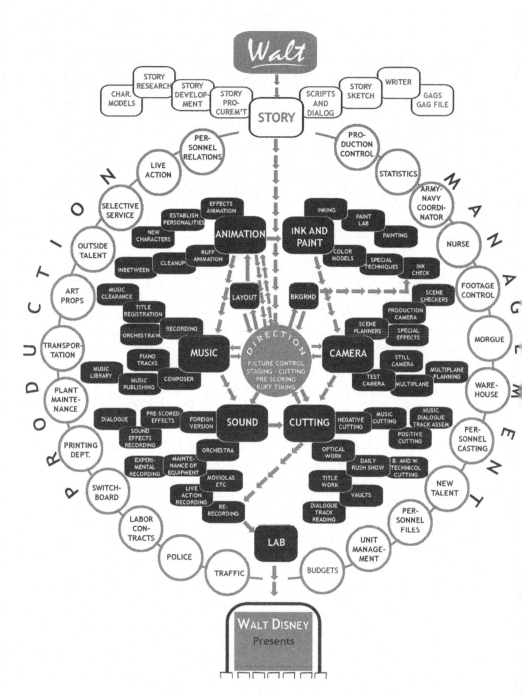

Replica of a flowchart of the Disney studio, from a 1943 employee handbook.
A handful of the items are particular to that year, but most are consistent
with the workflow in the late 1930s.

PART II

TURMOIL

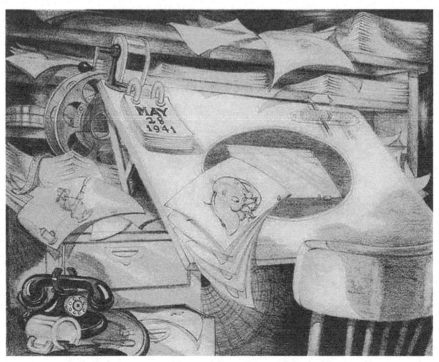

A drawing by an anonymous Disney artist during the Disney strike.

16 | A GROWING DIVIDE

IN THE SIX WEEKS between *Snow White*'s roaring Hollywood premiere and its 1938 general release, the Disney studio truly felt like a place of wonder. The screening was proof that this film of theirs would last the ages. Now the critics were loudly and unanimously raving about it. Columnist Westbrook Pegler called the film the happiest event since the armistice that ended the Great War. Walt Disney was hailed as a genius. The months of unpaid nights, mornings, and weekends had paid off. Now all that the employees had to do to collect their promised bonuses was to wait for the ticket sales.

It was particularly gratifying for the old-timers who had worked with Walt since the early days. Chief legal counsel and senior vice president Gunther Lessing was one of them. Oddly, he had stumbled into the film industry by accident.

Born in 1886 of a German-Jewish father in Waco, Texas, Gunther Lessing graduated from Yale Law School in 1908 and earned the top score on the Texas bar exam. He left to work in El Paso, situated near the Texas-Mexico border, and established himself as a "high-priced lawyer." There he built a reputation of both legal competence and Mexican cultural fluency. In January 1914 Lessing began working with two powerful entities: the Mutual Film Corporation (which had just signed D. W. Griffith to produce *Birth of a Nation*) and the leader of the Mexican Revolution, General Francisco "Pancho" Villa. Lessing brokered Villa's exclusive $25,000 contract with the studio interested in dramatizing his life. He continued working with Villa as his personal attorney, a source of humor and pride that Lessing would often mention during his years at the Disney studio.

However, Lessing had his secrets. In 1917, after he opened a law firm with two partners in El Paso, he was sued by his own employee, attorney Eugene S. Ives. Lessing had contracted Ives to handle a case in Arizona for $350. Ives had worked overtime, unpaid, to successfully reduce their clients' bail by $1,000. Following the assignment, Ives demanded a higher fee from Lessing and brought him to court. His grounds were what is known as *quantum meruit*— a deserved compensation that goes beyond a legal agreement. Ives lost the case, even under appeal: the requirements of his compensation were constrained to his contract, nothing more. This ruling would eventually dictate how Lessing maneuvered the Disney studio's bonus plan.

Although Pancho Villa was assassinated in 1923, Lessing stayed close with the Mexican revolutionaries. He witnessed actress Dolores del Río participate in the rebellion of late 1924 to early 1925. Del Río was a Mexican silent film diva and one of the first great foreign-born stars of Hollywood. In July 1927 Lessing signed a four-year, $35,000 contract as del Río's personal attorney.

For a time, Lessing and del Río had an amiable working relationship. She, Lessing, and their mutual spouses—Jaime and Loula—attended Hollywood parties together. That's when Lessing first met with Walt Disney, at the time a young cartoon producer who had just lost production rights to his Oswald cartoons. Around 1928 Lessing began working for Walt as a part-time legal consultant. It was Lessing who helped Walt protect the copyright of Mickey Mouse.

Lessing continued to work for del Río in various capacities, including handling her and Jaime's amicable divorce in 1928. However, the stock market crash of October 1929 and Jaime's sudden death from surgery complications shook her. She attempted to curtail Lessing's contract, and paid him $4,000 for services rendered. Lessing sued her anyway, for "lack of gratitude and appreciation" and the $31,000 balance.

While del Río was sucker punched by these events, Lessing's situation was more stable than most. He started working for Walt Disney full time on January 1, 1930.

Del Río spitefully reached out to support Lessing's despondent young wife. Loula was trapped in a miserable marriage, accusing her husband of throwing water in her face at a party, dragging her around by her ear in front of their friends, and turning her ten-year-old son against her. In July 1930 Lessing foisted a second lawsuit on del Río for encouraging Loula to divorce him. During the separation, while Lessing sent Loula and his stepson a paltry forty

Gunther Lessing and Dolores del Río in a press photo taken April 1928. The photo appeared in a *New York Daily News* story on July 24, 1930, under the headline CHARGES DOLORES DEL RIO TURNED WIFE AGAINST HIM.

dollars a month, del Río supplemented the sum from her own pockets. This enraged Lessing further.

While testifying publicly against del Río, Lessing argued that he protected her against hypothetical bits of bad publicity. He went on to openly discuss examples of her overt sexuality and sexual proclivity. This lawsuit vilified del Río as a "home wrecker" in the press. According to del Río's biographer, "Lessing's legal action seemed designed to destroy her."

Lessing won a $16,000 settlement against del Río in December 1931. Loula was granted her divorce from him in April 1932.

In all the press about the del Río case, Gunther Lessing was never linked to Walt Disney Productions. The Disney artists remained oblivious to Lessing's sordid connection with this empowered movie starlet.

And that was just how Lessing wanted it.

The Disney artists who had just completed *Snow White* jumped into the next big project, *Pinocchio*, brimming with confidence. Art Babbitt began working on the Geppetto character, doing some animation tests in his opening sequence as a bald, roly-poly sourpuss. The design had already been approved, and Geppetto's personality was deduced with Stanislavski's "character analysis" in mind: since Geppetto lived alone, he would be used to getting his way, but since he wished for a son to love, his rough exterior would belie a heart of gold.

True to the source material, young animator Frank Thomas began experimenting with Pinocchio as an obnoxious and clunky puppet. Thomas was among the newly minted art-school graduates hired between 1933 and 1935 and who were climbing the ranks at incredible speed.

After months of story conferences, *Pinocchio*'s working script was progressing. It included a Grandfather Tree, an ominous town solider, a nightmarish Bogeyland, and a birthday party finale.

Of course, the Disney studio continued producing shorts, which brought in a steady revenue stream and reinforced the branding of its cartoon stars. By New Year's 1938 Babbitt was just beginning his animation for the new Goofy and Donald cartoon, *Polar Trappers*. Although Babbitt had already been crowned a Goofy specialist, Goofy's animation direction for this cartoon was assigned to Woolie Reitherman, probably because Babbitt was occupied with Geppetto and Reitherman had some experience animating the Goof. Babbitt was assigned two long establishing scenes of Goofy lazily preparing a walrus trap and a walrus stealing his bucket of fish.

However, Babbitt's brief sequence cuts abruptly to the first of Reitherman's many scenes. Under Reitherman's pencil, Goofy zips straight into a fast-paced cartoon chase. Racing in skis and wielding a lasso, Goofy becomes an emblem of sportiness. Reitherman's Goofy has eyes that are wide open and alert, and movements that are quick and impulsive.

Babbitt would have just started to notice a trend: the younger artists were slowly taking the most coveted assignments. The top artists who had initially elevated Disney animation—men like Babbitt, Norm Ferguson, Fred Moore, Dick Lundy, and Bill Tytla—were beginning to be eclipsed by the art-school graduates. In the depths of Babbitt's gut was born a realization: he and his peers were replaceable.

After his conversations with Gunther Lessing in December, Babbitt spear-headed a company-wide group to block an IATSE takeover. Around the start of January, with Lessing's knowledge, Babbitt met with the Los Angeles regional directors of the National Labor Relations Board (NLRB). The board made it clear that if this group was going to exist at Walt Disney Productions, it required a few things:

- Its own constitution.
- A president.
- An elected executive board.
- A list of demands.
- Membership from the majority of Disney employees.
- Recognition from the company as its employees' sole bargaining organization.

One of the NLRB's regional directors, William Walsh, gave Babbitt a list of attorneys and suggested that the meetings be off company time and property. Babbitt and his colleagues who made up the temporary executive board, including Norm Ferguson, selected Leonard Janofsky, lawyer for the Screen Writers Guild with experience in NLRB cases.

Babbitt held the first executive board meeting in his and Marge's home. Fourteen Disney employees from different departments made up this board and attended the meeting. As with his home-hosted figure drawing sessions, Babbitt was quick to take initiative. Janofsky introduced himself as the group's legal counsel, and employees drew up a constitution and bylaws for Janofsky to review and revise. They also chose a name for their group—the Federation of Screen Cartoonists.

Gunther Lessing was also in Babbitt's house that night. He spent the evening not participating in the meeting but talking with Marge in the parlor, pouring some drinks at the bar, and adjourning to the fireplace. This was the last time Lessing was invited to such a meeting. Lessing's presence in the adjoining room reveals that he had planned to attend but was excluded at the last second. The only new element was Janofsky, who could see that the group was attempting to form a union, and therefore management was forbidden to participate. Lessing had tried to shape the group as a loosely knit social organization to his own liking, but now it was evolving outside his control.

Around Monday, January 24, Babbitt placed a notice on the company bulletin boards: "A mass meeting will be held in the Hollywood American Legion Auditorium, Thursday night, Jan 27th. Your future in this business is concerned—so it is imperative that you be there WITHOUT FAIL. Supervisors and production heads excluded." At the bottom of the flyer it read, "Persons not employed in this studio will not be admitted."

At "8 PM sharp," Babbitt and Janofsky led the meeting at the auditorium, laying out the Federation's purpose, according to its constitution: "To bargain collectively for its members, with Walt Disney Productions, Ltd., with respect to rates of pay, wages, hours and other conditions of employment." If any member of the Federation had a grievance against the company, that member would communicate it to a representative on the executive board. That board member would be empowered to bargain with management on behalf of the employee, and any settlement would be voted on at a Federation meeting.

The executive officers were chosen, and Babbitt was elected president. Members of the executive board were appointed among employees from every department. The demands were typical of a Hollywood union in 1938 but also emphasized resistance against the Bioff-held IATSE union:

1. "Higher pay for lower-salaried brackets."
2. "A forty hour five-day work week."
3. "In case of lay-off, two weeks' notice."
4. "A stipulated period of apprenticeship, varying with the need of different departments."
5. "The blocking of outside intervention, be it the Producers Association, the IATSE, or anyone else interfering with the employees' rights."
6. "The recognition . . . of a Grievance Committee to hear, judge, and correct the injustices suffered by any of our members."

Though the employees were not resounding with complaints, each of these demands was enticing to many Disney employees, for different reasons:

1. While some top-level artists like Babbitt were earning high salaries, lower-salaried Disney employees had become the lowest-paid in the industry. A Disney inbetweener earned $22.50 a week, whereas an inbetweener elsewhere earned $28 a week. Starting Disney painters earned $16 a week and inkers $18 a week. By contrast, an entry-level set-painting job in Hollywood started at $35 a week.
2. While some other sites had adopted a five-day workweek, Disney artists were expected to work half-days on Saturdays.
3. The Disney artists had witnessed their share of sudden layoffs.
4. A period of apprenticeship could be endless, or it could end with a termination. Inbetweeners were brought in for a "tryout period," fifteen at a time, after which all but three might be fired. During the Ink & Paint Department's tryout period, someone was fired every Friday. Remembered one inker, "Everyone was so scared and worried they could hardly relax enough to do their work."

The Federation membership quickly signed up 550 of the eligible employees. On Monday, January 31, the Federation of Screen Cartoonists announced itself to Disney management in a letter. It stated its purpose, explained that it represented a majority of Disney employees, and requested recognition as the studio's union.

Two days later, the Federation received a mixed message from the company. There was approval: "The purposes of your organization appear to be laudable and that we do not object in principle to bargain collectively with our employees." But there was also resistance: "There are other organizations that claim jurisdiction on the premises. We believe that you ... should settle the question of jurisdiction before approaching us for recognition or meetings."

This required extra legwork from Babbitt and his colleagues. The Federation would need certification from the NLRB—a *charter*—so it filed a petition with the NLRB on February 11. The NLRB responded on February 16, stating that it was waiting on a decision for a different case—one involving the Screen Writers Guild—that would determine the outcome of every motion picture case that was still pending. Babbitt had to wait.

There was suddenly a lot of waiting at the Disney studio. *Pinocchio* had serious problems, and Walt could feel it. "One fear is constantly before us," said Walt then, "the fear that our next effort will not be regarded by the public as highly as the last." Walt's own pursuit of excellence set him up for indomitable pressure.

The script needed work, and the characters needed revision. More than sixty seconds of finished Geppetto animation were discarded. The writers started from square one again, and *Pinocchio* was moved from the Animation Department back to the Story Department. There was now less for the animators to do around the studio. Bill Tytla began work animating the sorcerer for *The Sorcerer's Apprentice*. Babbitt was instructed to keep busy as best he could. His friend Dick Lundy was directing a new Donald Duck short called *The Autograph Hound* and gave Babbitt some scenes to animate.

During slack periods, temporary layoffs were expected. Higher-level artists had a clause in their contracts that allowed for layoffs up to four weeks without pay. Even so, the studio chose to keep Babbitt on.

Ever since the Bioff-led IATSE announced its plan to pursue all Hollywood crafts, those crafts rose up to block the IATSE. Hollywood alliances were formed.

Walt Disney Productions stood apart from the rest of the animation industry, but the smaller studios were hell-bent on blocking IATSE too. The independent animators' union called the Screen Cartoon Guild sought to unite artists from all studios, just like other unions. It held get-togethers with guest speakers, which were "open to all cartoonists in the animated cartoon industry whether members of the Guild or not."

The Guild went so far as to approach the artists of the Disney studio, even claiming to have signed up some of them there. That would make the Guild the third union to try to organize Disney animators, after the IATSE and the Federation.

But the IATSE was the common enemy of both the Guild and the Federation. On Friday, February 18, committee members of both the Guild and the Federation met and agreed not to interfere with each other. "We have one common objective," the Federation wrote, "to keep the IATSE out, and we're going to do it, cooperatively."

———————————

In a bright and smoky country club ballroom, the Disney artists danced, drank, and laughed. A red-hot swing band played as the female vocalist crooned. It was March 12, and the Federation of Screen Cartoonists had sponsored its first social event. It was the closest thing to a wrap party that the *Snow White* crew had, and Babbitt had organized it. This party might have stood as the only party the studio was to hold. That was not the impression Walt wished to cultivate, and he began to brainstorm another, bigger celebration of his own.

17 | THE NORCONIAN

WORK RESUMED AT THE DISNEY STUDIO on Monday as usual, and Babbitt flipped his drawings of Goofy in the new Mickey-Donald-Goofy cartoon, *The Whalers*. He animated nearly every Goofy scene in that cartoon and, as usual, took up huge quantities of screen time. Now he liberally used live-action reference for Goofy, choreographing his movements before his pencil even touched the paper.

Babbitt was proud to have developed this technique, but he was the only animator who relied on it for the shorts. As the younger art-school graduates like Frank Thomas and Woolie Reitherman continued to climb up the studio ladder, Babbitt struggled to remain relevant.

He wasn't the only one. Norm Ferguson, the Pluto specialist who had introduced personality animation to the Disney studio, sometimes found himself unable to draw without incredible effort. Fred Moore, the Mickey Mouse specialist who discovered squash-and-stretch, often found himself in a depressive rut, needing emphatic compliments or sometimes turning to alcohol. Bill Tytla, the most experienced fine artist of the cohort, became so sensitive that a slight critique on his drawing ability could crush him for "a week, maybe two."

Meanwhile, the younger animators seemed to glide effortlessly through their assignments. When *Ferdinand the Bull* went into production, puckish art-school graduate Ward Kimball handled the bullfighter scenes with impish delight. For the parade into the bullring, Kimball caricatured Disney animators as the banderilleros. Fred Moore's caricature waddled in like a toddler. Tytla's caricature (a picador) looked like a Cossack on a horse. Babbitt's caricature marched in like a pugilist, jaw protruding and fists swinging.

In life, Babbitt and Tytla were drifting apart. Bill and Adrienne married on April 21, 1938, and he chose Joe Grant as his best man. Grant had worked his way up since 1933 and now was head of the Character Model Department. Following the wedding, the Tytlas began making plans to move to La Crescenta, California.

Babbitt's closest friendship was disintegrating before his eyes.

The *Snow White* artists patiently awaited their profit-share bonuses as the film made huge returns all over the world. In May, Walt and Roy made enough money from *Snow White* to pay back their bank loans. For the first time in two years, the studio was out of debt. Walt immediately bought a new house in North Hollywood for his parents, Elias and Flora. Next, Walt would give his staff the greatest party they had ever seen.

On May 10 a new story outline appeared on the bulletin boards. It looked like all the other outlines for short cartoons still in the story phase. This "short" was called "Walt's Field Day." Beneath that was written, "Characters: Entire studio personnel and one guest per person. Locale: Lake Norconian Club. Time: June 4, 1938—from 10:00 AM on."

The memo laid out plans for an adults-only day outdoors, followed by a dinner and dance. Eight Disney employees volunteered for the Field Day Committee to help organize the event, including Ward Kimball, Hal Adelquist, and Art Babbitt. It appeared to be the perfect time for Walt to announce the distribution of the *Snow White* bonuses to his employees.

Saturday, June 4, the Disney employees and their friends drove the ninety minutes to the luxurious Lake Norconian Club. It was furnished with fifteen badminton courts, fifteen Ping-Pong tables, twenty-five horses for riding, ten horseshoe pits, a lake for boating, a pool for swimming, and grounds to play all sorts of games. A handful of donkeys grazed in the fields.

All day there were organized competitions in golf, badminton, Ping-Pong, horseshoes, swimming, volleyball, baseball, touch football, foot races, and rowing, with trophies promised to the winners. Then came the cocktail hour, followed by a lavish dinner and dancing in the grand ballroom with a live orchestra. The Disney employees had booked the hotel rooms to capacity.

Party at the Norconian, June 4, 1938. Marge Babbitt is at center, in front of artist Willis Pyle.

At 11:30 that evening, the band paused as head story man Ted Sears took the stage. He announced the winners of the day's events. There were cacophonous cheers. Then Walt himself took the stage—the moment that everyone had been waiting for. Those late hours and unpaid overtime on *Snow White*, the success of the film, all added up to those promised bonuses.

Walt began by outlining the company's new direction toward feature films. He addressed the exciting new productions in the pipeline, including *Bambi* and *Pinocchio*. He said he hoped that this day would invigorate everyone for the work that lay before them. And with a closing pleasantry, he took his seat.

There was confused, nervous applause. The live band resumed its set as scheduled. The Disney employees looked at one another, wondering where the bonuses were and if this party itself was the bonus. The room was now tainted with shattered expectations. The drinking increased. The tension grew. "For two years, all of us had been under terrible pressure, working long hours day and night to finish *Snow White*," remembered one of Babbitt's inbetweeners. "Something just snapped."

Someone rode one of the horses into the hotel lobby. Other drunken men and women climbed onto the field donkeys and tried to ride them. And still others began throwing each other into the pool, fully clothed.

Soon, one artist recalled, "there were naked swim parties, people got drunk and were often surprised what room they were in and who they were sleeping next to when they awoke the next morning." Another artist recalled couples swapping partners. Fred Moore drunkenly tumbled out of the hotel's second story balcony onto a shrub, unscathed.

Walt and Lillian Disney drove off, disgusted, leaving the wake of chaotic employees behind them. He never mentioned the party again, and in his presence, neither did they.

The talk about eventual bonuses did not die down, but there was work to be done. *Pinocchio* desperately needed an overhaul, and Art Babbitt, Bill Tytla, and Fred Moore were all called in to redesign Geppetto.

New voice actors were cast. German-born actor Christian Rub would play Geppetto. Babbitt listened to the recording of Rub's voice—soft and kindly— and began sketching.

He realized the animators had been going about Geppetto all wrong. The character was *not* a crotchety hermit but a soft-hearted papa. Babbitt injected the warmth of Rub's voice into his new designs, giving Geppetto a full head of hair, a mustache, and a leaner, bent frame. He submitted the designs, to the supervisors' approval. Hal Adelquist, now the chief assistant to *Pinocchio* director Ben Sharpsteen, requested Babbitt lead a meeting on Geppetto's redesign with the animation assistants.

The changes in Babbitt's design of Geppetto had one striking aspect: whether conscious or not, Babbitt had redesigned the character with the physical characteristics of his own father.

In July 1938 Dave Hand proposed an intricate new lecture program to Walt: the low-level artists would attend lectures by the mid-level artists, the mid-level artists would attend lectures by the top-level artists, and the top-level artists would be lectured by professional artists (including muralist Diego Rivera, writer Alexander Woollcott, and architect Frank Lloyd Wright.) In addition, a Development Board would be formed to give written critique of each Disney artist, thereby sharpening their specializations. Walt gave it his OK.

During that year, one of the supervising directors on *Pinocchio* offered Babbitt a promotion—from supervising animator to sequence director. But Babbitt passed on the offer. He preferred doing his own animation with his assistants, not managing a cadre of others. Nonetheless, as a supervising animator (along with Tytla and Moore), he now shared the same rank as the younger art-school graduates like Frank Thomas and Woolie Reitherman.

On June 28, 1938, the *Los Angeles Examiner* had announced that Walt Disney would distribute 20 percent of *Snow White's* earnings to his eight hundred employees, each bonus representing about twelve weeks' wages. The artists were ecstatic.

By the end of the summer, the trade papers were reporting that *Snow White* had grossed $2 million, on the way to being the most successful film of its day. However, Roy Disney posted a curt memo on the bulletin boards discouraging taking the trade papers' figures too seriously. "That was a tactical error," recalled an animator, "because we all knew that, in this area at least, trade papers are fairly accurate."

Neither Roy Disney nor Gunther Lessing offered either a bonus delivery date or an amount. Word spread that the bonuses were never coming at all.

Finally that summer the *Snow White* bonuses were distributed. Compared to the fat bonuses for the short cartoons, the *Snow White* bonuses were a pittance. Some of the artists received an amount equal to or smaller than they had received for the shorts. Some artists received none at all. "There was more confusion and hostility," an artist recalled. Even Walt's most loyal animators thought this was poorly managed.

Babbitt earned no bonus for *Snow White*. Whatever formula that had earned Babbitt large bonuses on shorts was now gone, without explanation.

In late August, *The Whalers* was released, prominently featuring Babbitt's Goofy animation. Babbitt received no bonus for that either.

While the bonus fiasco flickered through the animation ranks, Walt was consumed with other, grander things. In his office, he and Roy held maps and construction plans, budgeting them against the company checkbook. Walt envisioned an animation campus, a streamlined plant specifically built for cartoon production—the only one of its kind in the world. On August 31, he and Roy put their first deposit down for a fifty-one-acre plot in Burbank. This would be the site of the new Disney studio.

By early September 1938 *Pinocchio* was back on track. Jiminy Cricket had just been added, and Pinocchio himself was reshaped to be much more likeable. The story was still an epic narrative, but the completed storyboards now fit Walt's recipe for movie magic.

By the end of September, Walt was selecting music for a new feature film he was calling "The Concert Feature." The idea for the *Sorcerer's Apprentice* short had expanded the previous March into a pastiche of classical music–inspired animation. Famed conductor Leopold Stokowski would enthusiastically conduct the Philadelphia Orchestra to accompany the animation. Employees walking through the main building could hear the classical music played throughout the hallways as ideas were brainstormed and stories crafted.

The studio chose classical pieces that were rich with visual opportunity. Different ideas filled the pushpin boards for each musical number, including Tchaikovsky's *Nutcracker Suite*. Eliminating the Christmas motif, story artists began interpreting the melodies through nature. Thistles and orchids would perform the Russian Dance, and lizards would perform the Chinese Dance while mushrooms acted as lamplighters. (The lizards would eventually be replaced by mushroom dancers.)

The artists often had to halt their progress to attend an anti-union "information seminar" by Vice President Gunther Lessing. He repeatedly warned the staff about joining an independent union like the Screen Cartoon Guild. He said that the animation artists "on the outside" of Disney walls needed unions to protect them because they were untalented and lazy. Many of the Disney artists who heard this had once worked "on the outside" and still had friends in those studios. They also had no personal investment in Lessing, whose way of speaking was "too slick, too facile, and too arrogant." To previously uninformed staff, these seminars began educating them about the Guild's existence.

The Guild was growing its numbers and succeeding in signing up animators where the IATSE had not. Bad press also weakened the IATSE—on September 7, Willie Bioff was charged with having accepted a bribe in 1936 from Joseph Schenck, the 20th Century-Fox mogul. Even at the time of the transaction, it had alarmed the public, not only because of its enormous sum of $100,000 but also because of the pretext—this was a loan toward an alfalfa farm.

The charge opened up an examination of all of Bioff's business dealings going back to his 1936 arrival in Hollywood. A regional labor board director began to investigate. Bioff immediately retreated from his post as IATSE's West Coast representative and relocated to New York, biding his time until things cooled down.

Bioff's self-imposed exile did not stop the IATSE from claiming to represent Disney employees, even while the Federation of Screen Cartoonists claimed them. On September 21, the National Labor Relations Board finally investigated the Federation's petition for recognition and issued a legal hearing. Notices for the hearing were sent to all the unions that had ever staked a claim at Disney—the IATSE, the Federation, and the Screen Cartoon Guild.

Lessing responded to the notice on behalf of the Disney company: He denied that the Federation—the group that he and Babbitt had formed—represented the majority of the employees, and therefore it could not be recognized. He argued that enforcing the National Labor Relations Act would deprive some Disney employees (i.e., management) certain civil rights. He asked that the petition be dismissed.

It was not. The National Labor Relations Board hearing took place on October 24. Lessing represented the Disney company, and Leonard Janofsky and Babbitt represented the Federation. Seven separate attorneys represented various local branches of the IATSE. The Screen Cartoon Guild did not attend, honoring its noncompetitive agreement with the Federation.

Of the 675 total employees at the company at that time, 602 of them worked in animation production. Janofsky produced the Federation's 588 union membership cards.

A final verdict would arrive in the months to come. Until that verdict, Lessing refused to recognize the Federation as the Disney studio's union.

———————————

On October 25 Dave Hand submitted his final draft of the "Development Program Plan of Operation"; it would hold classes on subjects like Story Construction, Timing, Pantomime, Composition, and Caricature. There were three skill levels. Group A—the highest—had nine names, including Bill Tytla, Fred Moore, and Norm Ferguson, as well as younger art-school grads like Frank Thomas and Woolie Reitherman. Babbitt was placed in Group C.

Management did not share Hand's low opinion of Babbitt. On October 27 Babbitt's contract was renewed at $200 a week, still among the highest-paid artists at the studio.

In November, a nineteen-year-old named Bill Hurtz had just completed a year of training under Don Graham. He was thrust into Babbitt's animation unit, and for $25 a week he worked as one of Babbitt's animation assistants. Hurtz was terrified and a little starstruck. He remembered first seeing *Three Little Pigs* years ago in a local cinema and reading Babbitt's name under the art displayed in the lobby.

———————————

Walt Disney was increasingly dubbed a manufacturer of happily-ever-afters. He had revived the orphaned Snow White from her coffin and was currently bestowing Pinocchio the soul of a real boy. These make-believe children touched death. The theme of tragedy and redemption hung heavy in Walt's heart, even before the events of Saturday, November 26, 1938.

The new house he had bought his parents was a death trap. The furnace had a gas leak and had been poisoning Flora and Elias Disney. They both collapsed at the house from asphyxiation. Walt's father was barely alive when the ambulance arrived.

Walt's mother, however, was already dead.

It was the worst event that Walt had ever experienced. The news was quietly passed to the staff who worked closest with Walt, which would have included Babbitt. Babbitt knew what it was like to lose a parent under tragically avoidable circumstances. His own father's injury and premature death had hardened Babbitt against the travails he encountered in life.

Unfortunately, the same would prove to be true for Walt.

18 | A WOODEN BOY AND A WORLD WAR

ON NEWSPAPER STANDS THROUGHOUT HOLLYWOOD, the trade paper *Film Daily* reigned among top industry rags. The January 12, 1939, issue was emblazoned with the front-page headline CRITICS VOTE "SNOW WHITE" 1938's BEST. Below the headline was the list of the year's "Ten Best," displaying a vote count for each. Ranked at number two was Frank Capra's *You Can't Take It With You*, with 372 votes. *Snow White* had collected 419 votes.

Walt bought up several copies of this issue to distribute among his choice staff, accompanying a personalized memo. On February 4 he gave one to Art Babbitt.

"Dear Art," wrote Walt, "Since the critics have voted Snow White best picture of 1938, I thought you might like to stow away the attached copy of *Film Daily* with all the other mementos you may be saving for your grandchildren. Anyway, I think we should all be very happy that the picture's been selected as 1938's best.—Walt"

It seemed a thoughtful gesture, but in the aftermath of the bonus fiasco, it may have been a tactical attempt to keep the peace.

On Thursday night, February 23, at the Biltmore Hotel in Los Angeles, Hollywood gathered for the eleventh annual Academy Awards. *Ferdinand the Bull* won for best short cartoon. A special Oscar was also presented to Walt for *Snow White and the Seven Dwarfs*. Child actor Shirley Temple presented the tuxedoed Walt Disney with the golden statuette, alongside seven little statuettes. "Why, I'm so proud I think I'll bust," Walt said for the newsreel.

133

Construction began in February 1939 on Walt Disney's new Burbank studio, and production on *Pinocchio* was going at full steam. Babbitt continued handling a small unit that animated Geppetto. Sequence director Norm Ferguson, skilled in vaudeville-inspired pantomime, led the unit for Honest John the fox and Gideon the cat. Bill Tytla supervised Stromboli, a character who reflected Tytla's experience with fiery foreigners. Fred Moore supervised the boyish Lampwick, a veiled self-caricature.

Walt began to feel that Babbitt's animation of Geppetto was too analytical, too closely based off his live-action reference. Even Babbitt's assistant, Bill Hurtz, could see that Babbitt was getting "trapped in" the "mold" of live-action reference. Meanwhile, Fred Moore's style was considered too "cartoony." Sequence director Wilfred Jackson and Walt watched their animation in the sweatbox and agreed to have the two work on some Geppetto scenes together, in hopes to balance out their strengths.

Geppetto's vocal performer, German-born Christian Rub, doubled as the live-action model for the character. Rub gained a reputation among the animators for being "an irascible, nasty old guy" and "always spouting the glories of Hitler." The animators decided to teach him a lesson; as Rub stood on a raised platform simulating Geppetto's tilting raft, half a dozen men quietly gripped the platform and on cue, "gave Christian a ride he'd never forget."

Babbitt directed Rub's vocal sessions, and the seasoned actor repeatedly hammed up his performance. Babbitt kept correcting Rub for his overacting until Rub had had enough. "I have been doing it this way for over forty years!" he protested.

"Fine," said Babbitt. "Now we are going to do it correctly."

While the Geppetto design straddled the line between human and cartoon, the Blue Fairy's design was proportionately human, modeled by Marge in a dress and fake wings.

The young art-school graduates carried the rest of the picture. While Jiminy Cricket was handled by Ward Kimball, Pinocchio himself was supervised by Frank Thomas and Milt Kahl. Eric Larson led the unit handling Figaro the kitten. (Kahl and Larson had animated the woodland creatures in *Snow White*.) Woolie Reitherman led the unit for Monstro the Whale. Although Les Clark had been animating at the studio longer than nearly anyone, he was not assigned his own unit on *Pinocchio*. Walt began noticing the huge advancements in the art-school grads. One day he stopped one in the hall to compliment him on his drawings of the wooden boy. The animator, Ollie Johnston, was taken aback. Walt was not known to compliment artists to their face. "I was just trying to draw like the other fellows did," he stammered. Walt replied, "I don't give a damn where you get it, just keep doing it!"

Of all the creative departments at his studio, it was his animators who impressed Walt the most. Walt could dominate a story meeting or direct an editing session, but he relied entirely on his animators to bring his visions to life. "My only regret is that I can't draw better," said Walt at that time. "All I am is a movie-picture producer."

As *Pinocchio* pushed through, Walt periodically surveyed the progress on his new Burbank studio. It was nothing more than a construction site, but Walt's vision was crystal clear. Over the next few months, he drove his employees out there one group at a time. "Walt was excited about the new building even though it was out in a treeless wasteland of nothing but tumbleweeds," remembered one artist. "Nevertheless, when Walt asked what we thought of it our reply was 'Great, Walt!'"

Walt had the image so clear in his mind, it never occurred to him that he was the only one who could see it.

Breaking news from Europe in March 1939—Germany broke the Munich Agreement that it and Italy had signed with France and Great Britain. The Nazi regime began an eastward takeover of Czechoslovakia. On March 15 from Prague, Adolf Hitler proclaimed the Czech lands were now under Nazi rule.*

---

* *Snow White* may have left Prague's theaters, but a Jewish Czech art student named Dina Gottliebova could still rely on her memory. Her ability to render scenes from *Snow White* would eventually save her life in Auschwitz. As an inmate of the notorious Nazi death camp, she would paint a mural of *Snow White and the Seven Dwarfs* on the wall of the children's barrack. It would lead her to being brought to Dr. Josef Mengele to paint portraits of some Roma prisoners before their murders—and save her and her mother from extermination. Eventually, after the war, she moved to Paris, where she met and fell in love with Art Babbitt.

On April 12, 1939, Fascist Italy invaded Albania to the east, with an army of one hundred thousand soldiers and six hundred warplanes. The Albanian king was forced into exile, and the country was claimed in the name of Italy.

On May 22 Germany and Italy signed the Pact of Steel—a ten-year alliance of political, economic, and military cooperation.

In the spring of 1939, the Federation of Screen Cartoonists was still in limbo. Without certification from the National Labor Relations Board, Federation meetings became more irregular, and Babbitt stopped planning functions. Members stopped paying their monthly one-dollar union dues, and interest in the Federation waned. Some Disney artists began drifting to Screen Cartoon Guild meetings. They witnessed young animators from other studios speaking up, including one Warner Bros. cartoon director, Chuck Jones.

Goofy and Wilbur premiered in March, and Woolie Reitherman handled most of Goofy's animation. Babbitt had animated three sections of Goofy being outwitted by a frog and received no bonus for his work. The assignment was minor, so he wasn't necessarily due a large sum. But he was beginning to feel the effect of the bonus drought on his wallet. Additionally, *The Autograph Hound* was revised, director Dick Lundy was demoted back to animator, and Babbitt's animation was cut.

In May 1939 the company hit a milestone beyond everyone's expectations. *Snow White and the Seven Dwarfs* officially became the highest-grossing film of all time, earning $6.7 million. No additional bonuses were distributed.

On Tuesday July 25, the National Labor Relations Board finally responded, granting a charter (i.e., certification) to the Federation of Screen Cartoonists. The trial examiner had counted all the Federation membership cards and found that they represented the majority of the 602 Disney production artists. The IATSE, despite its claims, could not provide evidence that it had signed up any Disney artists. Babbitt immediately began planning the next steps, rallying Disney artists through bulletins with new Federation of Screen Cartoonists letterhead.

While industry papers dedicated increasingly more ink to union updates, they were eclipsed by the growing war in Europe. On August 23, Germany and Russia signed the Stalin-Hitler Pact, otherwise known as the German-Soviet Pact. On September 1 Germany invaded Poland from the west. Two days later, France and Britain declared war on Germany.

Meanwhile, Walt Disney was preparing to move his entire staff to the new Burbank studio. It had cost him $3 million—an enormous sum. By comparison, Hollywood's next largest building project that year was the Warner Bros. $700,000 studio renovation. In the two previous years Warner Bros. had released more than one hundred feature films. Disney had released one.

There was talk about how war would affect the studio, whether escapism would increase ticket sales or if Europe's closing market would decrease them. The answer came quickly: production control manager Herb Lamb stopped all new raises to assistants in the studio. "War scare, you know," he said.

At the end of September 1939, in the Hollywood High School auditorium, the Federation of Screen Cartoonists held elections for a new executive board. Babbitt stepped down as president, and animator Bill Roberts was elected to fill his post. Babbitt was elected vice president. Every department submitted demands; a charter was drawn up that night. "No demands were outrageous. No attempt was made to dominate or interfere with studio policy," said one Federation member in 1941.

After October 4, Federation attorney Janofsky presented Roy Disney with the Federation's list of demands, but Janofsky reported that Roy refused to negotiate. Later that month Roy agreed to meet with the Federation's executive board at a local restaurant. He told the union men, point-blank, that he had no use for unions.

Federation representatives from every creative department at Disney met to vote on their next move. One idea was to give Roy a deadline by which to sign, and if he missed the deadline the Federation would file a complaint with the National Labor Relations Board. Another was to dissolve the Federation altogether. Instead, they voted on a third option: wait for the studio to realize that a contract was in everyone's best interest.

Babbitt was feeling pinched in his bank account from the sudden disap-
pearance of bonus payouts. On October 19 he borrowed $200 from the com-
pany—one week's pay. On October 27 he borrowed another $200.

Neither the war in Europe nor the union talk slowed down the studio.
The female-dominated Ink & Paint Department worked in a mad rush for
Pinocchio's premiere in February. The "girls are getting pretty much on edge
due to long hours," noted one artist. Animation continued on "The Concert
Feature," now called *Fantasia*, for its release in one year. Development was
well underway for *Bambi*, while *Peter Pan*, *The Little Mermaid*, *Alice in Wonderland*, and a dog film called *Lady* were in their early story stages. It was all
part of Walt's grand vision.

And his vision was impervious to what was happening under his feet.

19 | DREAMS SHATTERED

ON THE CRACKED PAVEMENT of Hyperion Avenue, the tall gates of the old Disney studio still loomed, though the interior was mostly empty. Dust collected on the vacant linoleum floors. On January 4 and 5, 1940, the animators had boxed up their belongings. The camera operators and a few managers stayed behind to complete postproduction.

The new Burbank studio lot had been carefully designed. All the structures were built to precision and laid out on a grid. The new animation building was built opposite the studio theater, which could fit hundreds of employees at a time. But Walt also provided amenities unheard of anywhere else. The lot had an auto service station, and a coffee shop that delivered milkshakes to order at the artists' desks. There was a gymnasium for top employees on the upper floor of the animation building. Every structure on the lot was cooled by industrial air-conditioning—a rare luxury in 1940.

The interior of the new studio was stylishly designed in a mid-century modern motif, and every room had original, custom-made furniture of polished wood and leather. The animators' desks had an adjustable lever and new light disk, surrounded by three levels of shelves for paper. Around the edge of each shelf was a thin metal rim for the animators' cigarettes to rest lest they burn the wood. Along either side were drawers and cabinets for their materials. The animators discovered that the curved handles of the drawers doubled as beer bottle openers, and the lower cabinets were the perfect height for a fifth of scotch.

"You can't imagine what fun it was to work at Disney's," wrote one artist in September 1941. "There was a university atmosphere about the place, a youth and eagerness as of a high school, as if the grounds were a campus and the workrooms were study halls. Every day was a 'new' day. If you had an idea you could shout 'Eureka' down the halls and you'd be listened to and get paid for your idea. . . . Walt had the habit of sudden firing. But by heavens, you weed a garden, don't you?"

Indeed, Walt had ultimate power on the lot, and his mood was inconsistent. Even his admirers called him many-faced, a "beloved benefactor Mr. Nice Guy" one minute and "Ebeneezer Scrooge" the next.

Babbitt's animation room was a comfortable workspace at the end of a hall. He had a full-sized animation desk, wall-to-wall carpet, and his own Moviola for pencil tests. Babbitt liked his room, and Walt liked his animators knowing how prized they were.

But Babbitt made an unsettling discovery. While all full-fledged animators had wall-to-wall carpeting, animation assistants had carpet that fell short of the wall by a few feet. Animation trainees had no carpet at all. In Babbitt's estimation, Walt had delineated a class system, which Babbitt had loathed since his boyhood in Sioux City. He also discovered that the company athletic club, called the Penthouse Club, was only open to male artists earning $100 or more per week. Walt no doubt saw the Penthouse Club as an incentive, and asked Babbitt why he wouldn't become a member. "As soon as you make it accessible to everyone," Babbitt said, "I'd be happy to join."

Babbitt and the rest of the Federation met that month. Janofsky helped revise a contract, and the negotiating committee delivered it to the management. Again, it was ignored.

Nonetheless, Babbitt worked as hard as ever. After driving back to the house that he shared with Marge, he retreated to his personal workspace and his own animation desk and continued to animate. Marge watched him sit at his desk night after night as she sat in the house alone. He was now thirty-two, and asked Marge to start a family with him. Marge had trained her whole life to be a dancer, and she was not ready to trade her dream for the life of a housewife. She hammered her point home by accepting a touring vaudeville show, with herself billed as the model for Snow White. The show would also include tap dancers, the Three Stooges, and musical humorist Cliff "Ukelele Ike" Edwards, fresh off his gig voicing Jiminy Cricket. The tour started in January and would run for eight weeks.

As Marge's show travelled from Chicago to Buffalo, her hotel rooms were bombarded with messages from Art asking her to come home. He called and wrote letters constantly, until he asked her if they should divorce.

The tour was cut from eight weeks to three. When it was over, Marge bought a one-way ticket to New York City and stayed.

Theatergoers were eager for the latest animated feature by Walt Disney. After waiting two years for a follow-up to *Snow White*, they crammed into their seats to see *Gulliver's Travels*.

Of course, this was not a film by Disney but by the Fleischer studio—the same studio that had created Betty Boop and Popeye. The Fleischers had not only borrowed the European fantasy format from Disney but also used several of his former artists (including story man and voice actor Pinto Colvig).

While this confusion likely helped the Fleischers' ticket sales, it hurt Disney's. Audiences for *Gulliver's Travels* were underwhelmed. The Fleischers had some technical advances up their sleeves, like the occasional three-dimensional rotating background, but most of the characters lacked personality. With *Gulliver* still in theaters, Disney's *Pinocchio* was released on February 23, 1940. Critics were excited about the film, but moviegoers disheartened by *Gulliver's Travels* did not flock to *Pinocchio* the way they had to *Snow White*.

The same month of *Pinocchio*'s release, Babbitt received a contract renewal. It was for $200 a week—the same salary he had been earning since December 1936. This contract was also one page shorter; it excluded the clause about a bonus system.

Trade papers reported that *Snow White* had grossed $8 million. But Disney was also now going to trade shares publicly, and this was promulgated with Wall Street–style finesse. "Walter Elias Disney is about to become 'big business,' turning from his 17 years of self and private financing . . . to public financing to the tune of some $3,800,000 of, probably, a six per cent preferred stock convertible into common stock on a share-to-share basis," reported the *Motion Picture Herald*. "The investment bankers are on the way in at this very minute."

Within the studio, while the lower-level animators continued on the shorts, the top animators worked on *Fantasia*. Babbitt's pièces de résistance in the film were from Tchaikovsky's *Nutcracker Suite*: the Russian Trepak and the Chinese Dance. Both were designed in pastel by artist Elmer Plummer. Plummer had painted thistles and orchids for the Russian Trepak, and short, plump mushrooms with wide rice-farmer-style caps for the Chinese Dance.

The sequences in *Fantasia*'s *Nutcracker Suite* were conceived to be artistic explorations of gradation, repetition, unity, contrast, and harmony. However, Babbitt turned the Chinese Dance into something more. He created a tiny mushroom child whose personality jumped off the screen.

Babbitt would describe the littlest mushroom (later given the name Hop Low by the studio when the character proved popular) like a latent self-portrait. "It was the story of one character who was constantly out of step with all the others," he explained, "and he never did quite get into the crowd. Except there was one occasion—I think it was the scene where he marches toward the camera, and then on back, as if he were reviewing his troops—which gives you an indication of the little guy's cocky character." He blithely added, "He is not aware—or refuses to accept—that he is at fault; that there is something wrong with him."

It was at this time that a feud between Plummer and Babbitt began. Babbitt ignored Plummer's model sheets that uniformly turned the mushroom caps into rice-farmer hats and instead varied the sizes and shapes of the mushrooms. Disgruntled, Plummer told Babbitt's assistant Bill Hurtz, "These old-timers are on their way out. They're not keeping up with the times." Hurtz was left to shuttle the drawings to and from Babbitt's and Plummer's rooms as each corrected the other's artwork. The animated result became a bizarre morphing of mushroom shapes that lasted for a solid minute. The inconsistency even passed Walt's critical eye. In the sweatbox, Walt only gave one note: instead of the little guy bowing on the final beat, have him miss the beat and bow after. Babbitt made the change, keeping the littlest mushroom out of step through to the end.

On March 18 the studio utilized their big new theater and screened a work-in-progress reel of *Fantasia*. Babbitt's mushroom scene received high praise from the other animators. "He deserves it," remarked a witness. The next day, the animators were still talking about the scene. Babbitt responded glibly, "Well now maybe Walt won't fire me!"

Work on *Bambi* was still moving through the pipeline. It was going to be a tour de force of animation and Disney's "A" picture.

The "B" picture, *Dumbo*, was significantly cheaper. Whereas *Pinocchio* cost $2.6 million and *Fantasia* was costing $2 million, *Dumbo* would cost less than $650,000. It would run just sixty-four minutes and be animated in a loose, cartoony style that was more facile. The title character wouldn't even speak.

In March the Disney studio animators attended an initial lunch meeting for *Dumbo*. Lead animators would have included Babbitt, Bill Tytla, and art-school grads Ward Kimball and Woolie Reitherman.

Fred Moore, once the studio's star animator, was not invited. In his room, he yelled and drank from his whiskey stash. His assignments had gotten smaller as the features grew more sophisticated. His drinking had also gotten worse. His friends in the studio often saw him curse himself at his desk and drink throughout the day.

On March 25 Walt pulled up to his studio to see the operators of his air-conditioning system on strike, wielding picket signs reading ENGINEER ON STRIKE and UNFAIR TO ENGINEERS. Police officers patrolled the gate, each armed with two pistols and tear gas bombs.

Walt called one of the officers over. "What the hell are those guys doing out there?" he demanded.

"They're on strike, Walt," said the officer.

"For Christ's sake," said Walt, "tell 'em to get back to work; we'll have a meeting tonight!" He drove through the gate, and the striking engineers returned to work.

Back at the original Disney lot on Hyperion Avenue, the cameramen also had grievances. Gunther Lessing called the five members of the Federation's negotiating committee—including Babbitt and Bill Roberts—to settle the issue. The committee had not met in several months, having voted to not put pressure on the management. Now they were being asked to placate the cameramen.

"I found that it was a matter of salaries and that the fellows weren't getting raises," said Roberts in 1942. Subsequently, Roberts went to the Camera Department representative and acquired a salary schedule for their future raises. He took the schedule to production control manager Herb Lamb and production engineer Bill Garity, who agreed to put the salary schedule into effect. "However," said Roberts, "the union wasn't very active, and none of us were very active in pushing the thing." Soon, the cameramen's grievance was forgotten.

———————

One of Walt's proudest claims was that his company never had to answer to stockholders. That changed at the start of April. To compensate for a newly growing debt, 755,000 shares of Disney stock were sold publicly, raising $3.5 million. The sum roughly amounted to the cost of the Burbank studio. Roy could be overheard grumbling, "Christ, that bastard never owned anything in his life. Just when he'd about get ready to make the 18th payment on his car, he'd buy another. Now he's bought a new studio."

Meanwhile, the war in Europe was obliterating movie ticket sales there. On April 9, the Nazis invaded Denmark and Norway. The allied resistance of France and Britain braced to halt a larger German invasion, just as they had in the Great War.

By mid-April, *Pinocchio* was still far from breaking even. "'Pinocchio' I hear, is laying a financial egg, may be lucky to meet production cost," wrote national columnist Walter Winchell. Walt Disney Productions was once again sinking in debt. Production work on *Bambi* slowed. Babbitt joined Fred Moore, Wilfred Jackson, Ward Kimball, and Norm Ferguson for lunch. They talked about bad story ideas and the issuance of Disney stock, but everybody seemed to be worried about the fate of the studio.

Cuts had to be made, and employees started to be laid off. On April 23, the animators learned that Johnny Cannon's contract was not being renewed. Cannon had been one of Disney's first animators, predating them all. It was sobering news, especially for those who were questioning their own job security.

On May 9 the Nazis invaded the Netherlands and, on May 16, Belgium. German tanks proceeded unhindered through the Ardennes Forest at the Belgium-Luxembourg border. The invasion of Western Europe had begun.

Only another quick, inexpensive film could keep the studio afloat. In mid-May, Walt desperately pitched to his story team a *Jack and the Beanstalk* feature starring Mickey Mouse: "The main idea is that we are trying to get a feature out of here in a hell of a hurry . . . our European market is shot—which you're all aware of, and we have to get something out of here that can go out and make some money on just the American market alone." Walt calculated that the war was cutting the studio's profits by 40 to 45 percent, and he told his artists that to avoid further layoffs everyone would have to cut corners.

"I felt responsible to every one of them," said Walt in 1942, breaking down in tears. "In the spring of 1940 I was about going crazy—"

At the time, the company employed nearly twelve hundred people. Walt met with the bank and board of directors. "It was obvious that the representatives and stockholders demanded that I reduce my staff to less than half immediately . . ." he said. "I tried to find another way. I tried to increase my output of short subjects. . . . I fought as long as I could to keep these people there."

Then the mass layoffs began. From May through June, employees were let go by the hundreds.

"Our personnel is to be cut, between 300 and 400 people, in the next few weeks," wrote one artist on May 26. "It has begun already, and last week the axe fell on about 25, and this Saturday 50 people were released. What makes it nerve-wracking is that the people who are being canned are simply those who are not working on anything vital at the moment, more or less regardless of ability. . . . And every other studio will be in the same position, so that there will be practically no chance of finding another artist's job."

"We are all fighting mental battles now," wrote another artist on June 4.

By mid-June, Herb Lamb told the staff that the studio was still over budget. In lieu of more layoffs, the Disney staff accepted a company-wide pay cut.

On June 17, 1940, the French military surrendered to Germany, and the Nazis marched through Paris. As Washington raced to prepare for war, US citizens began to experience rising prices of food, gas, and other basic expenses. Income taxes were scheduled to increase. Compounded with the Disney pay cuts, it was nearly impossible for the average employee to save money.

Babbitt had even more to contend with. He filed for divorce from Marge on June 21.

That summer, Babbitt and Woolie Reitherman animated sky-bound Goofy in *Goofy's Glider* (directed by Jack Kinney). In Europe, the summer-long Battle of Britain was fought in the sky, as the Royal Air Force defended the United Kingdom from German warplanes.

20 | HILBERMAN, SORRELL, AND BIOFF

IN 1947, SIX YEARS after the Disney strike, Walt Disney sat before the House Un-American Activities Committee. Two chief investigators faced him.

"Have you at any time, in the past, had any Communists employed at your studio?" asked one investigator.

"Yes," said Walt, "in the past I had some people that I definitely feel were Communists."

Walt named four people that day. Dave Hilberman was the only artist he mentioned. The other three were the business managers of the Screen Cartoon Guild. One of those three was the strike organizer Herbert K. Sorrell.

Up to 1940, Hilberman, then twenty-nine, had been happy at the Disney studio. He had been Bill Tytla's assistant and a talented layout artist, but he witnessed the mass layoffs in disbelief. Hilberman may have been the Disney artist most viscerally affected by the layoffs.

Born and raised in 1911 in Cleveland, Ohio, Hilberman attended the Cleveland School of Art for three years before joining the Cleveland Play House as a stagehand. Soon he became friends with locals who were members of the John Reed Club, an association of "leftwing artists, writers, musicians, part of the anti-fascist movement then." In 1932 at age twenty-one, he signed up for a one-week club trip to Communist Russia. Something about the trip hooked Hilberman, and he extended his stay for six months.

Disney strike leaders pose with heads of the Screen Actors Guild. Standing (left to right): George Bodle, Herb Sorrell, Kenneth Thomson (founding member of SAG), Bill Tytla, and Noel Madison (founding member of SAG). Kneeling: Dave Hilberman and Art Babbitt.

Hilberman enrolled in a program at the Leningrad Academy of Art, a Communist state-sponsored school that provided its students with a monthly stipend, housing, and art supplies. He earned extra money working backstage at three Leningrad theaters. Doing so, he discovered that Communism promoted racial equality such as he had never witnessed. "Between scenes, a White and Negro character appear at opposite ends of the proscenium arch and sing tunes as overtures to the next scene," he wrote during that time. "Between acts the Negro singer came out to the audience and made a direct appeal to them to fight against race discrimination."

When he returned to the States, Hilberman told a Cleveland reporter that "he finds America dull and lifeless. . . . In Leningrad there was more fun and laughter. . . . Here, he finds, people are too serious-minded."

In July 1936 during Disney's nationwide talent hunt, he was recruited with about forty other artists. Hilberman listed his Leningrad training, and at the time, Walt Disney considered the experience to his credit. He started at an entry-level position earning twenty dollars a week.

The Disney studio contrasted greatly with Leningrad. At Disney there was little artistic freedom; the pay was nearly half of what he could get as a set painter. Hilberman must have been struck by the difference, because it was around this time that he joined the Communist Party. In December 1937 it was Hilberman who picked up the issue of *Time* magazine and showed the article about Bioff to Babbitt.

By early 1938 Hilberman was earning ninety dollars a week as a top layout man, and he was the first production layout artist to start working on *Bambi*. By 1940 he was supervising six others. When it came to talking with management, including Roy Disney, Hilberman was the spokesperson for forty other layout artists.

When the layoffs began that summer, everyone was on unsure footing. "You were about as good as Walt's eyebrow was that day," remembered one artist. Everything changed for Hilberman when he learned that his friend, *Fantasia* layout artist Zack Schwartz, was among those being laid off. Hilberman beseeched his superiors to reconsider, making a case for Schwartz's talent and efficiency. "The powers that be wouldn't hear of it," he later said. "There was a situation where, having satisfied the director with the quality of your work, having [people] pitching for you, it still didn't count. Which meant that you had absolutely no job security. This created a real uncertainty and a fear among the people."

The firings seemed to be unjust, but there was no independent entity to hear the artists' grievances. There was no one who could bargain collectively with the management on behalf of the employees. There was no bona fide union.

To Art Babbitt, the studio's policies began to reek of injustice. In mid-August 1940, he was shocked to learn that his experienced animation assistant, Bill Hurtz, was still earning only a top inbetweener's salary of $25 a week. Hurtz requested $27.50 a week—the starting salary for an assistant. Babbitt penned a vitriolic note and sent it to Walt, who paged Babbitt to his office. Babbitt stormed in. Walt told him to mind his own business, and that if he or anyone else didn't like the way the company was run, they could quit. Babbitt retorted that if the studio could not afford to give Hurtz a $2.50 raise, Babbitt would pay Hurtz out of his own pocket. Walt must have weighed the consequences. At the end of the day, Hurtz received his raise.

But the studio was hurting. In the last year, it had lost $1.25 million, about 12 percent of the company's total worth. Walt was not one to squirrel away cash; he had reinvested everything back into the studio. To cut costs, several projects still in development were placed on hold, like *Alice in Wonderland* and *Peter Pan*. Walt needed something cheaper and faster, and he swiftly began developing another feature film—one that would be only partially animated, only partially in Technicolor, and just 72 minutes long. Called *The Reluctant Dragon* after its cartoon centerpiece, it would be a whimsical tour of the Disney studio on film, interspersed with cartoon sequences.

Around late August Babbitt was put on the cartoon *Baggage Buster*. In the short, Goofy tries in vain to handle a magician's steamer trunk. Once again, Babbitt utilized live-action reference. He enlisted Dick Lundy to model Goofy's movements, and Babbitt filmed him in front of the studio soundstage for several minutes over a few days. Walt showed up one day, brimming with enthusiasm. He said he had a new idea for a Goofy series. In Walt's hand was a manual titled *How to Ski*. The Goof, said Walt, could star in an entire series of "How To" shorts. Babbitt saw that Goofy was evolving into an active sportsman—thanks to Woolie Reitherman.

As Babbitt was animating, he grew tense and insecure. The inspired looseness that once came so easily to him was gone. "Suddenly I had stiffened up in my animation," he later reflected. "It's like somebody getting stage fright—on a stage or in the movies. And my work began to look and feel metallic. It had a hardness to it. . . . I wanted my characters to live, and they weren't really living." He was doing what the teacher Don Graham had warned everyone against; he was tracing, not caricaturing. Babbitt followed the live-action reference so closely that Goofy's hands even had five fingers instead of four.

Director Jack Kinney was unsatisfied. He said, "Mr. Babbitt required live action to be shot on all of his pick-up animation, that he would follow very closely. In fact, for my money, it was too close." Walt remembered telling Babbitt, "'You can't use it as a crutch; it should be for inspiration only.' . . . It got to a point where all of his work was stiff."

Walt didn't need to tell this to the art-school graduates like Woolie Reitherman, Ward Kimball, or Frank Thomas. Nor did they appear to have any interest in unions.

Vice President Gunther Lessing was in a panic. It was around early September 1940, and he had learned that the IATSE had signed up seventeen cameramen—the majority of the department. These were the same cameramen who had voiced grievances earlier that year. Lessing, flanked by Herb Lamb, called Babbitt, Bill Roberts, and the rest of the Federation's negotiating committee into his office.

The committee hadn't met since Lessing's attempt to placate the cameramen six months before. Roberts called two of the cameramen up to Lessing's room. He asked what had happened to the schedule for salary increases that he passed to Herb Lamb and Bill Garity. The cameramen said that no raises were distributed.

Lessing demanded to know what the Federation would do about this IATSE infiltration. Roberts replied, "We can't do anything, we don't have a contract with anybody."

Lessing drew up some figures for salary increases. He told the committee members to find those cameramen and lie to them: say that the Federation had negotiated the increases. Roberts was shocked. Management "didn't want it to look as if the outside union (the IATSE) had forced them in any way to make these adjustments that had long ago been suggested," he said.

Babbitt was incensed, saying, "What you are trying to do is get me to stooge for you, and I won't do it for you or for anybody else." Roberts suggested an idea: since Lessing had the names of the cameramen who signed with the IATSE, he could transfer them all to another department, thereby making the union membership for camera operators moot. If that failed, he could simply fire them. Babbitt jumped in: "If you do that to them," he said, "I personally will report it to the IATSE, because if you are capable of pulling a trick like that on those men for joining the IATSE, you are capable of pulling the trick on any one of us."

The meeting ended. Later that day, the Federation committee reconvened in Roberts's room. They agreed not to revive or persist with the Federation but simply to "let it die."

Outside the grip of the IATSE, it seemed that nearly every craft in Hollywood had a union or two fighting for representation. These included:

- The Art Directors Guild (ADG)
- The American Federation of Musicians (AFM)
- The American Federation of Radio Artists (AFRA)
- The American Guild of Musical Artists (AGMA)
- The American Guild of Variety Artists (AGVA)
- The Artists Managers Guild (AMG)
- The Motion Picture Costume Makers (MPCM)
- The Screen Actors Guild (SAG)
- The Screen Directors Guild (SDG)
- The Society of Motion Picture Artists and Illustrators (SMPAI)
- The Society of Motion Picture Film Editors (SMPFE)
- The Screen Publicists Guild (SPG)
- The Screen Writers Guild (SWG)
- The Screen Office Employees Guild (SOEG)

(The list does not include unions for other trades, like engineers, electricians, drivers, and service workers.) Around Hollywood, one out of every five working professionals was a union member.

Across the nation, unions were growing and competing for members, while parent organizations scrambled to represent them. The IATSE was one such organization, and by late 1940 it had to compete against two monoliths: the Congress of Industrial Organizations (CIO)—previously called the Committee for Industrial Organization—and the American Federation of Labor (AFL).

The CIO was a midwestern giant, focused mainly on factory unions like those of the automotive, steel, and rubber industries. The AFL dominated the coasts, prioritizing craft unions like those in entertainment and publicity. After the Federation of Motion Picture Crafts dissolved, the AFL absorbed the Hollywood Painters Union—which had won the 1937 strike.

That victorious strike caused a swell of Hollywood unionism. In its aftermath, one leader emerged as the hero of Hollywood labor: Herbert K. Sorrell.

Tall, heavy, and broad-shouldered, Sorrell looked like a prizefighter who could get things done. Sorrell was born in 1897 in Deepwater, Missouri, a state rife with labor disputes. There was great railroad-worker strike in 1877, followed by a general strike of several different types of laborers in St. Louis. In 1897 the pastor of St. Louis's Central Christian Church said, "The burning questions of today are those of social righteousness" and declared that capitalists had built "a system of industrial slavery."

From an early age, Sorrell was exposed to the ravages of union wars. Sorrell's father was a factory worker and a leader of a successful company strike. In 1900 a great streetcar-workers strike in St. Louis turned violent, ending with two hundred laborers injured and fourteen dead. When Sorrell was a boy, his father led another strike but failed. "I heard him say many times, 'If you can't pull the men up with you, pull out and leave them,'" remembered Sorrell.

Sorrell spent his adolescence earning "a man's salary" in manual labor and defending himself against bullies. In 1917 Sorrell was a riveter in a shipyard. When the United States entered the Great War that April, Sorrell went out on strike. It was a crime to stop industrial labor during wartime, and in lieu of jail time he opted to be drafted. By the time he got his papers in order (under an assumed name), the war was over.

As a young man, he was a professional boxer. He had the nose of someone who had endured many blows to the face. In the early 1920s Sorrell founded a painting business in Oakland, California, becoming an employer himself. "I hold no prejudice against employers or people who hire men to do the work. It is a necessary thing, and, having been one, I feel that I know that end of it," he said. In 1923 he sold his business and traveled to Hollywood for a set-painting job at Universal Studios.

In 1925 Sorrell attended a union meeting held, as he recalled, by the Brotherhood of Set Painters and Scene Decorators because they promised free beer— and "because I could see that was one way that we could raise the standard of living in the studios. I joined the union that night."

One day the following year, Sorrell's employer demanded to see everyone's union card. When Sorrell proudly presented his, he was immediately fired. Everywhere Sorrell sought work, his union status led to his termination. Sorrell began crashing film shoots in the streets of Hollywood. He introduced himself as a union organizer and asked the cameramen for their union cards. If they couldn't present them, he smashed their cameras.

On November 29, 1926, the first Studios Basic Agreement was made with Hollywood labor, prohibiting discrimination to union members. Sorrell gladly returned to work painting Hollywood sets.

During that time, he followed the news that George Browne and Willie Bioff had taken control of the IATSE. In 1937 Sorrell helped create the FMPC to block the IATSE from signing up members. In April he was one of the picket captains who fought in the big Hollywood strike of 1937. "As soon as we went out, Bioff and Browne said we were Communists," said Sorrell. He blatantly ignored the city ordinance that picket lines could not cross a driveway, since every studio gate was a driveway. Outside Paramount Pictures, Sorrell used his intimidation tactics to drive strikebreakers from the lot. Sorrel was soon appointed the business agent of the Painters Union, competing with IATSE for members and influence. While other unions caved to IATSE's pressures and bribes, Sorrell's Painters Union refused to break the strike. Eventually Bioff sent Mafia goons to fight the FMPC strikers. Sorrell and his men surprised the goons at their hotels and pummeled them. "I am not pulling any punches," he said later. "We had to fight for everything we got."

After the strike was settled, Sorrell confronted Willie Bioff about who had jurisdiction over a group of forty-eight scenic painters. The ex-boxer towered over the squat IATSE kingpin, and Bioff gave up without a fight. During settlement negotiations, Sorrell learned that Bioff was standing in the way of the painters negotiating a 20 percent raise (instead of only 10 percent). Sorrell went to see Bioff in his "illustrious setup" of an office. "Bioff got all white, and he sat down and he got sick," recalled Sorrell. "So he did not get back to work for several days." The scenic painters got their 20 percent raise.

After the Painters Union won the strike, other crafts sought to align with them. Herb Sorrell had made a name for himself. He would shortly be called "studio labor's No. 1 leader."

Sorrell's efforts appeared to work, and Willie Bioff left town in 1938. On August 4, 1939, after nearly a year, Bioff suddenly returned to Hollywood on a secret flight. He threatened movie producers and demanded closed shops (requiring every craftsman to be a union member), potentially swelling IATSE numbers.

While Bioff regrew his influence, Sorrell was building his. He fought to strengthen the Painters Union like he was amassing an anti-IATSE army.

In October 1939 Bioff and the IATSE won a 10 percent raise for their film technicians. Herb Sorrell, however, fighting on behalf of the Painters Union, won a 15 percent increase for its studio painters. Some days later, Bioff received a letter from a studio manager to revoke the IATSE 10 percent raise. Unbelievably, Bioff accepted (along with a likely bribe) and tried—unsuccessfully—to meet with his representatives to cancel his own union's wage increase. The news put Bioff's true allegiance under scrutiny yet again.

Outside the Disney studio, the Screen Cartoon Guild was making strides. At the end of October the National Labor Relations Board declared the Guild the legal representative for cartoonists at Warner Bros., MGM, and Universal Pictures. Warner Bros. was the home of Porky Pig, Daffy Duck, and a wily gray hare to be christened Bugs Bunny. MGM was working on its first cartoon starring a cat-and-mouse duo soon named Tom and Jerry. Universal produced cartoons starring Andy Panda, and in a year would debut Woody Woodpecker.

But National Labor Relations Board certification did not require studios to recognize the Guild as a bargaining entity for their employees. That was at the discretion of studio management. And to management, Hollywood unions stank of the IATSE and Willie Bioff.

Conservative journalist Westbrook Pegler had been spending weeks preparing to take down Willie Bioff with his syndicated column Fair Enough, known for its anti-union, anti–New Deal rhetoric. Now Pegler went to new investigative lengths, traveling to Chicago to uncover Bioff's police records and interview law enforcement officers. He published his exposé on Bioff on November 22, 1939.

With characteristic bravado, Pegler wrote, "Willie Bioff, the labor dictator of the entire amusement industry of the United States and Canada, and sole arbiter, on the union side, of problems affecting 35,000 men and women of mechanical crafts of Hollywood, was convicted of pandering in a trial before Judge Arnold Heap of the Chicago Municipal Court in February, 1922." Pegler revealed Bioff's 1922 conviction for running a brothel and serving only one week of his six-month sentence. He also explained Bioff's ties to the Capone gang.

That very day, the court of Chicago's Cook County issued a warrant against Bioff, right when Bioff was scheduled to lead union negotiations. Bioff conveniently framed Pegler's exposé as an anti-union smear. "It looks like a plot to discredit me on the eve of negotiations with film producers," Bioff responded. "For fifteen years I was around Chicago and immediately available if they wanted me."

From late November through December 1939, Bioff and his lawyers futilely fought his extradition. Bioff was finally sent to prison on February 20, 1940, to complete his original six-month sentence. "I would call my plight persecution," Bioff declared. "Maybe I have been doing too much for the working man. I think the big interests are after me." He also blamed opposing unions, "and the Communists."

This gave George Browne, Bioff's accomplice, license to send a Communist-hunting senator to Hollywood to set up a "Congressional Committee to Investigate Un-Americanism." The move was designed to weaken all non-IATSE unions.

Herb Sorrell did not let this witch hunt go unopposed. He stated publicly that this senator would do better to investigate Willie Bioff than potential Communists in Hollywood. Enlisting famed writers Dorothy Parker and Donald Ogden Stewart, Sorrell helped lead a demonstration against the fearmongering senator.

Hollywood relished Bioff's absence. *Variety* wrote, "Since he left here to return to Chicago and pay his debt to society, Hollywood labor affairs no longer have been turbulent. The people of the industry were not compelled to sit on the anxious seat because of what Willie might say or do."

On September 20, 1940, Willie Bioff completed the balance of his sentence. A car drove up to the Chicago prison around a gaggle of reporters positioned out front. Then it veered to the unoccupied side entrance, picked Bioff up, and whisked him away. As it drove off, Bioff threw a typed statement out of the car window: "I hope those who are responsible for my incarceration are satisfied," it read. "I have paid my pound of flesh to society."

He immediately flew back to Hollywood to expand his empire.

21 | THE FEDERATION VERSUS THE GUILD

OF ALL THE MANY CRAFTS IN HOLLYWOOD, animation was the last to unionize. As Herb Sorrell testified later, "The cartoonists throughout the industry were very much underpaid." Perhaps it was because animation was a newer enterprise, or the themes were commonly filled with risibility and fantasy. Or because, as Robert D. Feild wrote in July 1941, Disney's animation "is to most people still a mystery while the artist himself is an enigma invariably associated with a Mouse." Whatever the reason, labor organizations noticed this. (By September 1940 even the CIO had approached animation artists at Disney and MGM.)

The Screen Cartoon Guild—newly renamed the Screen Cartoonists Guild—needed an advantage. Bill Littlejohn, a high-ranking MGM animator, was president of the Guild. An MGM assistant animator, Cuban-born Pepe Ruiz, was its financial secretary. They approached the Painters Union, which was part of the AFL and of which Herb Sorrell was the famed business agent. The Guild arranged to become an affiliate of the Painters Union, which provided two invaluable resources: the support of the AFL, with its thousands of members across the country, and Sorrell himself.

Sorrell went to work. Given that Littlejohn and Ruiz worked there, Sorrell approached MGM animation first. They signed up the MGM animation artists with the Guild, collecting union cards with signatures.

Sorrell took the stack of signed union cards to MGM producer Fred Quimby, argued for the Guild's representation, and challenged MGM's

156

Screen Cartoonists Guild leader and MGM animator Bill Littlejohn. Image captured by striker Ray Patin.

proposed pay scale. He was met with what he called "the usual opposition." On Wednesday night, September 18, the MGM cartoonists voted to strike in one week if they didn't get representation. The threat made front-page headlines.

MGM was not the only animation studio under Sorrell's scope. As MGM animators were voting to strike, Sorrell reached out to one Disney artist who, he had heard, was the mouthpiece for forty other artists: Dave Hilberman.

Hilberman was distraught about the sudden mass layoffs. He invited a dozen coworkers to his home and pitched them the benefits of an independent, industry-wide union. They, too, had grievances that could only be addressed through collective bargaining. The most important was job security.

First, Hilberman needed proof that the majority of Disney employees wanted the Guild to represent them. He needed membership cards. Acquiring signatures would take time. Hilberman printed blank cards and distributed them throughout the Disney studio. The ones that came back with signatures he forwarded to Sorrell and Littlejohn.

The Guild triumphed on September 21 when MGM signed a union contract. The agreement stipulated a 100 percent closed shop as well as a forty-hour workweek, paid overtime, and a $4 increase in starting salaries. Animators and layout artists would start at $85 a week, assistant animators at $30 a week, inbetweeners and inkers at $22 a week, and painters $20 a week. The new MGM wages were all greater than those at Disney. The Guild's victory was also front-page news. Suddenly, Guild membership cards at Disney started coming back to Hilberman with signatures.

The country was becoming more pro-labor every day. On October 24, 1940, a federally mandated forty-hour workweek went into effect. Nicknamed the Wages and Hours Act, this law guaranteed overtime pay for any nonspecialists. The following Monday, October 28, Walt Disney Productions released a memo stating that overtime would soon be paid for hours over forty per week for employees who weren't considered specialists. This would curtail the Saturday half-day. The memo somberly concluded that the act "will add a further burden of overtime payments to the losses already suffered through the curtailment of foreign revenues."

The artists, however, were thrilled. "For the first time in five-and-a-half years I would receive overtime! I was elated," remembered one of Walt's loyal artists. "But any pleasure I got from the new law was spoiled by the usual rumor of Christmas layoffs."

By November the studio had assigned the last of the lead animators for *Dumbo*. Bill Tytla would animate the title character, inspired by his own two-year-old son, Peter.

Ward Kimball, a fan of southern music, was assigned the crows. Fred Moore was given the boyish and appealing Timothy Q. Mouse. Babbitt was assigned the singing delivery boy, Mr. Stork. To animate him, Babbitt caricatured voice actor Sterling Holloway's overgrown hair and half-lidded eyes.

The rest of the studio was working on cartoon shorts and a slew of features: *Bambi*, *The Reluctant Dragon*, the *Jack and the Beanstalk*–inspired "Mickey Feature," *The Wind in the Willows*, and a follow-up to *Fantasia*.

Babbitt's work was sharply interrupted late one morning in early December with an urgent message on the dictograph (the Disney company loudspeaker). Walt required to see the five committee members of the now-defunct

Federation. When the group, led by Bill Roberts and Babbitt, arrived in Walt's office, they faced Walt, Gunther Lessing, personnel director Hal Adelquist, and personnel manager Hugh Pressley. Walt was clearly agitated as he passed around a letter he had just received. It was from the Screen Cartoonists Guild, stating that the Guild had signed up a majority of Disney artists and that it was requesting a meeting to gain recognition at the studio. (According to evidence, this majority was an accurate count.)

Babbitt described the conversation in great detail two years later: Walt was desperate for the Federation to reorganize in order to block the Guild (as it had with the IATSE), and he offered to sign a closed-shop agreement immediately.

Babbitt said that he would be ashamed to face the Federation members after a year and a half of negotiation refusals. Walt replied that if people on the outside told him how to run his business, he would do everything he could to resist them, and that if necessary he would close down the studio. He instructed Babbitt to call up the Federation's attorney, Leonard Janofsky, to get to work laying out demands for a closed-shop agreement. Babbitt refused, confident that Janofsky wouldn't work on behalf of management.

The meeting had not gone as Walt had hoped, and he was cautioned (presumably by Lessing) not to discuss labor issues with his employees thereafter.

At 10:00 AM the next day, Bill Roberts called the other ex-Federation negotiating committee members into his room, ready to revive the Federation. Babbitt, however, thought that using the Federation to block a bona fide union was "a dirty trick." As far as he was concerned, he was through. Two of the other four committee members, including Norm Ferguson, agreed with Babbitt; one member was neutral, and only Roberts opposed.

Acting on his own, Roberts contacted Janofsky. The attorney said that he refused to work with the Federation any longer. When Babbitt heard this, he told Roberts that Janofsky certainly suspected that the Federation was a studio-dominated "company union"—a sham.

Within a few days, Roberts found a new lawyer—one who had handled an auto accident case for a coworker—and scheduled a Federation meeting at his home on Monday night, December 16, 1940.

That night at Bill Roberts's house, sixteen representatives across every creative department gathered to discuss the possibility of reorganizing the Federation. A stenographer recorded the meeting.

After Roberts briefed everyone, Babbitt spoke up. "I had no intention of being here at all tonight because if anyone was thoroughly disgusted, I have been," he said. "Right from the start we have always maintained that not only were we trying to keep out an outside union, but we mentioned the specific outside union and that was the IATSE. We never said anything about trying to keep out unions in general. I have always made it very clear that my own personal standpoint has been that I have no bones to pick with unionism."

With his flair for pomp, Babbitt then read two sections of the National Labor Relations Act—one pertaining to workers' rights to organize without interference, the other against company-sponsored unions.

"I don't feel vindictive about the thing," Babbitt continued. "I think it's a misunderstanding on everybody's part. If Walt had taken the trouble to find out what we were doing and why we were doing it, the contract would have been signed a long time ago. . . . I would have liked to have said to Walt, 'Well, you're the boss—whatever you say goes,' and then I'd be a good boy. But still at the same time I feel I owe an obligation to all the people that have been foolish enough to follow me into this thing, and I can't feel that it's right. I really can't."

"Then you're for the other union?" one of the artists asked him.

"I'm not for any union," said Babbitt.

"But you're against *this*—what do you want to do?" asked the artist.

"We are going through a social change, and it is inevitable that there will be union organizations," said Babbitt. "Every day the studio is dealing with electricians' unions, actors' unions, musicians' unions—but aside from that, assuming that I was wrong, assuming that there wasn't that change taking place, I can't have confidence in what Gunther Lessing says today after all the times we have been stalled and pushed around and made fun of. . . . I'd like to oblige Walt, and I'd like to do what he wants us to do because all in all he's been pretty square, but I don't think that this [reviving the Federation] is going to do him any good or us any good."

There was impassioned debate on both sides of the issue. "If this other thing gets in," said one artist, "maybe the studio will go broke."

"As swell as Walt has been in the past," said Babbitt, "I'm not polishing any apples, I've got my foot in too far—he's never taken the trouble to see the other side. He's firmly convinced that all unions are stevedores and gangsters. It has never occurred to him that he might find a decent person to deal with. . . ."

I do think Walt is very much in need of a little education along those lines. Now isn't the time to do it. I think his feeling is so strong against these other unions, and one of the first things he can do to stop them is reorganize this Federation."

The artists began comparing the salaries between Disney and MGM, and there was genuine concern with the discrepancy among the inkers, painters, inbetweeners, assistants, and junior animators.

"Personally," said Roberts, "I'm convinced of this, that Walt all along has shown a tendency to neglect the people in those jobs, and I think some work would have to be done on them if we ever tried to start this thing. I think that's the first thing we'd have to do, because Walt isn't interested in them. He's interested too much in what he called the 'creative and inspirational help.' And he isn't interested and doesn't respect those jobs where there is tedious but absolutely necessary work and hard work."

Babbitt responded, "I'm actually under the belief that the guys that signed with another union signed because they were discontented, and I'm sure it wasn't all salary."

"What would it be if it wasn't salary?" barked Roberts. "Fresh air? Opening the windows or something?"

The answer, of course, was job security. "You know everyone that gets fired has a grievance," replied Babbitt. "That causes a lot of dissension, and it's something like that that makes the guys want to join a protective organization."

At the end of the meeting, the members voted to decide whether to hold a studio-wide meeting to revive the Federation or to let it remain inactive. Fourteen members voted to revive the Federation. And so the motion was carried.

As Babbitt drove home, he was left to wonder if anyone else agreed with why Janofsky had quit—that the Federation was, in fact, a company-dominated sham. He had read them the National Labor Relations Act, and he voiced the need of an independent grievance committee. He could feed them facts and figures, but like Goofy trying to close a magician's steamer trunk, there was just no helping it. Disorder was on the horizon.

22 | THE GUILD AND BABBITT

BABBITT REFUSED TO PARTICIPATE any longer in the Federation, which was now campaigning to sign up as many Disney artists as possible. Bill Roberts, still acting as president, had prepared new blank membership cards.

Technically, Roberts himself was now a supervisor, ranking him among management and therefore ineligible to join a union. Nonetheless, studio supervisors soon appeared with stacks of Federation membership cards and handed them to the lower-level artists, including one of Babbitt's assistants. This coercion was deliberately in violation of the National Labor Relations Act. If the Federation wouldn't take labor law seriously, perhaps someone else would.

The Screen Cartoonists Guild got wind of these coercive tactics and soon sent orders to the studio to cease and desist. On the afternoon of January 4, 1941, Roberts had a secret meeting with a few of Walt's most loyal supervising artists at one participant's home. There was a Guild spy at the studio, he said, and the group debated who it could be. They suspected Norm Ferguson.

On January 9 the Guild began its campaign to organize Disney. Sorrell and the AFL drafted flyers, printed at the AFL's expense, and gave the flyers to newsboys hired to distribute them at the Disney gate. These papers answered questions like "How can I show an interest in the Guild without endangering my job?" and "If I have already signed a Federation card does that bind me to vote for it?" (It didn't.) The flyers also emphasized how affiliation with the AFL strengthened the Guild. The handouts invited all Disney employees to an evening seminar on Thursday, January 16.

The afternoon before that seminar, the Federation convened in the local high school auditorium. To everyone's exasperation, nothing was accomplished, and no plans were laid out. "What a bunch of amateurs," commented one artist.

The Guild's meeting included several speakers: AFL representative Aubrey Blair, Screen Cartoonists Guild attorney George Bodle, and Guild business manager Herb Sorrell, as well as representatives from the Screen Writers Guild and the Screen Office Employees Guild. By the end of the meeting, it was confirmed by the press that a "big majority" of Disney workers had signed up with the Guild.

This did not sit well with Walt's most loyal artists, including director Wilfred Jackson and a group of the art-school graduates, like Woolie Reitherman and Frank Thomas. They sought help from their boss, though Walt resisted. "I explained to them that it was none of my concern, that I had been cautioned to not even talk with any of my boys on labor," Walt said in 1947. The delegation said that they did not want to follow Herb Sorrell, and they proposed a studio-wide election to vote for their preferred union.

AFL representative Aubrey Blair. Image captured by striker Ray Patin.

An election, Walt concurred, would be a clear decider. The Guild agreed to this and filed a petition with the National Labor Relations Board asking for one. A resolution appeared to be imminent.

Meanwhile, Walt was preparing for the general release of *Fantasia*. It was advertised as a once-in-a-lifetime experience, accessible in only select theaters in the United States and with premium ticket prices. The studio had conceived of a new auditory experience called "Fantasound." Special speakers installed around the theater played recordings of eight synchronized audio tracks. Chief engineer Bill Garity traveled to twelve major cities across the United States to supervise the installation of Fantasound units in those theaters. Over lunch, Walt told a group of his loyal animators that installing the Fantasound system cost $1,200 per theater but that union trouble with engineers in New York inflated the cost to $25,000. "He doesn't mind the employees of the studio getting together and organizing," wrote one of the animators at the time, "just so long as they aren't told what to do by some outside bleeder." (The twelve Fantasound units would end up costing the studio $480,000—around three-quarters of the cost of *Dumbo*.)

At the editor's bay, *The Reluctant Dragon* feature required some live-action reshoots. It was for a sequence in an animation room where Norm Ferguson, Fred Moore, and Ward Kimball ham it up. The script had Kimball on camera drawing Mickey, but a rewrite changed the character to Goofy. On January 23, Babbitt was brought in as a hand-double to draw Goofy. In the completed film, the live hand in the brief shot is Babbitt's.

By the end of January, Disney management executed a new tactic to settle labor disputes. They put a labor specialist, a bombastic bootlicker named Anthony O'Rourke, on the company payroll.

Since 1934 O'Rourke had been an impartial chairman of the International Ladies Garment Workers Union, drafting agreements between employers and employees. He professed having settled three to five cases daily. He said, "I told Mr. Walt Disney . . . that I would attempt to straighten out the confused labor conditions existing there, on two conditions: The first one was that I would decide all the cases in the same way that I act as impartial chairman for the Garment industry; and, second, that the decision would be final and binding. . . . Mr. Disney said, 'That is exactly what I want.'"

Soon a flyer appeared on the Disney bulletin boards advertising open meetings with "guest speaker Anthony G. O'Rourke" for all creative employees. At the foot of the flyer, its sponsor was printed in bold: THE FEDERATION.

In these meetings, O'Rourke described his system for judging labor disputes, which he called the "impartial machine." It consisted of a five-person court—two representatives from management, two from the employees, and an "impartial chairman." "It insures just and equitable treatment of all grievances—large and small," O'Rourke stated. This was accompanied by a reminder that the National Labor Relations Board had already designated the Federation as the sole union for Disney employees.

In Hollywood, Columbia Pictures's animation studio, Screen Gems, began negotiations with the Guild for a union contract. The Guild represented the forty-four artists at Screen Gems and, with MGM, two of the top six studios. Still unorganized were Warner Bros. animation, George Pal Studios, Universal Studios animation, and Disney. These six shops employed roughly 1,500 animation artists, including around 630 at Disney alone. Immediately, the Guild began its second campaign for Disney membership.

Babbitt was seething more than ever. The hiring of O'Rourke revealed that the Federation and the Disney company were in cahoots. He coolly decided how to return fire at the Federation, Lessing, and the studio all at once. And he had the ear of the AFL.

On February 3, the AFL filed a charge of unfair labor practice with the National Labor Relations Board against Walt Disney Productions, declaring that Disney "interfered with, restrained and coerced its employees and dominated and interfered with the operation and administration of the Federation of Screen Cartoonists."

Herb Sorrell withdrew the petition for an election. He argued that since the Federation was a company-dominated union, it was illegitimate. If the Federation unit at Disney did not disband, the AFL threatened to place Disney on the Unfair/Do Not Patronize list, prompting a boycott of Disney films and merchandise. The Labor Relations Board opened an investigation to determine the legitimacy of the Federation.

This propelled the right-wing, Hearst-controlled press (like the *Los Angeles Examiner*) to call Sorrell a Communist. Gunther Lessing ensured that Walt saw this, and soon Walt was convinced. He held a meeting with his Personnel Department, noting, "I know that the head of the Painters' local is a Communist. That is why they came out in the papers and gave him hell after he said they would boycott us."

———————

The relaxed campus culture of the studio was slipping away. Tight budgets had caused the company to monitor the artists by the minute. Adelquist called it the "Control System." Female secretaries, called "Control Girls," stood outside each animation unit with time cards tallying the hours spent working and the hours spent idle. This was to determine the cost of each film, and the artists were trusted to fill them out accurately. The time cards were sent to the Time Office and processed on an early IBM machine. Idle time was reported to Adelquist, who saw that Babbitt consistently left his "idle time" space blank.

The studio reported a $140,000 profit in the first fiscal quarter, thanks to revenue from *Fantasia* and with three more feature films—*Dumbo, The Reluctant Dragon*, and *Bambi*—slated before the year's end. On paper the studio looked financially sound.

Nevertheless, on Thursday, February 6, Walt's office issued an urgent memo to all employees: "Statistics prove that the footage output of the plant for the past six weeks has dropped 50%.... The Company recognizes the right of employees to organize and to join in any labor organization of their own choosing, and the Company does not intend to interfere in this right. HOWEVER, the law clearly provides that matters of this sort should be done off the employer's premises and on the employees' own time.... This is an appeal to your sense of fairness and I trust it will be sufficient to remedy the matter. Sincerely, Walt."

This memo rankled even some of Walt's more loyal artists. One remembered, "This appeal to our 'sense of fairness,' coming from the man who had reneged on his promise to pay us twenty percent of his profits from *Snow White*."

Additionally, it didn't appear that the company truly recognized the right of employees to join in any labor organization of their choosing. Gunther Lessing stated publicly that same day, "The Federation of Screen Cartoonists was certified to us two years ago by the labor board as bargaining agent for the employees and until the NLRB certifies someone else we will continue to recognize it."

It was clear what the Disney Guilders had to do. If Lessing was claiming to obey the Labor Relations Board's old ruling, then they needed a new ruling. The Guild had to get certified by the Labor Relations Board.

That night the Guild held a mass meeting at Hollywood's Roosevelt Hotel studio lounge. Speakers included Aubrey Blair of the AFL, Guild attorney George Bodle, Herb Sorrell—and Art Babbitt. What made this meeting momentous, however, were speeches by two of the country's most celebrated thinkers, Donald Ogden Stewart and Dorothy Parker. (Both had protested alongside Sorrell in February 1940, and both were members of the Screen Writers Guild.)

Parker's speech held particular punch. She talked about working for the women's suffrage movement more than two decades before, and recently fighting a company union alongside the Screen Writers Guild. "I think the two words *company union* form the filthiest phrase in the language," she said. "Our Screen Writers Guild is going strong now. But—it took more than seven years. That's what I wanted to say. That's the ugly warning. Don't throw away seven years."

Just as the Screen Cartoonists Guild had an MGM unit and a Warner Bros. unit, the leaders of the meeting planned to form a Disney unit. The next meeting was scheduled for the following Monday, February 10, at 8:15 PM.

On Monday morning, Disney management posted a memo on the bulletin board: "IMPORTANT MEETING TODAY! Place: Theater. Time: 5:00 o'clock. Subject: Talk by Walt." All production staff were required to attend.

As the artists entered the large theater, Walt positioned himself near a microphone, where he was being recorded. At thirty-nine years old, Walt did not consider himself a public speaker. There was nervousness in Walt's voice as he read from his fifteen-page script:

"In the twenty years I have spent in this business, I have weathered many storms." Walt then talked about his life of struggling to make animation "one of the greatest mediums of fantasy and entertainment yet developed."

Babbitt was in the audience. He, too, had been part of the medium's development—from the art education that evolved into a Disney art school, to the character analysis that endowed characters with personality, to the live-action reference that analyzed movement.

Then Walt described how the war in Europe had eliminated half the market. "There are certain individuals who would like to blame the executives of the company for not foreseeing this calamity that was caused by the war in Europe. I think that is unfair. I ask you to look at what happened to France. I ask you to look and see what England and America are doing now, frantically trying to prepare themselves. If *they* didn't know, with all their ways of finding out, the true condition of things over there, how can anyone hold *us* responsible?" Walt went on to describe how much paid vacations and sick leave were costing the company.

Walt had spoken to his artists from the lens of a businessman, and they filed out of the meeting feeling more polarized than ever. What Walt did not express to his artists were his own feelings about the future. He didn't level with them. *Pinocchio* and *Fantasia* had yet to recoup their costs, and the studio was quickly sinking back into debt.

There was a huge turnout at the Screen Cartoonists Guild meeting that night, with the Guild counting more than 250 Disney members. The official Disney unit of the Guild was formed and its officers nominated. Babbitt was nominated for chairman. The deciding election for officers would be held by mail-order ballots to be opened during a meeting on February 18.

Soon after the nomination was made public, Lessing invited Babbitt to his home for dinner. "We had a drink or two and talked a little bit about everything," said Lessing. Then he asked if Babbitt was going to accept the Guild's nomination. Babbitt replied that he would.

Lessing told him that the lower-ranked people he was fighting for weren't worth it. He added that if Babbitt were smart, he would make sure that he suddenly became too "sick" to accept, or just go away for a few days. Otherwise, Lessing cautioned, he was going to get himself into a lot of trouble.

Trouble or not, the Guild was rising in numbers. Walter Lantz, the animation producer of Universal Pictures, was preparing to sign with the Guild. There was one hiccup, though: half of Lantz's artists had formed a company union called the Walter Lantz Employee Association. This was oddly parallel to Disney, except that with Lantz, negotiations progressed steadily, and the Guild triumphed without a strike.

On Tuesday, February 18, at the big Guild meeting, Babbitt was elected chairman of the Disney unit. Hilberman was elected secretary. (In addition, the vice chairman was airbrush artist Phyllis Lambertson, and treasurer was animator Tom Armstrong.) A tentative union contract was discussed and submitted to the committee.

Another issue was also discussed, settled, and put into action—and it would not bode well for Lessing and Babbitt's friendship.

———————

Gunther Lessing must have thought he was doing great as a labor specialist. Starting Monday, February 24, he put forth a new pay scale for the Ink & Paint Department. (The wages still started at $16 but could grow by $2 or $2.50 every three months to $37.50—barring termination.)

Then on Wednesday, February 26, Lessing found a shocking carbon-copied letter on his desk. It was from Guild president Bill Littlejohn and addressed to the head of the Painters District Council, requesting severe action against the Disney company. Littlejohn charged Disney with refusing to negotiate with the Guild, deliberately scheduling work meetings in conflict with Guild meetings, and attempting to revive a defunct company union. Therefore, the Guild asked the council to adopt the resolution to put the Disney company on the official Unfair/Do Not Patronize list of all AFL affiliates throughout the country. It was another boycott threat.

Lessing immediately called Howard Painter, the Federation's new lawyer, and asked if the Guild's Disney unit had authorized this. Painter didn't know, so Lessing summoned Babbitt into his office and asked him directly. Babbitt replied that he knew nothing about it. Lessing asked him if a boycott was a fair tactic, and Babbitt played dumb. Later that day, management officials called Babbitt into a conference, and Babbitt repeated his response.

The next day at the studio, Babbitt had a different story. He told a Federation chairman (possibly Bill Roberts) that twenty-five members of the Guild's Disney unit, including himself, had approved the resolution.

This infuriated the Federation supporters, and bulletins from both the Federation and the Guild bombarded the bulletin boards. The Disney company posted a bulletin headlined, IS DISNEY BOYCOTT IN HANDS OF MGM GUILD? Another read, ARE THESE 25 TO JEOPARDIZE YOUR FUTURE AND THAT OF YOUR 1100 FELLOW EMPLOYEES?

Lessing's handbills may have been meant to sow doubt in the Guild's leaders, so Babbitt posted a bulletin of his own: "CALM DOWN BOYS!! Mr. Lessing is a nice guy and a very smart attorney. He should be able to recognize his own tactics." As opposed to all of his previous posts, this one was boldly signed ART BABBITT, adding a derisive "P.S. May I compliment the Federation on its very close cooperation with the studio attorneys."

Now when Walt saw Babbitt pass by, his eyes followed Babbitt. Walt whispered to his staff that this top animator had become a "Benedict Arnold."

23 | DISNEY VERSUS THE LABOR BOARD

HOLLYWOOD CULTURE IN EARLY 1941 was a tenuous balance of glitz and social upset. Labor news was everywhere, and on a daily basis—one only had to pick up the trade papers. Strike threats were commonplace, used strategically to achieve a union contract. Nearly always a strike was averted by a company's use of poise and diplomacy. Unfortunately, Gunther Lessing possessed those two qualities in increasingly short supply.

At the Academy Awards on February 27, 1941, *Pinocchio* won awards for best score and for the song "When You Wish Upon a Star." As for the Best Short Subject: Cartoons category, Lessing had not sent in a single submission. He was bitter that the Academy had not accepted *Fantasia* for this year's competition, though it had premiered in November. The Academy said it could be submitted next year, but according to the rules, *Fantasia*'s general release in January 1941 disqualified it among the films of 1940. As a result, the winning short cartoon was MGM's *The Milky Way*. Directed and produced by ex-Disney employee Rudolph Ising, it beat out the first cartoons to star Bugs Bunny and Tom and Jerry. Disney had won the Academy Award in this category every year until now; this event forecast a changing tide in Hollywood cartoons.

Back at the Disney animation rooms, Bill Tytla helped Ward Kimball on his dancing crows for *Dumbo*, and Kimball, in turn, attempted to help Fred Moore on Timothy the mouse. Kimball found his efforts to be futile, reflecting, "Fred is so used to success that when a real problem faces him he doesn't know what to do." A sketch cropped up of Fred yelling, "Help! I mean it; I used to knock this stuff out right and left."

171

In one of Moore's sequences, Timothy becomes intoxicated after falling into a bucket of spiked water. Moore struggled with animating the drunken Timothy and ended up digging into the studio's reference library ("morgue") for Babbitt's animation of Abner the drunken mouse. Moore watched the reel and flipped the original drawings. He even pinned some of Babbitt's drawings to his desk as he worked.

Babbitt was fighting his own demons as well. His assignment of Mr. Stork had taken weeks longer than expected. When he was nearly finished, he informed the supervisors that he was ready for his next scenes. However, for the first time in years, there were none to be had. Additional *Dumbo* assignments for Babbitt had mysteriously dried up. In the wake of mass budget cuts, Babbitt's job was only as stable as his deliverables. If there was not enough work to justify employment, an artist would be laid off, as many had before.

Babbitt called Walt's office from his office phone. As Babbitt recalled in 1942, Walt told him that he was so hard to get along with that none of the directors wanted to work with him. It was a surprise to Babbitt. Except for Sam Armstrong (director of *Fantasia*'s mushroom sequence), Babbitt had never had difficulty with directors. He immediately went to each director's room one by one to ask them point-blank if this was true. Bill Roberts, Wilfred Jackson, Ben Sharpsteen, and all the others denied that they told Walt this.

Ultimately, Babbitt was given a *Dumbo* sequence, but one far below his skill level—clowns silhouetted against a circus tent. Three such sequences were in the film, with the other two assigned to junior animators. In Babbitt's sequence, the clowns decide to organize, singing that they're "gonna hit the big boss for a raise."

Babbitt said nothing about it. He had already been warned by Guild attorney George Bodle and the Labor Relations Board's field examiner, George Yager, to watch his step. He hunched over his animation desk, squinted his eyes, and drew.

"The artists in the cartoon industry at last have a Union!" read the March bulletin from the Screen Cartoonists Guild. "Because the industry is young, the artists who compose it have lagged behind, rather than kept pace with the organization of the employees in the other fields of motion picture entertainment. The actors, the writers, the publicists, etc., have long been organized. We were the last!"

At the following general-membership Guild meeting on Monday, March 3, announcements were made: the Labor Relations Board had said that it would take six to nine months to complete its investigation on whether the Federation was company dominated. What's more, the Guild had the rightful claim to the majority of eligible employees, since the Federation's tally wrongfully included employees not eligible, such as supervising animators and directors. The Disney unit put the boycott resolution to a vote and unanimously decided to place the studio on the Unfair/Do Not Patronize list if the studio refused a cross-check. This cross-check would tally Disney's total artists against the Guild's list of Disney artists, to confirm if the Guild had the majority.

The cross-check had to be conducted by an impartial third party. Lessing agreed to a cross-check under the condition that the "impartial third party" was the Labor Relations Board. However, the Labor Relations Board was unavailable for six to nine months. "The NLRB has its hands tied," protested the Guild, "It has a case pending before it now regarding the legality of [the Federation] and is therefore unable to be impartial."

Meanwhile, accusations of being a Communist continued to bombard Sorrell. He was prepared to extricate himself from negotiations and resign from the Painters Union altogether, but the union voted to reject his resignation.

Sorrell stayed on, much to the relief of the Guild members. But the allegation was a blemish that would only fester with time.

While the battle raged between the Guild and the Federation, the studio put eyes on its artists. At a meeting with Personnel, Walt discussed designating "efficiency experts" to curb expenses. He suspected Babbitt of earning more bonuses than he deserved. "There might be an animator, like Babbitt, who is getting more work because he hasn't properly completed the work going to [his] clean-up [assistants]," he told them, "and still, we have the problem of keeping him busy. This plan of ours will stop the racketeers." Whether true or not, suspicion of animators exploiting the bonus system permeated the studio.

Two men from Personnel, including Hal Adelquist, became the efficiency experts and began patrolling the corridors. They popped in and out of rooms to reinforce the new "speed up" order for employees to obey. As one of the more loyal artists remembered, they were "on a scouting expedition throughout the studio to report to [Walt] any information they could glean and also report any infractions of working rules." These rules forbade any union talk on company property or company time. "Whenever those two men . . . came into our rooms, we 'clammed up.'"

Certain animators (including Les Clark and Fred Moore) complained to Adelquist that Babbitt had been spending a lot of time in their room talking about the Guild. On March 12, Adelquist summoned Babbitt to his office for a meeting. His secretary kept stenographic notes.

"A few complaints regarding you personally have come to my attention," said Adelquist. "I want to refer you again to Walt's memo to please carry on union activities either at lunchtime or after five-thirty. It has come up that you have been going through the unit, talking to the fellows—"

"They'll have to prove that," said Babbitt.

"There's no intention to prove anything, Art," said Adelquist.

"When I go to the coffee shop," said Babbitt, "if I talk to anybody, I do it there. People on both sides are guilty. [Animator] Dan MacManus can tell you that he took one and a half hours of my time last week. Yesterday [animator] Berny Wolf came in and spent almost an hour with me."

"I'll want to call all those boys and remind them of Walt's memo," said Adelquist. "I'm not taking sides, only complaints have come to me that you personally have been going into the rooms and talking to the boys during working hours."

"Yes, I've done that," said Babbitt. "I don't deny it. But when I go into a room, like Bill Tytla—I see him every day—I never stay more than five minutes. Same with Les Clark."

"You understand what I mean," said Adelquist.

"Both Bodle and Yager in the Labor Board have cautioned me, so I have been extremely careful," said Babbitt.

"If the boys do drop into your room during company time, I would appreciate your telling them to make it after business hours," said Adelquist. "We are in such a condition right now that the thing we need is production. We need it so badly that if we don't get it, there won't *be* any unions. The more time you take away from the man who should be contributing work is bad. We don't want to discontinue the coffee shop and those privileges, but if we don't get out the work, we're going to have to. If it were someone else from the other union, I would tell him the same thing and ask him to be fair and honest about it."

"I have no excuse for myself," said Babbitt, "but I am more or less in the position where I am under scrutiny by everybody. Everyone who is not on my side is bound to criticize me."

"If you fellows, on your respective sides, could only agree that the working time here at the studio should be consumed in working—and any other discussions should be after hours," said Adelquist. "What I wanted to talk to you about was that I'd appreciate you fellows cooperating with Walt. That's the one thing he asked for . . . for the men to give him a fair deal. He doesn't care what happens off the lot."

"I'm inclined to believe he doesn't give a damn what happens off the lot," Babbitt retorted.

The discourse intensified and for a minute the secretary lost track. Adelquist addressed Babbitt's belated delivery of his Mr. Stork scenes, linking the delay to the hours Babbitt spent talking to colleagues and making flyers. Babbitt argued that it took longer because he was striving for quality.

Adelquist de-escalated the conversation. "There have been complaints that you personally have solicited for unions during company hours and have been taking other people's time," he said.

"That's true."

"I just wanted to caution you about it," said Adelquist. "I'm only asking for your sense of fair play on the thing. If fellows do come in to your room to ask questions, tell them you are busy but would be happy to talk to them on your own time. I'd tell the same thing to the opposing interest."

This closing statement was Adelquist's attempt to appear fair and transparent. But his actions increasingly demonstrated something else—that he would do whatever it took to curry Walt's favor.

Babbitt, in an attempt to placate his ex-groomsman, posted a sign on his office door reading, DO NOT DISTURB; IF YOU WANT INFORMATION ATTEND TONIGHT'S MEETING.

That month, the Guild gained the support of the Central Labor Council of the San Fernando Valley. At the following Guild meeting on Monday, March 10, more than 400 attendees witnessed the induction of 150 animation artists, most of whom were from Disney. The Guild began sponsoring twice-weekly sketch classes, as well as talks by California's deputy labor commissioner.

For unknown reasons, Babbitt started bringing a loaded .22-caliber pistol to work at this time. Known as a "plinking gun," this model is often used for target practice, such as the skeet-shooting that Babbitt had done in the California desert. Babbitt used it as an overt intimidation tactic—an apparent move out of Sorrell's playbook. He kept the gun in the top drawer of his animation desk, barely covered with a piece of paper. He didn't hesitate to open the drawer and gauge others' reactions.

Unsurprisingly, this did not go over well. On the morning of March 22 the Burbank police charged Babbitt with carrying a loaded weapon without a permit. While in jail (with bail set at $200), "one of the girls" from the Guild brought him an apple—a token of support from the hundreds he represented. He pleaded guilty, his thirty-day sentence was suspended, and he was placed on parole.

Meanwhile, Walt Disney Productions was desperately searching for ways to stay afloat. On Friday, March 21, Disney's Airbrush Department was discontinued. Those artists were offered a one-month tryout in the Ink & Paint Department—which incensed many, since Ink & Paint tryouts had always been three months. A conference was held on Saturday between Gunther Lessing and AFL leaders Blair, Bodle, and Sorrell. Negotiations took place, to no avail. The conference would not be the last, though that day would be the Disney studio's last working Saturday.

That following Monday, March 24, Roy Disney called a five o'clock meeting for the key artists from the Layout, Background, Direction, and Animation Departments. Some months before, unions had successfully pushed the US government to regulate a five-day workweek through the new Wages and Hours Act. Roy outlined a forty-hour, five-day workweek for all employees who were considered nonspecialists. To save the studio money, Roy announced salary cuts across the board and an elimination of luxury items. He asked that people start work punctually at 8:30 and put in an honest eight hours every day. Director Dave Hand suggested posting an oversized thermometer on the wall gauging the film footage progress.

Babbitt accepted the standard 15 percent pay cut for high earners, from $200 a week to $170. Everyone signed an acknowledgment of their salary cut with a percentage proportionate to their wages. "God damn," Fred Moore protested, "why don't they weed out the dead wood!" The term *dead wood* began circulating more among the non-Guild employees. Ever since the hiring spree for *Snow White*, many newer low-level artists were seen as weighing down the studio. They had circumvented the arduous tryout period and were considered lazy and complacent.

To decide which craftworkers in Hollywood qualified for the forty-hour workweek, a Wages and Hours Act hearing was held on March 25. Hollywood studio managers argued against representatives of fourteen Hollywood unions. The Screen Cartoonists Guild was included among the unions that argued for its workers' rights. The Federation was suspiciously absent.

———————

On Monday, March 31, four Guild committee members met with Gunther Lessing to voice grievances. These concerned the treatment of the ex-airbrush artists, unfair salary cuts for inkers and inbetweeners, and nine effects animators slated for layoffs who wanted a trial period in character animation. Lessing asked that the complaints be presented in written form, and the Guild members did so. Lessing then required that the Guild resolve this with O'Rourke and his impartial machine. When asked who in the impartial machine would cast the deciding vote, it was revealed that it was O'Rourke himself, a management employee. The Guild, aghast, canceled the meeting.

The artists weren't the only thorns in Lessing's side; the Editing Department was also fed up with prolonged contract negotiation. Its union, the Society of Motion Picture Film Editors, had been certified for nearly two years. On March 27 the union had filed an unfair charge against the company, along with other unions that Walt Disney Productions failed to recognize: the Transportation Drivers Union, the Studio Plasterers, and the Film Technicians/Laboratory Workers. They all aligned with the Screen Cartoonists Guild, their union leaders working in tandem, and with the American Federation of Labor (AFL) representing them all.

On the night of Tuesday, April 1, the AFL prepared to lead hundreds of Disney employees to go on strike in a week's time. The news made the front page of *Variety*. The Guilders said that Gunther Lessing had refused to meet or even answer their telephone calls. Walt's own supporters pressed Walt to bring in a more experienced conciliator or even lead negotiations himself.

On Wednesday, April 2, Lessing agreed to negotiate with the various union leaders of the AFL. He explained that the delay was a big misunderstanding and that he desired to follow the same protocol as the other studios. At this, the Labor Relations Board stepped in and called an "armistice," averting the planned strike. Lessing subsequently issued a memo to all Disney studio personnel, falsely reporting that "there has been no evidence received by the Disney management to support the gossip about a strike."

While Blair, Bodle, and Sorrell prepared to confer with Lessing, the Disney vice president didn't waste time. A few days later, fifteen studio security guards were deputized as members of the Burbank police force at City Hall. The maneuver, not uncommon in Hollywood, gave Disney guards the legal authority to use force and make arrests.

Lessing, accompanied by Herb Lamb, met with AFL and Guild union reps on Wednesday, April 9, and Friday, April 11. Lessing advocated for an election, all the while flaunting his experience at Herb Sorrell. "He would say he was the legal counsel for Pancho Villa," said Sorrell, "and I'd say, 'Pancho Villa never won anything legal in his life.'" Infuriated by Lessing's inflexibility, the AFL rescheduled its labor strike for the following week.

On Tuesday, April 15, Lessing requested more time to consider the union demands. The AFL complied and agreed on a temporary "truce." Lessing had a new strategy: buy time for the Federation to assure its legitimacy. That Friday, the Federation strengthened its platform by electing a new board of officers.

Walt joined the meeting with the AFL on Monday, April 21. Herb Sorrell brought a stack of Guild membership cards, claiming to have the majority needed, and demanded that Walt sign a union contract. "I told Mr. Sorrell that there is only one way for me to go and that was an election," recounted Walt six years later. "And that is what the law had set up—the National Labor Relations Board was for that purpose. He laughed at me and he said that he would use the Labor Board as it suited his purposes. . . . I told him that it was a matter of principle with me, that I couldn't go on working with my boys feeling that I had sold them down the river to him on his say-so, and he laughed at me and told me I was naïve and foolish."

Sorrell challenged Walt to make a deal or he would turn the studio into "a hospital filled with workers beaten in a union war." He said, "This could be turned into a nice hospital or dust bowl." The threat of razing the studio to a dust bowl crossed the line. The meeting was a bust.

Lessing then appeared to step aside as Disney's union negotiator, replaced with an experienced labor attorney named Walter P. Spreckels. Spreckels was the regional director of the Labor Relations Board in Los Angeles, but now that he was Disney's labor negotiator, his seat at the board was filled by longtime labor specialist William Walsh.

While Spreckels scheduled his first conference with the negotiation team of Blair, Bodle, and Sorrell (for Monday, April 28), Walsh tackled the Disney issue from the local Labor Relations Board office. Walsh no doubt remembered Babbitt from 1937, when Babbitt had consulted with Walsh during the Federation's founding, and Walsh had given Babbitt a list of labor attorneys. Now Walsh addressed the February complaint against the Federation's legitimacy. Instead of waiting for a formal hearing in Washington, Walsh

Walter Spreckels (left) in 1939, sharing the results of a unionization ballot at Gilmore Stadium, Hollywood.

called for an immediate conference—a local, unofficial hearing in his Los Angeles offices.

The conference was held on April 29 at 1:30 PM. Gunther Lessing and Federation attorney Howard Painter stated their case against Herb Sorrell and Art Babbitt, referencing Sorrell's "dust bowl" threat. Lessing and Painter had far more legal experience than their opposition, but Babbitt's testimony tipped the scales. Specifically, Walsh ruled that because the Federation was codeveloped by management, it could never be independent, "and much of the responsibility for this must be laid at the door of Gunther Lessing." Walsh ruled that the Federation was indeed company-dominated and therefore illegitimate.

Painter and Lessing leapt from their chairs, calling the Guild members "white-livered cowards." Painter demanded that Walsh consider the newly elected Federation board. Instead, Walsh recommended that the Federation disband voluntarily, saying he had no doubt that Washington would agree with his ruling.

At the studio the next day, Dave Hilberman waved the latest edition of *Variety*, which reported the conference, and shouted the news. Babbitt spent lunchtime gloating, walking through the studio campus warmly greeting his fellow Guild members. In his office, Walt wired each Labor Relations Board member in Washington requesting a hearing as soon as possible.

The Federation stubbornly refused to concede. On May 1 a Federation bulletin appeared on the boards with the headline BUT MR. BABBITT, WE DON'T FEEL COMPANY DOMINATED! To combat any doubt, the next morning, Guilders distributed handbills outlining the events of the conference. This infuriated Howard Painter. He circulated a two-page bulletin that same day, invalidating the decision and scorning Babbitt in all caps. He wrote, "THE VERY OFFICER TO WHOM WAS INTRUSTED THE WELFARE OF THE FEDERATION NOW CONTENDS THAT THE FEDERATION WAS DOMINATED BY THE COMPANY." The bulletin concluded that the matter would be taken to the federal level.

It wasn't an empty threat; Walt announced that if a strike was called and "any violence occurs," he would close the studio. It is telling that Walt automatically named violence among labor tactics. He had become conditioned to fear unionists. Just as Babbitt's opinions had become extreme, so had Walt's. Top attorneys at Walt's company—Gunther Lessing, Anthony O'Rourke, and Howard Painter—blamed the discord on Babbitt. As Babbitt described in 1942,

Walt confronted Babbitt in the corridor of the main animation building and said that if Babbitt didn't stop organizing his employees, he would throw Babbitt "right the hell out of the front gate."

This exchange, if true, was oddly prophetic. That is exactly what the studio did.

24 | THE FINAL STRIKE VOTE

AROUND MAY 3, 1941, three days after Walt's first request for a hearing, the National Labor Relations Board responded and set a hearing for May 19. Walt took a brief vacation and left his lawyers to sort the rest out.

The Disney employees had diverged into warring factions. Disney labor relations consultant Walter Spreckels circulated a page-long bulletin on Monday, May 5, acknowledging the divisiveness at the studio and summarizing the upcoming hearing. "If the Board finds the Federation to be a legitimate labor organization, you may be required to express your choice between the Guild (A. F. of L.) or the Federation; if the Board finds against the Federation you may be required to vote for or against the Guild. Whichever way the Labor Board rules, Walt will abide by the law."

There was still a lot of work to be done at the studio. After delays, *The Reluctant Dragon* was set to release on June 6, but poor *Dumbo* still had a ways to go. Although 90 percent of *Dumbo*'s animation was complete, only 30 percent of its cels were inked and painted, and just 10 percent of those cels had been photographed. *Dumbo*'s August 15 release would add much needed revenue, if the studio could finish it in time. *Bambi* was also expected to be released in early fall, and the "Mickey Feature" around Christmas. (Eventually all of these would be exponentially delayed—*The Reluctant Dragon* until late June, *Dumbo* until October, *Bambi* until 1942, and the "Mickey Feature," as part of *Fun and Fancy Free*, until 1947.)

The studio received a paltry bump in its finances on May 8, when it sold the old Hyperion Avenue studio for $75,000. The birthplace of all Disney animation from Mickey and Minnie Mouse to *Snow White* would henceforth be a thing of the past.

On Friday, May 9, at 9:15 AM, Blair, Bodle, Sorrell, and Babbitt met with Spreckels at Herb Lamb's request. They discussed the possibility of a Guild grievance committee. No agreement was reached at the meeting, and so the AFL *again* called a strike for the following week. The threat worked. Over the weekend, Spreckels met with Blair, Bodle, and Sorrell and agreed to meet with a grievance committee, but pending the upcoming hearing. The strike was averted. Sorrell was impressed with Spreckels's fairness and credited him with being the sole reason the strike threat was cancelled. He said that it would be easy to reach a final agreement as long as Spreckels continued to handle the negotiations.

That week, when Walt returned from his vacation, things began to change. On Thursday, May 15, the Federation circulated its final bulletin. "The certification from the NLRB outlived its usefulness as we knew it would one day," it read. "And so—fellow members, the Federation passes into oblivion."

That day, without warning, Disney management reneged on Spreckels's earlier deal to recognize a grievance committee. This flip was a shock to the Guild, which made a plea for the studio remain neutral and to report any negotiation interference to Spreckels. However, Spreckels's role had become strictly ornamental.

The next day a new bulletin appeared. "Today marks the introduction of a new Union for the employees of Walt Disney Studio," it read. "Its name is the American Society of Screen Cartoonists ... ASSC has a clean slate ... JOIN TODAY." The names of the chairpersons, as well as the PO box, were the same as the Federation's.

A labor crisis suddenly struck the Warner Bros. animation studio. The AFL had been in negotiations with animation producer Leon Schlesinger for weeks. Schlesinger, overweight in a tight suit and curly toupee, normally led his animators with good-natured laissez-faire. He was a businessman, not an artist, and his creative direction was little more than saying, "Put a lot of jokes in it."

Over the weekend of May 17–18, the Guild's Warner Bros. unit (led by Chuck Jones) made Schlesinger an ultimatum: sign a union contract now or

Under the mask of the American Society of Screen Cartoonists, strikers claim is a company union.

A drawing by an anonymous Disney striker depicting how the new Disney union, the ASSC, was just a rebranding of the previous company union, the Federation of Screen Cartoonists.

suffer a strike on Monday. Rather than complying, Schlesinger issued a lockout. On Monday May 19, his 185 workers arrived at the door to see a sign reading STUDIO CLOSED ON ACCOUNT OF STRIKE. That afternoon, Schlesinger met with Herb Sorrell, Chuck Jones, and the rest of the Warner Bros. cartoonists' negotiating committee. "We tried very hard to make a deal with Mr. Schlesinger and we offered him the same deal we had with MGM," said Sorrell. "Schlesinger did not comply." That evening, at the behest of the AFL, the Los Angeles Central Labor Council placed Schlesinger's studio on the Unfair/Do Not Patronize list.

The lockout went into a second day. On Tuesday evening, Sorrell and Schlesinger met again. Schlesinger complained that the Guild was financially killing him. Sorrell told Schlesinger, "Raise the price to Warner Brothers. They have to pay it." Schlesinger looked at the contract again—and pointed out that the agreement was for $2,600 more than it was two days before. Sorrell explained that each day, he was increasing the demands for all the lowest-paid staff, "and it would cost him $1,300 a day for every day he prolonged the opening." Schlesinger grabbed the contract with a "give me that" and signed.

"Now," said Schlesinger, "what about Disney?"

The Disney hearing took place as scheduled on May 19. At the local Labor Relations Board office, a trial examiner from Washington presided over Walt Disney Productions and the Screen Cartoonists Guild. Gunther Lessing, not Spreckels, represented the company.

Lessing produced pamphlets stating that the Federation had disbanded, therefore the Labor Relations Board was "trying a dead body." The trial examiner reminded Lessing that the "body" being tried was Walt Disney Productions, not the Federation, and that if Lessing confused them, then the two couldn't be far apart after all.

Lessing agreed to a consent decree (a settlement without any admission of guilt), and the hearing was adjourned.

Suddenly, on May 20, roughly twenty-four Disney artists received an ominous memo. Due to "circumstances beyond the control of this studio . . . your release is effective as of 5:30 PM this afternoon." Attached were two weeks' salary in lieu of notice. Walt met with the group in his office, explaining that the layoff was an unfortunate side effect of world conditions and offering them letters of recommendation. The artists glanced at one another. Of the people laid off that day, seventeen were Guild members, including five Guild officials. It was certain that the Personnel Department had cherry-picked them to be terminated. The non-Guilders had informed Personnel whenever an artist was spotted at a Guild meeting.

The Disney animators—Guild members and not—called the mass firing a "Blitzkrieg." The timing was inordinately suspicious. Due to the layoff, the population of Guild members at the studio now possibly inched below half, though Lessing denied any discrimination. Rumors of another mass layoff began to spread, and Disney artists began to suspect that the axe would fall on "Babbitt and his Guild followers."

A day or two later, Babbitt led a lunch meeting in the studio animation building. It was an introduction to the Guild for the tyros working as apprentices and in the Traffic Department (i.e., messenger boys). Hal Adelquist got wind of the meeting and informed Gunther Lessing. Lessing interrogated four of the youths, asking to identify those in attendance. They refused to name names.

The union election was also imminent. Walt Disney released a statement on Thursday, May 22. "My employees . . . are free to join any organization, and we will bargain collectively with the union or organization so chosen." On the same document, Disney's new publicity manager claimed that the ASSC now had the majority of artists. Guild members objected that a member of management was speaking on behalf of the ASSC.

That night, at an emergency meeting at the Roosevelt Hotel, the Guild voiced its complaints. Its members felt that the creation of the ASSC was a signal that Disney had broken faith with them—that despite the Guild's many concessions postponing its strike threats, the company had only been stalling.

Bill Hurtz was now a Guild officer alongside Babbitt. He remembered, "Art got me to one side and said, 'When I nod at you, get up and make a motion to strike.'" He did, and the motion passed. They would schedule a strike vote for May 28 if Walt refused to meet with them.

Guild president Bill Littlejohn wired Walt Disney: "The union committee was instructed unanimously to meet with you personally on Monday, May 26, for the purpose of obtaining recognition. . . . Failure to grant a meeting will result in recommendation that the union take action to protect the interests of its members."

In his office, Walt was coordinating the June 6 release of *The Reluctant Dragon*, the production of *Bambi*, and the completion of *Dumbo*. He was making plans for a grand research trip to Latin America. He replied that he was too busy to meet.

On Monday night, in the Blossom Room of the Roosevelt Hotel, the Disney Guilders voted 315 to 4 to strike. The six hundred Guild members voted unanimously to approve the strike, set for 6:00 AM Wednesday, May 28. The Guild immediately appointed different committees to handle the details, including publicity, pickets, and office. The Guild also announced that the Los Angeles Central Labor Council would meet on Tuesday afternoon to move forward with a national Disney boycott.

Late Tuesday morning, Walt again addressed his entire staff in the studio theater: "I believe it only fair to tell our employees that in the event of a strike the studio will remain open. .... I desire that it be made plain to all my employees that they are free to join any union which they may select or prefer. We always have been ready, are now ready, and always will be ready to bargain collectively with any appropriate bargaining unit designated by a majority of the employees by secret ballot in an election held for that purpose. I'm sorry," Walt concluded, "that's all that I can say. Thanks." Walt left the theater to a tremendous ovation.

Babbitt was not at the meeting. As he exited the studio restaurant, the chief of studio police took hold of his arm and handed him an envelope, telling him it was bad news. The envelope contained two notices on Disney studio letterhead. The first stated that conducting union activities on company time and property "disturbed the morale of the employees and has seriously interrupted and disturbed production operations," thereby violating his employment contract.

The second letter was a single paragraph: "Walt Disney Productions . . . hereby terminates all of your right, title, and interest in said contract and terminates your employment thereunder forthwith." It was signed "Gunther Lessing, Vice President." Babbitt was to clear out immediately.

Babbitt was granted permission to pack his things and load his car in front of the animation building. The chief and another officer flanked him. With slow and deliberate showmanship, Babbitt loaded his car as the mass of Disney employees left Walt's meeting from the theater directly opposite the animation building. Babbitt shouted that he had been fired. Some helped him load his car, and others called out that they would see him on the picket line the next day.

As Babbitt drove off, he called out, "I'll be back!" People who had applauded Walt minutes before now cheered for Babbitt. Some inkers sobbed. Fred Moore began running around in a panic.

Bill Tytla paced the building's steps with a worried look on his face. He had found his calling at the Disney studio, but he had joined the Guild to support Babbitt. Like it or not, the line in the sand had been drawn.

25 | STRIKE!

THE PRESS CALLED THEM "LOYALISTS." But there were many reasons why hundreds of nonstriking Disney artists drove to work the morning of May 28, 1941. *Dumbo* and *Bambi* would not be completed without them. They also shared a gratitude toward Walt, who not only had hired them during the Depression but also had provided them with an opulent new studio. Besides, what kind of tyrant insisted on being addressed by his first name?

The first thing they noticed as they approached the studio was a seemingly endless line of cars parked by the curb leading to the front gate. What they saw at the Disney entrance was a spectacle they had not anticipated.

About five hundred men and women were on their feet, walking in a large circle in front of the entrance. Nearly one in ten carried wooden picket signs, many painted with cartoon characters.

IT'S NOT CRICKET TO PASS A PICKET, warned Jiminy Cricket.

I'D RATHER BE A DOG THAN A SCAB, chided Pluto.

I SIGN YOUR DRAWINGS / YOU SIGN YOUR LIVES, taunted a caricature of Walt.

MICHELANGELO, RAPHAEL, LEONARDO DA VINCI, RUBENS, REMBRANDT ALL BELONGED TO GUILDS.

The number 600 showed up a few times, too, referring to the total number of Disney artists. A strike handout reported that one sign read, ONE GENIUS AGAINST 600 GUINEA PIGS. Another had, SNOW WHITE AND THE 600 DWARFS.

The Disney strikers outside the main gate on South Buena Vista Street.

Art Babbitt (left) surrounded by strikers outside the Disney studio.

Traffic entering the studio slowed to a crawl. As each car inched through, the strikers hooted and hollered, calling each strikebreaker a "scab" and a "fink." A sound truck was parked nearby, providing a portable PA system to the person at the microphone. Bystanders and non-strikers were handed flyers titled AN APPEAL TO REASON—its title borrowed from the Socialist periodical that Walt's father used to read.

"The salaries of the Disney artists average less than those of house painters," read a press bulletin. "The Disney girl inkers and painters receive between $16 and $20 a week. On *Snow White*, the much-publicized bonuses did not even compensate the artists for the two years of overtime they worked. *Snow White* made the highest box office gross in history—over $10,000,000.00. All the other major cartoon studios in Hollywood have Screen Cartoon Guild contracts. The Disney Studio is the only non-union studio in Hollywood." The strikers were demanding a 10 percent wage increase across the board, a 25 percent wage increase for the lower bracketed artists, and the reinstatement of the nineteen animators—including Babbitt—who they argued were fired for union activity.

The Disney carpenters, machinists, teamsters, and culinary workers refused to cross the picket line. Electricians, cameramen, sound men, and film editors also refused. One striker photographed each "scab" who drove through. Atop a hill in the eucalyptus knoll across the street, a striker in a beret and smock stood at an easel painting a landscape of the ordeal. On the ground, there were "guys pouring their individual speeches into the ears of those on the fence," wrote one non-striker that day. "I was struck with the magnitude of it all."

"The average age was less than 25," said Herb Sorrell in 1948. "They became the most enthusiastic strikers I have ever seen in my life." Some strikers leaped onto car bumpers; other rocked cars side to side. Once embattled drivers were through the gates, they were greeted with cheers and claps from a welcoming committee of nonstriking inkers and painters.

The strikers had each been given two- or three-hour shifts, ensuring a twenty-four-hour picket line. They were mostly inbetweeners, animation assistants, inkers, and painters, but among them were also story artists, effects artists, background painters, and animators. Bill Tytla and Art Babbitt stood out as the highest paid on strike.

The previous night, the Guild had voted to include supervising animators among its membership. This made not only Babbitt and Tytla eligible to strike but also all other top animators. Babbitt was on his feet rallying alongside the other strikers, shouting to non-strikers by name, including Ward Kimball. "I felt terrible," Kimball journaled that day. "Friends on the inside waving to me to come in. Friends on the outside pleading with me to stay out; Jeezus. I was on the spot!"

Inside the studio, loyalists were worried. "How the hell can Walt run a studio without us?" asked Norm Ferguson. As non-strikers passed the gauntlet of pickets, strikers warned them that once the union won, it would fine them an amount equal to their salary plus $5 per day, plus a $100 penalty. Ferguson told his fellow non-strikers, "Any agreement made will have to involve protection for you guys or Walt wouldn't sign, so stay on and receive your salary!" With nearly all the assistants and inbetweeners outside, the animators pitched in to do those jobs for each other. If the films weren't completed, the Bank of America might foreclose. Right now, everything was riding on *Dumbo*, the studio's "B" picture.

Relationships were severed. It was the end of Babbitt's friendships with nonstriking animators Les Clark and Fred Moore. Babbitt was also dating a blonde secretary named Nora Cochran before the strike; she was unsympathetic.

The strike took its toll on those who couldn't choose a side. Novice animator Walt Kelly (future creator of the comic strip *Pogo*) had friends on both sides, and he packed up and left altogether. He claimed it was to care for his ill sister, but privately he left his friends this note:

> For years I have reached for the moon
> But the business now is in roon
> So I don't hesitate
> To state that my fate
> Is to take a fug of a scroon!

After 10:00 AM, the strikers dispersed to the adjacent eucalyptus knoll. Sorrell recalled that "from 10 to 11 or 11:30, we would talk to them on a loud speaker system, and of course they could hear in Disney's what we were saying across the street."

Every emphatic slur and enthusiastic cheer that erupted from the PA system echoed in the Burbank studio. Walt was still seen smiling at lunchtime. "I'm going to see this to the end," he said. "I told 'em I'm willing to hold an election, but they refuse, it's their funeral!"

Walt was fixated on having a secret-ballot vote to determine the majority, but there was good reason for the Guild to deny an election. The Disney company, it was rumored, was fudging the numbers, counting its non-artist employees as artists. The studio released a statement that there were only 309 absences out of 1,214 total employees that day, and that there would have been fewer if not for the threat of union goons. The strikers knew that of those 1,214, there were hundreds of employees—from accounting to security—who were ineligible for an animators' union.

Caricatures of Disney strike leaders by a member of the strike. Top row: Pepe Ruiz, Herb Sorrell, Art Babbitt. Middle row: Dave Hilberman, unknown, Bill Tytla, Chuck Jones. Bottom row: unknown, Bill Littlejohn.

In truth, no one seemed to agree on how many artists were on strike and how many were not. Bill Littlejohn figured 450 strikers out of 580 artists, while Babbitt counted 375 strikers out of 550 artists. The Disney strikers also reinforced their numbers with spouses and friends on the picket line. In actuality, it was an extremely balanced divide, with roughly 330 strikers out of roughly 602 artists. (The evenness of the split was confirmed later by the Guild's business agent.) It was what made the strike so adversarial. If just twenty strikers changed their vote in the heat of a company-led election, the union would lose.

Roy Disney returned that day from a New York business trip and released a statement debunking those number-fudging rumors and insisting on an election to prove it. Guild president Bill Littlejohn responded: "The request of the company for an election is made only for the purpose of beclouding the issues involved in our strike. . . . The Guild is striking against company unionism, intimidation, discrimination and persecution." At the local Labor Relations Board office, William Walsh sent his chief investigator, field examiner George Yager, to determine just which union had rightful claim of the majority, the Guild or the ASSC. Alas, Yager could not.

It was a dry day out in the Los Angeles heat, but those inside were sweating too. At around four o'clock, Walt called a few trusted artists to his office. He had hired a photographer that morning to take images of the strikers on the picket line. Those pictures were printed poster-sized and lined the walls of his office, the faces of the strikers clearly visible. Walt went from picture to picture, pointing at the faces with either incredulity or ire. Roy arrived to reassure Walt, while Lessing, ever confident, promised that the strike would dissipate within a day. Walt liked the sound of that, and went to the fridge in the corner kitchen of his office and poured everyone a glass of sherry.

As quitting time neared, the strikers swelled the gates again. Guild attorney George Bodle shouted over the loudspeaker, "Unless the Screen Cartoonists is recognized and five union officials reinstated, picket lines will be established in front of every theater showing Disney films."

That afternoon, the sound wagon announced that Leon Schlesinger had visited the picket line and stopped by to chat with Sorrell. Schlesinger was now sympathetic and offered to help. What if the Warner Bros. animators contributed to the strike? It would be subversive and unexpected—perfect for the artists behind Looney Tunes.

That night, some of the loyalists held an emergency meeting at Abraham Lincoln High School. There was fear, resentment, and a desire to protect the studio. They planned a "back to work" effort intended to woo the strikers. Each loyalist there was given names of three strikers to approach with promises of reinstated bonuses. Starting the next day, many of the strikers and their families encountered a loyalist at their front door or on the other end of a telephone line asking them to stop associating with the "wrong crowd."

This one-to-three ratio indicates there were significantly more artists fighting for the Guild than were fighting against it.

Babbitt surely noticed that this offer to reinstate the previously withheld bonuses was a familiar strikebreaking tactic. It had been Gunther Lessing's attempted strategy to win back the Disney cameramen from the IATSE.

As a leader of the strike, Babbitt's days were packed from dawn until dusk. He was there for the mass picket line from 7:30 to 9:30 AM, chiding arriving loyalists either on the microphone or with the crowd. He contacted several labor groups affiliated with the AFL to spread support for a Disney boycott. He checked on the material that came from the publicity committee at strike headquarters. Each evening, when he wasn't at the mass studio picket from 5:00 to 6:30 PM, he attended board meetings of other unions and appealed for support. His last task every evening was to plan for the following day with the other Screen Cartoonist Guild leaders, including Bill Littlejohn, Herb Sorrell, Dave Hilberman, and the head of the Warner Bros. unit, Chuck Jones.

During the day, the publicity committee drafted flyers and bulletins to distribute to studios across Hollywood. Women typed drafts, men operated the printing press, and everyone had copies to hand out to non-strikers, industry professionals, and theatergoers. There were also "chalk-talk pickets" at theaters, in which strikers sketched on a portable chalkboard while they educated the public about their cause.

The American Federation of Labor identified Disney as the only company in Hollywood not employing union labor. Littlejohn petitioned to other AFL unions, "Disney has long paid the lowest wages in the cartoon industry." But there was a distinction between the company and Walt. Even Sorrell said, "The workers tried in every way to reach an amicable agreement but Gunther Lessing blocked their every move to make a satisfactory deal with the company."

The biggest blow came from the Technicolor film-processing plant. Disney had had a relationship with Technicolor since 1932. Beginning in 1936, Disney used Technicolor for all its films. That Thursday, Sorrell visited the Technicolor processing labs and met with the head of the laboratory technicians' union. The technicians not only agreed to stop handling Disney film immediately, but they also threatened to strike if their managers forced the workers to handle a Disney film.

On Monday, the Disney strike had galvanized the unions representing electrical workers, cameramen, maintenance men, air-conditioning men, teamsters, lab technicians, and culinary workers. The Screen Writers Guild donated $350 to the strikers. The Newspaper Guild at the *Los Angeles Daily News* refused to print the *Donald Duck* comic strip. After a speech from Babbitt to the Screen Office Employees Guild, the members voted to offer their complete support as well.

Just as George Bodle promised, pickets marched at movie theaters playing Disney films. Called "flying squadrons," they got newfound public attention. Outside the Hollywood Pantages Theatre, actors Robert Taylor and Barbara Stanwyck talked to one of the strikers. The El Capitan Theatre, which was playing the new hit *Citizen Kane*, pulled the accompanying Disney cartoon almost immediately.

At the start of that week, the Labor Relations Board began to investigate the legitimacy of the American Society of Screen Cartoonists. The Disney company countered that the Guild signed up workers outside its jurisdiction,

Strikers as "flying squadrons" picketing a theater showing *Fantasia*.

specifically from the studio comic strip, the Traffic Department (i.e., messenger boys), and the studio art school.

As the leader of the art school, Don Graham was torn between his allegiances. Quietly, he left Disney, never to return. Without Graham, the art school and training program both dissolved permanently. The pioneering education program that had elevated Disney animation—the heart of the Disney golden age itself—had come to an end.

Among the loyalists were artists who did not follow either Sorrell or the ASSC. One of these employees called the US Labor Department from inside the studio, begging for a conciliation between the Guild and the ASSC. A conciliator came on Monday, but on Tuesday, June 3, he said his hands were tied because Disney refused to recognize the Guild.

Those non-strikers wrote a petition that day, addressed to the president of the United States. Fifty-seven nonstriking artists signed the petition requesting the National Labor Relations Board to intervene. The signers included men and women from every department, like supervision (Jack King), concept design (Lee Blair) and story (Carl Barks). Not one of the names was a lead animator from the cohort of art school graduates.

Outside the gates, support for the Disney strike surged as the Screen Writers Guild, the Extras Advisory Council, and the Society of Motion Picture Film Editors joined the strike. With the additional pickets, Sorrell launched a nationwide campaign "to drive *Fantasia* from the screen." Now *Fantasia* ticket-holders had to navigate through sixty to one hundred strikers at the theater.

Though *Fantasia* was in its twenty-second week, it was still far from breaking even. Disney extended its national run with cheaper, mono-track screenings, but this angered ticket-buyers who paid extra for the "once in a lifetime" experience of Fantasound.

The Reluctant Dragon was poised to bring in some much-needed income, once it was distributed to theaters on its June 6 schedule. But Sorrell met with Disney's distribution company, RKO. With the Los Angeles Central

Labor Council behind him, Sorrell threatened RKO with a boycott if it didn't cease distributing Disney films during the strike. RKO deliberated. And with Technicolor striking in sympathy, *The Reluctant Dragon*'s release was postponed three more weeks.

26 | THE BIG STICK

ONE WEEK INTO THE STRIKE, both sides were settling into their roles. The Disney strikers occupied the shady eucalyptus knoll opposite the studio's front gate. Those who were not on picket duty relaxed there in the folding chairs, hammocks, and six camping tents that spotted the hill. The off-duty Disney strikers kept their morale high with ball games, horseshoes, Ping-Pong, badminton, chess, checkers, archery, and sketching. They called the knoll "Camp Cartoonist."

The non-strikers called it "Skunk Hollow."

Donations had been rolling in all week, but Thursday, June 5, saw the formation of a makeshift soup kitchen on the eucalyptus grove. It served three meals a day on long picnic tables, built by the carpenters at the Warner Bros. animation studio. The culinary workers' union donated the services of a union chef, and for lunch served 511 hamburgers, 634 cups of coffee, and 29 pounds of coleslaw. "We served dinner at 6 o'clock after the mass picket line would go off, after the workers had gone through," said Herb Sorrell. "And then the musicians many nights would send down a truckload of musicians and they would play and these kids would dance in the street in front of the gates." When musicians weren't available for the dance, the car radios sufficed.

The spectacle was unlike any the press had ever seen. Screenwriter Dalton Trumbo dubbed it "Hollywood's favorite strike." Strikers rode donkeys and bicycles, donned roller skates, and dressed dogs with sandwich boards. Bill Littlejohn flew overhead in his biplane, a Luscombe Phantom two-seater, wiggling his wings above the strikers.

On those long summer evenings, the strike community gathered on the knoll to hear announcements from Babbitt, Hilberman, Sorrell, and other leaders. Cheers and applause closed out each meeting.

The strikers began receiving an internal daily newsletter called *On the Line* chronicling each day's successes. The bottom always contained a single-panel cartoon caricaturing Walt beside a sombrero-wearing crony he called "Gunny."

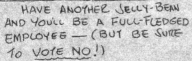

Drawings printed in the striker's daily newsletter *On the Line* lampooning Walt and "Gunny": (top, left to right) June 12, June 13, (bottom, left to right): June 18, June 20.

"Be sure and give Disney all the credit due to him," Babbitt told the press. "The man had foresight and a certain genius and it took plenty of guts for him to buck this industry and prove he had the real thing. But other things are more important than what Walt had. When Disney began to get the idea for this Burbank studio, he became a different man. From a man who worked closely and collectively with his workers, he got to be boss. Since that time, the policy toward his employees—his studio despotism—has been—well, this strike tells you what it has been."

Leon Schlesinger made good on his promise. The Warner Bros. animators, led by Chuck Jones, took time at the end of each day to prepare for the Disney strike. Thursday, June 5, saw the Warner Bros. animators decked out as an American Revolution fife and drum corps blocking all traffic along Riverside Drive.

A handmade effigy of the strike's true nemesis, Gunther Lessing, was hung from a eucalyptus tree, alongside another marked SCAB. Lessing addressed the strikers, requesting the effigy of himself for his office.

Not every striker remained devoted to the Guild or its methods. Hank Ketcham, who would later create *Dennis the Menace*, was a young Disney striker early on. "As serious as the issues were, it all struck me as infantile behavior," he remembered later. He chose to break ranks and return to work. "The loudest insults seemed to come from those whom I once considered my very good pals. It was a shattering experience for many; as in any civil war, the house was divided and close friendships evaporated."

One non-striker counted more than thirty-five Disney strikers coming back to work. Babbitt's rancor didn't help matters. Several strikers used the microphone with the portable PA system, but only Babbitt was poised in verbal attack mode. His behavior echoed a description of his mother: "If she had it in for you, God help you."

"Heard that this morning Babbitt, microphone in hand, called everybody a big gray rat," one non-striker wrote. "Didn't sit well with those within and without. Bad taste. More guys back today." If so, a roughly equal number must have joined. According to records, the number of strikers always stayed around 330.

Disney studio gag drawings of Art Babbitt on strike, by nonstriking artist Jesse Marsh.

Sometimes Babbitt wished the non-strikers each a loud and sarcastic "Good morning" by name, hoping to shame them. "Well here comes Milt Kahl," shouted Babbitt one morning. "His wife has to protect him by bringing him to work. Poor Milt!" Mrs. Kahl dropped off her husband, drove back around and returned fire at Babbitt, "You can't even keep a wife to protect you!"

Wives on both sides appeared ever supportive of their husbands. Word got out that wives of loyalists joined their husbands crossing the picket line and helped with work in the studio, pro bono. The wives of the strikers, on the other hand, formed a committee called the Women's Auxiliary and began organizing fundraisers, starting with a bake sale.

Bill Tytla remained with the strikers, without his wife, Adrienne. His presence on the knoll and at meetings held weight. Adrienne recalled, "There were phone calls, excited conversations, long meetings, bitter disappointment." When Tytla drove back to his home after a long day, he had to contend with a wife recovering from tuberculosis who was barely mobile. The two also had a young son, and Tytla had gone from being one of the highest-paid animators in the world to earning nothing. Adrienne sorely needed health care and childcare and could only feel "torn and ambivalent" about the strike.

The strike leaders were also concerned. Faith in their cause was only as strong as the group's conviction, and cracks were starting to show. Artists who were friends on opposite sides talked through the studio fence. This was vehemently discouraged, and the strikers' newsletter didn't mince words. "Those who have remained inside have been constantly bombarded with misinformation and false promises. . . . DON'T LET THOSE WHO HAVE BEEN FOOLED TRY TO FOOL <u>YOU</u> !!!"

The Los Angeles Central Labor Council, which was affiliated with the AFL, was trying its best to mediate. Now the council was prepared to finally place Disney on the Unfair/Do Not Patronize list. This potential boycott would be enforced by five million AFL members nationwide. Walt saw this as nothing more than a bullying tactic, waving a threat over his head like a wooden club.

The council committee consisted of president Harry Sherman, executive secretary-treasurer J. W. Buzzell, and representative Lew Blix. Walt agreed to an initial meeting with the council committee on Tuesday, June 10. Walt repeated his demand for a secret election to determine the winning union. The council demanded a cross-check—a name-by-name comparison between the lists of Guild members and Disney employees. Nobody budged.

Walt had a second meeting with the council in his office on Wednesday, June 11, the fifteenth day of the strike. With him were Roy and Gunther

J. W. Buzzell, executive secretary-treasurer of the Los Angeles Central Labor Council, in 1940.

Lessing. There were also four strikers who had not yet stoked Walt's ire, as well as a secretary transcribing verbatim.

"Mr. Disney," began Buzzell, "the fact that there is a strike here and a petition to put the firm and its products on the official Unfair list for the labor movement, under our law we are required to make every possible effort to reach an amicable, acceptable settlement of the difficulties before we take that kind of action."

"I think we have given you our answer before on that, Mr. Buzzell," said Walt. "We are just back where we were when we first started to negotiate."

"It's probably true," said Buzzell. "Our purpose in making this visit is to attempt to see if we can't change your mind."

"To me," said Walt, "it's the guy with the big stick standing there, trying to make me change my mind. No other way to look at it. No other answer to it. To be very frank, with me you will agree on that, won't you?"

"I will agree that unless you do it, we are going forward with [the boycott]," said Buzzell, "and there isn't anything the Labor Council can do except to say to these people we'll go as far as we can. It is not our desire. We'd rather settle things than fight. But we have to."

"As long as the big stick settles it," said Walt, incredulously. "Conditions are not going to improve by the moves that you think are your weapons. But if that's what it must be, that's what it must be, and I fought for principles before, and I'll fight for them again. I have never been yellow—I have never been a coward. I might have been foolish at times, but I sort of have a faith, a faith that kind of pulls you through a lot of these things. When it comes to a compromise of this sort, to me it isn't a compromise. It's just laying down. To me it's one of the most un-American things that can be done."

Walt continued, "It happens to be, in my opinion, a minority that's claiming the right to bargain. Now what they are after is the truth, and that's what we have got to find—the truth of the thing. Who is the majority? In a case of that sort, it should be determined in the proper way . . . and you want to take the big stick and beat them into thinking your way."

The strikers boiled it down to the one thing they needed. "You simply say we have a majority," one said.

"The cross-check is definitely unfair," said Walt. "People have signed your cards *under pressure*."

"That's your opinion, Walt," said another striker. "We don't believe that."

"I have a right to my opinions just as you have to your opinions," said Walt. "The one way to really find out—the one way to prove it—is to put it up for a vote. And the very fact that you refuse to go to a vote just convinces me that you haven't got a majority. And for that reason I will fight all the harder on the thing—"

Buzzell replied, "I'm not saying we're doing it for the purpose of making threats. . . . It is the natural course of events, and if we do it, we shall endeavor like any other fight. If we have to fight, we're going to throw all the punches we can, and duck all we can, and kick when we can."

This analogy confirmed the deeply held suspicions that Walt had been harboring since he was a boy. "I know the usual union methods, Mr. Buzzell," Walt said. "I've been brought up through my life with them. My dad was beat up by a bunch of union people one time." Walt's emotional inner child—that remarkable insight that produced masterpieces of family entertainment—was now navigating union negotiations.

Lessing heard the boxing metaphor and played to Walt's fears, saying to Walt, "It must mean that they attempt to carry out the threat to turn this studio into a dust bowl or a hospital."

"I don't see anything unfair about a cross-check," said a striker. "I'd say so many people signed Guild cards—they must have signed them because they wanted to belong to the Guild."

"What is unfair about a secret election?" asked Lessing.

"I think if we held an election it would still exist under that condition of coercion," said the striker. "Walt points out they will go in and vote secretly. A lot of people even in a secret vote both haven't the guts to vote the way they want to."

"The only coercion I know is that the Guild has threatened them," said Lessing. "I never pass the picket line without somebody either taking my picture or my name."

"It's not the union or things like that that we are fighting," said Walt, "it's the methods of determining who should be that bargaining agent."

"You're asking us to submit to an election," finished Buzzell. "There's five or six very valid reasons why we don't. I presume you have played poker. If you've brought a hand and showed your hand, you wouldn't submit to dealing the cards over again to find out if you had it right. And we ain't going to either. That's what it amounts to."

That was that. At noon the next day, the Central Labor Council officially placed Disney on the Unfair/Do Not Patronize list. The nationwide Disney boycott had begun.

On Thursday afternoon, June 12, nearly all the loyalists ditched work early to avoid the strikers. When the picket line surged again at 5:00, the street was almost empty, except for a small group. They were dispersed by a parade of marching Warner Bros. animators, this time with costumes and props à la the French Revolution. Several of them dressed like executioners and carried a hand-crafted guillotine on their shoulders. On it lay the effigy of Gunther Lessing, its neck under the blade beneath a sign reading, SEVERANCE PAY OR SEVERING HEADS? Others carried the sign bearing the adapted French battle cry, "LIBERTÉ, FRATERNITÉ, CLOSED SHOPPÉ."

Support for the strikers had grown. The *Los Angeles Herald Express* had pulled the Mickey Mouse comic strip, and telegrams of encouragement came in from the newspaper guilds of Cleveland and San Francisco. The publishing union, Allied Printing Trades, refused to publish Disney comic books. Cash donations kept rolling in.

Some of the nonstriking inkers and painters, tired of being harangued by the striker horde, sneaked into work though the studio's storm drain. The strikers got wind of this and gleefully called them "sewer rats."

The feelings about Walt varied among the strikers. Some of them maintained no ill will against the company. Others, like Babbitt, spoke with histrionics, radicalizing the strike into a class war. Walt would learn just how hot the blood ran.

On the morning of Friday, June 13, Walt Disney met with the labor relations council for the Motion Picture Producers Association, Pat Casey. The meeting was as fruitless as the others. "Another appeal to reason terminated in a deadlock as a result of the now well-known Disney stubbornness," blasted the strike bulletin. In the afternoon, the company prepared for a press screening of *The Reluctant Dragon* on the studio grounds. When the journalists arrived, they were blocked by a massive demonstration, as one of the strikers improvised a "Man on the Street" radio program over the PA microphone.

Walt was not about to give the strikers any more fuel for their demonstrations. Like the day before, he dismissed his employees early, this time to reconvene for a staff meeting at the high school auditorium. The loyalists were all gone by the time the evening pickets assembled.

When the strikers learned where the loyalists had gone, they moved to the high school, sound truck and all. By the time the strikers arrived, many of the loyalists were already heading home. Walt was pleased with having won this battle. He sat in his blue Packard convertible and smiled, tipping his hat like President Roosevelt.

Babbitt grabbed the microphone and roared from the sound truck's loudspeaker, "Walt Disney, you ought to be ashamed." He said it again, emphatically: "Walt Disney, you ought to be ashamed!"

Babbitt ran down while Walt stopped and got out of his car. As Walt's feet hit the pavement he clenched his fists. "Why you dirty sonofabitch!" shouted Walt. Hundreds of voices booed and cheered. The crowds closed in on them. Before either man could take a swing, Babbitt was pulled away. Walt saw this, got back into his car, and drove off.

27 | THE 21 CLUB

THE GUILD CONTINUED HITTING WALT where it hurt—in his public image. "A bankroll can change a lot of things, including a nice kid from Hyperion," wrote the L.A.-based magazine *Radio Life* on June 15. "A lot of good guys and gals helped make Disney in a spirit of cooperation, and now it's mostly corporation. Maybe Disney ought to renovate his soul."

Walt considered this a smear campaign, but some supporters took things further. They formed a secret society, calling themselves the "Committee of 21" and hoisted an attack on the Guild.

The committee's first letter arrived on June 16 and was also sent to several non-AFL Hollywood unions. It was a lengthy, rambling diatribe of extremism and conspiracy theory. It warned that the strike was funded by Russian Communist groups and that Aubrey Blair and Herb Sorrell were using the Labor Relations Board "to pull the RED HERRING of 'Patriotic cooperation' to divert you from the certain failure."

The strikers wondered aloud who composed the Committee of 21. Some suspected it was Willie Bioff's goons. Bioff had been in the news a lot lately, having recently been extradited to New York to face an extortion charge. On Tuesday morning, June 17, Babbitt tried to reassure the strikers. They did their best to belittle the anonymous group, and printed a mock invitation: "The Committee of 21 meets, secretly, every nite. Bring your mask, 1 Junior G man badge, 1 Superman cape and a suitable holder to swing a red herring with."

Strike leadership presumed the anonymous group was composed of the high-ranking Disney artists who belonged to the studio's Penthouse Club.

— AND WE FURTHER FIND THEY ARE NOW DISCUSSING A FIVE YEAR PLAN!

One Disney striker's rendition of the Committee of 21, as seen in their daily newsletter *On the Line* on June 17.

Thus, the Committee of 21 earned the moniker the "21 Club." Their accusations now became associated with the most privileged Disney loyalists.

Nevertheless, Walt continued seeking a solution. He had hired an IATSE lawyer, Harold V. Smith, to mediate a strike settlement. Besides representing the IATSE soundmen, Smith was also chairman of the business agents' committee of the IATSE. Meetings between Smith and the Guild started on Monday, June 16. Smith proposed making the studio 80 to 90 percent Guild membership, barring an election, and a reinstatement of all employees, with *one* exception: Art Babbitt.

The Guild presented its counterproposal—a 100 percent Guild shop, barring a cross-check, and a reinstatement of all employees including Art Babbitt.

Guild attorney Bodle reiterated his willingness for an election under the auspices of the Labor Relations Board. However, the board could not conduct the election while charges of company domination against the ASSC were still pending. Then the Guild learned that the company was hiring art-school students to help finish up *Dumbo.* Babbitt wrote in a handbill, "The strikers feel [Walt] is now suggesting an election as a bid for public sympathy."

Meanwhile, Roy traveled back to New York on the weekend of June 14. He had one goal: meet with RKO and convince the company to distribute Disney films again.

Harold Smith met with the Guild representatives again on Wednesday, June 18. This time, Smith shared a new development from the studio: Disney loyalists were dismantling the ASSC. They were now organizing another company union, this one called the Animated Cartoon Associates (ACA). They claimed four hundred members and were prepared to call the Labor Relations Board to authorize an election. As if to strengthen its claim to legitimacy, this studio union pledged to have different board members than the last two.

———

Now in its fourth week, the strike was taking a toll on the picket line. There were a few glimmers of joy; four couples had been married since the strike began, including Bill and Mary Hurtz. The Women's Auxiliary had set up day care for the Disney strikers' toddlers. But some strikers who were living hand-to-mouth were getting behind in their rent. Others were relying on the strike soup kitchen for free meals. William Littlejohn wrote a letter to the Guild representatives desperately asking for help.

On June 19 Chuck Jones organized a parade of Warner Bros. animators delivering a truck of food for the Disney strikers, under the banner BUNDLES FOR DISNEY and a sign reading, LOOK FELLAS, MANNA! Jones brought up the rear staggering under a big sack of potatoes.

The Women's Auxiliary doubled their efforts. They organized an industry-wide art sale with the help of the women at Warner Bros. animation. The fundraiser would sell original sketches, watercolors, and ceramics throughout the week, from noon until 9 PM, for up to ten dollars each. Disney art teacher Gene Fleury helped organize the event. The women also planned a mammoth street dance and carnival fundraiser right outside the studio.

Guild meetings on the eucalyptus knoll were now focused on keeping spirits high. All strikers with special talents were encouraged to participate. An entertainment committee was formed. There were magic shows, costumed skits parodying Walt and "Gunny," and sing-alongs. One song in the tune of "Little Brown Jug" began:

I'm the Kansas City Kid
Do you know what I have did?
Fired Guild leaders up and down
And gave them all the run-around.

Chorus: Yo-ho-ho, you and me
                    Little red axe, how I love thee.

Screen Actors Guild members showed up for support. Actor John Garfield marched with a sign in the picket line. Frank Morgan, the Wizard of Oz himself, spoke with Bill Tytla atop the knoll.

Something ignited in Tytla shortly thereafter. He went rogue and tried to broker a peace with Walt, man to man. The details differ: Tytla either approached Walt at a café or telephoned Walt over the weekend. Either way, the mission failed. Some loyalists laughed at Tytla's "peace proposal," calling it "a wild, hairbrained idea." It was also a sign that the strike's united front was cracking.

Loyalists, including top creatives like Norm Ferguson, Fred Moore, Dick Lundy, and Wilfred Jackson, gathered in the Roosevelt Hotel on Thursday night, June 19. The meeting confirmed the disbanding of the ASSC and the establishment of its replacement, the Animated Cartoon Associates.

Suddenly they heard a ruckus outside the doors of the large meeting room. The meeting had barely begun when fifty strikers stormed the hotel, screaming from the lobby and pushing through the doors. A few of the larger loyalists held them off. A striker swung with a hand that had drawn *Dumbo* storyboards and was punched with a hand that had animated Mickey Mouse in *Fantasia*. A loyal character designer, Jim Bodrero, got between the two and yelled to have no bloodshed as others pulled them apart. The strikers remained in the lobby while the loyalists returned to their meeting. Norm Ferguson and Fred Moore were nominated for the ACA's steering committee. Bodrero was elected president. "Good meeting," opined a loyalist that day, "we had good unity." After the meeting, ACA members discovered that strikers had stabbed their cars' tires with ice picks.

The drama was too much for some officials within the Disney studio. Both the director of film distribution and the head of eastern publicity had resigned. Now, upset at the company's discriminatory layoffs, production control manager Herb Lamb quit as well.

———————

Around Wednesday, June 23, the Committee of 21 disseminated its second letter. "YOU ARE LOST, because the Public and the entire Union Labor Movement is alert to the Communistic issue your stupidity has exposed."

The Disney strike was starting its fifth week. The strikers were weakening, and it was starting to show. "We have been ragged by the vicious and unfounded accusations of the now notorious, if still anonymous, '21 Club,'" they wrote.

Chuck Jones once again led the Warner Bros. artists in a parade, this time staging a mock funeral. The men dressed in black suits; the women wore black dresses and veils and carried large prop candles. Six of the men (with Jones in the rear) carried a large, hand-crafted coffin on their shoulders like pallbearers. On the side of the coffin was elegantly painted "R.I.P.—F.S.C." Behind them, weeping widows in black dresses and black shawls over their heads carried signs that read, "A.S.S.C." and "A.C.A." The "mourners" placed the prop candles in stands and dabbed their eyes with handkerchiefs, wailing over Disney's three company unions.

Roy returned from New York on June 24. He had convinced RKO to distribute *The Reluctant Dragon*. The strike had delayed the film by nearly a month. *Dragon* finally premiered that Friday at Broadway's Palace Theatre in New York to a rousing, sold-out audience.

Saturday night, June 28, was the strikers' big street dance fundraiser. Festivities began at 8:30 PM; admission was twenty-five cents. Big-band music rang out along South Buena Vista Street and Riverside Drive. There were hot dogs and beverages, carnival booths, and a bonfire. One striker had a caricature station while another had a fortune-telling table. A third put on a medicine show, and others staffed a kissing booth. From the studio rooftop, Disney security flashed their searchlights down at them. It was a night of fun and optimism. Many, including attorney Bodle, was sure that the strike would be settled soon. By the end of the night the benefit had raised $570.

On Sunday the *New York Times* published a featured article on the Disney strike. It quoted strikers calling Walt an "egocentric paternalist," a far cry from his portrayal in *The Reluctant Dragon*.

Walt could take it no longer. That very day he drove to the San Fernando Valley. He had tried working with his own labor counselor (Walter Spreckels), an independent labor counselor (Pat Casey), the Los Angeles Central Labor Council (Messrs. Sherman, Buzzell, and Blix), and a business agent from IATSE (Harold Smith).

He had one last recourse for ending the strike on his own terms.

28 | WILLIE BIOFF AND WALT DISNEY

FOR A LITTLE MAN FROM CHICAGO, WILLIE Bioff held considerable power in Hollywood. By 1941 he controlled the workflow of thirty-five thousand people in the movie industry. Bioff could single-handedly order hundreds of studio employees to halt production or projectionists to stop playing that studio's films. It was a two-pronged attack that threatened most Hollywood studios with bankruptcy. Sound technicians, camera operators, electricians, property men, plasterers, utility workers, special effects technicians, and projectionists were all dues-paying members of the IATSE. As a wielder of unequaled power, Bioff had audience with the top brass of Hollywood.

One of them was Joseph M. Schenck, the chairman of the board of 20th Century-Fox. Schenck, a long-faced man in his sixties, had been making deals with Bioff ever since the Chicagoan arrived as IATSE's West Coast representative. That business relationship had been profitable for both. Bioff wouldn't call a strike, and Schenck would thank Bioff with gifts to his personal bank account. It was a perfect arrangement.

Then in early 1941 Schenck was arrested for tax evasion. The movie mogul had tried to claim a loss when filing his taxes in 1935 and 1936. His trial began on March 3 and was to run several weeks. When the prosecutor, US attorney Mathias F. Correa, began exploring Schenck's papers, he discovered something interesting—the extent of Schenck's generosity to Bioff. There were enormous sums changing hands in 1936 and 1937, including a gift to Bioff of $22,000 in stock shares of 20th Century-Fox, and his $100,000 "alfalfa farm" loan. If

Fox was just one of the major studios in Hollywood, then Bioff was earning far more than a labor leader's $3,000-a-year salary.

On around April 4 Correa started interrogating industry executives about their own gifts to Bioff. He discovered that the kickbacks were often in the form of cash (paid in $100, $500, and $1,000 bills) and dividends, but there were also Oriental rugs, draperies, furnishings, and other merchandise, as well as tens of thousands of stock shares. Some of the gifts were from known sources, like 20th Century-Fox and RKO, though many others were anonymous. On April 29, twelve days after winning his tax-fraud case against Schenck, Correa charged Bioff with tax fraud. Bioff had underreported $185,000 of earnings in 1936 and 1937 and owed $85,000 to the US government. It was the same charge that had landed Al Capone in prison years before. Now it looked like Bioff had followed in the footsteps of the big boss.

The IATSE leader was arrested and placed on a $5,000 bail until his trial. Bioff's court date was slated for July, but IATSE president George Browne was able to negotiate for a delay until September. It didn't really matter to Correa; while on bail, Bioff couldn't leave the state. For three more weeks Correa continued assembling a second, much larger case against Willie Bioff as well as against George Browne.

The news of that second case broke in the afternoon on Friday, May 23. Bioff and Browne were each indicted on charges of extortion and conspiracy. It was what Hollywood had been clamoring for. The story was so explosive that *Variety*, which had finished its morning print run for the week, rushed out a special edition that night. Willie Bioff and George Browne would have their day in New York federal court. A conviction could earn them each a thirty-year prison sentence. Bioff didn't relent. "You can say for me that I am completely surprised," he said. "I don't know anything about the charges contained in the New York indictment. I never extorted a dime from anybody."

Correa put off the income tax trial indefinitely to bring Bioff and Browne to trial for extortion and conspiracy. He also arranged to conduct the prosecution personally. On May 27 in Chicago, George Browne surrendered to a US marshal. Smiling cheerfully, Browne told reporters, "I never committed a crime in my life." The trial date was set for August 18 for both men.

At his arraignment at New York federal court the morning of Thursday, June 12, Bioff was charged with collaborating with George Browne to extort $550,000 from Warner Bros., Paramount, Loew's, and 20th Century-Fox. Bioff naturally pleaded not guilty. Correa voiced his fear of his own witnesses' safety, and the judge agreed, warning Bioff, "I want it clearly understood that if any witnesses are molested in any form, either by telephone calls or personal communications, bail will be revoked forthwith and the defendant incarcerated."

Bioff explained to the press that the real reason for union corruption in Hollywood was "members of the Communist party."

Bioff was asked about gangsterism in the film unions, but he refused to answer. A reporter asked, "Is that all you want to say?"

Bioff barked, "That's all!"

On the night of June 13, Bioff flew back to California and returned to his ranch in the San Fernando Valley. He was there waiting on June 29 when Walt Disney arrived.

Immediately following Walt's secret meeting in the Valley, the Disney strikers began seeing strange things. Anonymous lies were dropped to the press that the strike was already settled. SWEEPING VICTORY FOR CARTOONISTS IN STRIKE SETTLEMENT WITH DISNEY, read the *Weekly Variety* headline. Additionally, Walt Disney Productions released a notice that all strikers had to file an "application for reinstatement" within three days if they wanted to keep their jobs. This was on the heels of the Communism accusations made by the Committee of 21 against strike leader Herb Sorrell. The Disney strikers were shaken.

In the afternoon of Monday, June 30, nine guests arrived at Bioff's mahogany-paneled mansion. Four were top Disney management, led by Roy Disney and Gunther Lessing. The other five were representatives from the American Federation of Labor (AFL), led by Aubrey Blair.

In their alliance with Aubrey Blair and the AFL, the Disney strikers had overlooked one fact: George Browne, IATSE president (and Bioff's partner), had been elected the vice president of the AFL. This demonstrated just how far the IATSE's reach was.

Bioff's home suggested sensitivity and culture, but mostly opulence. It was surrounded by alfalfa flowers and contained a knotty pine library filled with rare books. There were expensive Chinese vases and a kidney-shaped swimming pool. It was not the typical home of a professional union representative.

Willie Bioff greeted his guests from Disney and the AFL, and together they drafted a proposal to end the Disney strike. Bioff always had the IATSE projectionists in his back pocket, and now was his chance to use them.

The Disney strikers were unaware of this AFL-Bioff-Disney negotiation. At the Screen Cartoonist Guild headquarters, Herb Sorrell, George Bodle, and the other strike leaders had prepared their own twenty-four-point proposal. These points included a pay scale with set increases, overtime pay, severance pay, a grievance committee, a screen-credit committee (Disney's short cartoons were the only ones in Hollywood without screen credit), twelve days of sick leave, a union label on all Disney films, full retroactive pay for strikers, and a guarantee of fifty weeks of employment per year. Further was this stipulation: "Female employees shall receive equal pay for equal work and shall be accorded equal opportunity for advancement with male employees." When Herb Sorrell read the terms, he received thunderous applause.

At 6:30 that evening, Aubrey Blair and the other AFL leaders arrived at the Guild headquarters. The AFL offered the Guild a blanket agreement that would affiliate them with the IATSE. As an act of good faith, the AFL promised that Disney would sign a contract within twenty-four hours, or else all IATSE theater projectionists would stop running Disney films. But there was a catch: Herb Sorrell and George Bodle had to withdraw from negotiations. If they failed to agree, the AFL would sever its support for the Guild, the Painters Union with which it was affiliated, and the Disney strike.

Sorrell had been loyal to the Guild, going so far as to donating some of his salary to the Disney strike. Now, however, it looked like his presence was obstructing a possible settlement. For the sake of the strike, he said he would bow out. "If the IATSE had a method of settling it, it would be all right, and [I told them] that I would retire from the picture," said Sorrell. "I only wanted to see them get what they had coming, and I did not want any part of it." (Babbitt alone voiced a counterproposal: for the loyalists to be levied a 50 percent penalty on the salary they earned during the strike. Just like his epithets at the microphone, this would have denigrated the non-strikers.)

The strikers accepted Sorrell's resignation and agreed to the terms of the contract. Babbitt and the other Guild negotiators rode in two of the AFL leaders' cars to the signing location. All previous AFL meetings had been held at the Roosevelt Hotel, but the cars did not stop there, instead continuing toward the San Fernando Valley. The strikers inquired where they were going. Only then did the AFL leaders reveal that the contract would be signed at Willie Bioff's ranch.

At the next opportunity, the Guild members in one car leaped from the vehicle and returned to Guild headquarters.

The two Guild members in the other car did not bail. One of those two was Babbitt. Soon he found himself pulling up in front of Bioff's mansion, where he saw Willie Bioff flanked by Gunther Lessing and Roy Disney.

Bioff had heard that Babbitt liked the outdoors, and he offered Babbitt his full salary if he were to stay out of the way, and "go camping" indefinitely.

Babbitt rejected the offer. He said he had enough money.

Bioff grew furious. He demanded that Babbitt go along; otherwise Bioff would "take over" the Guild and the entire Disney studio.

Babbitt didn't budge.

With negotiations at a deadlock, Babbitt was driven back to the Guild headquarters.

That night the strikers held an emergency mass meeting. For the first time, strikers were pulled off the twenty-four-hour picket line. Sorrell chose to be absent. "I did not show up at the meeting that night, purposely," said Sorrell, "and everyone wanted to know where I was. Aubrey Blair told them that I had got disgusted with the strike and that I was through."

There was considerable conflict and confusion as to why Bioff was involved at all. Booing filled the room. When it was time to vote on the AFL-Bioff proposition, the strikers unanimously rejected it. They voted "not to enter into any agreement to which Bioff was a party."

———————

Roy Disney, Gunther Lessing, and chief engineer Bill Garity drafted an open letter to be published over Walt's name, and placed a full-page ad in *Variety* on July 1:

To My Employees on Strike:

I believe you are entitled to know why you are not working today. I offered your leaders the following terms:

(1) All employees to be reinstated to former positions
(2) No discrimination
(3) Recognition of your Union
(4) Closed Shop
(5) 50% retroactive pay for the time on strike—something without precedent in the American labor movement
(6) Increase in wages to make yours the highest salary scale in the cartoon industry
(7) Two weeks' vacation with pay

I believe that you have been misled and misinformed about the real issues underlying the strike at the studio. I am positively convinced that Communistic agitation, leadership, and activities have brought about this strike, and has persuaded you to reject this fair and equitable settlement.

I address you in this manner because I have no other means of reaching you.

WALT DISNEY

The next day, *Variety* printed another full-page ad with key words in bold:

Dear Walt:

Willie Bioff is not our leader.

Present your terms to **our** elected leaders, so that they may be submitted to us and there should be no difficulty in quickly settling our differences.

Your Striking Employees.

Inside the studio, Roy Disney and Gunther Lessing called a company-wide meeting, informing the staff that the Guild rejected their offer. Lessing emphatically blamed the Guild, saying, "Every time we think there is a chance of a settlement they come back with outlandish proposals to upset everything. . . . They're just using this Bioff stuff as a stall and an excuse."

Some strikers traveled to Herb Sorrell's home. They wanted his help in fighting Bioff, and they hoped to woo Sorrell back to the strike. In doing so, they would risk losing the AFL's valuable support not only for Sorrell but also for the Painters Union and the Guild. Sorrell agreed to rejoin the strike.

The strikers had facts to set straight and distributed handbills of Donald Duck and Mickey Mouse emphatically stating, "Disney Artists Still on Strike Despite Rumors" and "The Boycott is Still On!" As loyalists entered the front gates, the strikers handed out flyers that asked, "Do you know about the 'negotiation' meeting for which Walt and his new 'chum' waited in vain last night? . . . Bioff is our common enemy!" The strikers had an updated slogan: "Walt Cannot BIOFF Us!"

A Disney strike flyer from July 11, 1941, caricaturing Walt and Willie Bioff.

Bill Littlejohn released a statement from the Screen Cartoonists Guild: "The strikers were never offered the terms advertised in the papers by Disney. Apparently the terms had been discussed only by Disney and Bioff." The company revoked the closed-shop offer it had made. "We're going ahead and make cartoon comedies without the strikers," Lessing said. "Whenever we have met the union demands they have made new ones until the thing is ridiculous." However, this did not mean that Bioff was completely out of the picture.

The strikers sought support from all allies. To the Teamsters' Local 683, the Guild distributed a flyer stating, "If Bioff reestablishes his hold on motion picture labor it is the end of democracy, of honesty, and of decency in our trade union." Notices of support began pouring in. AFL-affiliated unions nationwide continued to honor the Disney boycott. The Screen Actors Guild derided the Disney-Bioff alliance and donated $1,000. Even the Milk Drivers and Dairy Employees donated $250. When news of Disney's collaboration with Bioff reached New York, clergy from Protestant, Catholic, and Jewish faiths wrote letters in protest.

Bioff used the situation to petition for a delay in his prosecution. For his part in the Disney labor dispute, he was (as his lawyer called him) an "indispensable man."

On the evening of Friday, July 4, crowds gathered in front of Hollywood's Pantages Theater and RKO Hillstreet Theatre for Hollywood's first screening of *The Reluctant Dragon*. These additional screenings would bring in desperately needed revenue while helping with the studio's public image.

Soon chauffeured vehicles pulled up. A car stopped in front of the crowded theaters' entrances, and out stepped Disney artists in formal eveningwear. Casually, the artists reached into the cars and pulled out their picket signs.

Disney strikers masquerading as chauffeurs continued to drop off other strikers dressed for a gala premiere. Picket signs with familiar Disney characters graced the air—along with new signs shaped like the Reluctant Dragon. The most elaborate sign constituted ten separate segments, requiring that many strikers to march in queue. It depicted an enormous dragon with the word UNFAIR across its side and Walt's caricatured head bearing the label THE

The Los Angeles premiere of *The Reluctant Dragon* at the RKO Hillstreet Theatre and its black-tie picket led by Babbitt, photographed by striker Kosti Ruohomaa, July 4, 1941.

RELUCTANT DISNEY. One striker impersonated a radio emcee and interviewed the picketers with a microphone. Strikers handed newly mimeographed leaflets with illustrations of a Walt-dragon refusing to sign a union contract. "Walt is still the RELUCTANT DISNEY!!!"

The reviews were also colored by the strike. *Box Office Digest* called *The Reluctant Dragon* an industrial film "to sell the stockholders." A half-page review in the *Weekly Variety* embedded this op-ed: "A curious coincidence is the relapse of 'The Reluctant Dragon'—planned two to three years ago—at this particular time, when Disney's studio employees are on strike. Dr. Goebbels couldn't do a better propaganda job to show the workers in Disney's pen-and-ink factory a happy and contented lot doing their daily chores midst idyllic surroundings."

The cover of a four-page leaflet distributed at theaters playing
The Reluctant Dragon.

Support for the strikers' anti-Bioff position rolled in like a tidal wave. At
the start of the following week, Babbitt addressed the strikers: "I would say
that our chances of winning are 100% because we have never been more solid!"

Pickets continued with doubled fervor. Strikers marched outside the Carthay Circle Theatre, where *Fantasia* continued its record-breaking run, and
outside the two theaters showing *The Reluctant Dragon.* The women of the
strike arranged a phone-calling campaign to Disney's switchboard and to theaters showing *The Reluctant Dragon.* "Keep their lines busy all the time," they
wrote. "Ask your friends to help you do just that."

Herb Sorrell remembered that the Disney company took drastic measures. "Mr. Disney, when he could not get any police from the city, decided to hire fifty private police from outside the city," he said. "We almost came to blows there." With the help of Burbank police, Sorrell had the private officers confined inside the property line.

Bioff's goons arrived, unmistakable in flashy clothes and torpedo-style cars, threatening the speaker at the strikers' microphone. A non-striker who saw this wrote "that anyone who tries to fight those [IATSE] leaders is risking his job and perhaps his life."

It was an uncomfortable situation for all parties. Bioff had his fingers in Walt Disney Productions; now he tried to dictate to Walt the terms of a contract with Disney employees. He used his signature ploy: threatening to stop all IATSE projectionists from playing Disney films. Artists on strike was one thing, but even his non-strikers knew that without projectionists, "Walt is helpless."

At that time, Walt tried to reason why he enlisted Bioff: "Believe me, he honestly tried to settle the thing peacefully. All he got out of it was a kick in the chin and I'm telling you the deal was not a bargain for me."

Then the colossus swooped in. Some strikers had reached out to the Congress of Industrial Organizations (CIO), the AFL's rival. The CIO had dominated the industrial unions of the Midwest but aspired to expand into entertainment crafts as well, and offered to back the Screen Cartoonists Guild both financially and morally.

Herb Sorrell politely turned down the CIO. For now, the strikers were still part of the AFL.

Clearly, Sorrell and the Guild were certain that Disney and the AFL would come to their senses and abandon Willie Bioff. That thought was soon dashed. On Tuesday, July 8, Bioff was spotted entering the building where the AFL's western director had an office. Shortly afterward, Roy Disney, Gunther Lessing, and Bill Garity also entered, followed by AFL representative Aubrey Blair, the IATSE's international representative, and heads of eight local unions under the IATSE's control. These unions—the Teamsters, the Soundmen, the Electrical

Workers, the Plasterers, the Laboratory Workers, the Utility Workers, the Projectionists, and the Cameramen—had all honored the Disney strike for six solid weeks. Their involvement accounted for ninety-eight souls on the picket line, according to the studio. (The Guild counted twenty-one.)

By the time the meeting was over, each of these eight local unions had been ordered to sign blanket contracts and return to work. As reported by the press, the IATSE's pretense for this act was "cleaning out Commies and curb any CIO muscle-in attempt." The Disney camera operators would resume filming Disney animation, and the laboratory workers would begin processing one hundred additional Technicolor prints of *The Reluctant Dragon*. In a final blow to the Guild, the AFL called off the Disney boycott. No longer would the AFL support the Disney unit of the Screen Cartoonists Guild.

The Disney strikers were in a panic. They feared that the IATSE might now issue a charter for their own cartoonists' union. The irony was head-spinning: the very purpose of forming an independent cartoonists' union had been to block Bioff at Disney, and now it appeared that Disney would use Bioff to block them—the independent union!

The Guild meeting that evening continued well past midnight. Sorrell and the leaders explained that this was a single hang-up and they expressed unwavering confidence in their eventual triumph. After all, the Guild still had Disney's twenty-six striking film editors on their side.

The next day, Wednesday, July 9, the IATSE ordered the film editors back to work. Filing past the pickets on Thursday, the editors apologized to the striking cartoonists.

"The defection of certain Bioff-dominated unions did not change the situation," announced Bill Littlejohn. "The demands of the union are the same as they were six months ago. We have never had an opportunity to present our proposals to Walt because he, in violation of the Wagner Act, has consistently refused to meet with his employees. Apparently Walt prefers to deal with Willie Bioff."

The National Labor Relations Act (or Wagner Act) listed five unfair labor practices. The Disney company had already been charged with three: coercing employees, dominating the formation of a labor organization, and discrimination in regard to tenure of employment. Now attorney George Bodle charged the company with a fourth: refusing to bargain collectively with the employees' representative.

While Roy Disney and Gunther Lessing were facilitating this defection, Walt was at a particular standstill. The US Office of Inter-American Affairs was prepared to bankroll Disney for its research trip to Latin America. This was part of the government's "Good Neighbor" program to combat the spread of Naziism in the Americas. It was a remarkably fortuitous deal. The group's arrival in Argentina was originally planned to coincide with *Fantasia*'s premiere in Buenos Aires, but the strike had delayed that. The federal government refused to move forward with the plan while the strike remained unsettled.

Desperately, Walt called a local government agent, US labor arbitrator Stanley White, to see if he could settle the strike. "The government wanted me to go to South America," said Walt in 1942. "That is why we agreed to arbitration."

As opposed to conciliation or mediation, arbitration would decide once and for all. Washington quickly dispatched White to the Disney studio. Walt was ready for the US government to settle it.

The Disney strikers carrying their ten-segmented RELUCTANT DISNEY sign, photographed by striker Kosti Ruohomaa.

29 | THE GUILD AND THE CIO

"STILL WITH CHIP-MUNK INTELLIGENCE, you go round and round on your Picket treadmill," read the latest bulletin from the Committee of 21. "Now you cling to the forlorn hope expressed in those in-FAMOUS LAST WORDS, 'Herbert Stewart (Communist Party Card #60622) Sorrell will win again like he did in 1937.' . . . Bioff has never compromised with 'the commies.' He knows (what you do not seem to realize) that to believe in or string along with a communist pledge <u>to-day</u> is to get a knife in your back <u>tomorrow</u>."

Sorrell's middle name was Knott. The Disney strikers responded by writing in their own leaflets: "We don't know, of course, but it begins to look as if someone in the 21 Club has been hitting the weed."

Sorrell had been labeled a Communist by the press, by the studio, and most recently by the AFL-supported IATSE. Now that the AFL withdrew its support from him and the Guild, he informed the CIO that he was ready to accept their help.

On Friday July 11, the CIO officially adopted a resolution to "extend full support to the Screen Cartoonists, Local 852," and to have every local CIO union follow suit. The CIO said that they had long been eager to move into the film industry, and now they moved fast. That evening, all CIO projectionists, encompassing fifty-five theaters, voted to cease screening Disney films. Representing between one hundred thousand and four hundred thousand unionists nationwide, the CIO also put Walt Disney Productions on its own Unfair list. A new boycott had begun.

Other unions stepped up. The Screen Actors Guild continued to honor the Disney strike. The local Machinists Union had unanimously voted to honor the picket line. Technicolor once again stopped processing Disney film. The

Laboratory Technicians Union, whose members worked at Technicolor, doubled its financial contribution to the strike.

Strikers' efforts intensified. A mass picket line outside the RKO Hillstreet Theatre turned into a "riot," requiring the police to be summoned and ending the run of *The Reluctant Dragon* at the theater after only seven days. All over the country, pickets surrounded theaters that tried to show *The Reluctant Dragon*. That weekend, the Disney strikers engaged in a "handbill blitz," reaching for public support like never before.

Sketch by striker Bob Totten given to his sweetheart, fellow striker (and future wife) Betty Smith, depicting how the weeks took their toll.

All the while, federal labor conciliator Stanley White was spending his days at the Disney studio assessing and examining, speaking with Disney strike leaders and Disney company executives alike. White wired a report to the Department of Labor in Washington, DC. On Sunday night, July 13, the director of the US Conciliation Service, Dr. John R. Steelman, wired a proposed settlement from Washington to end the strike.

The strike was on day forty-eight when on Monday, July 14, the US government offered to arbitrate. At their meeting on the knoll, the strikers unanimously voted to accept whatever the government decided. The Guild wired to Steelman, "We, as patriotic Americans, accept your proposal."

Within an hour of the strikers' vote, Walt Disney Productions rejected the government's offer.

Gunther Lessing blasted the Labor Relations Board, protesting that Steelman did not "possess full information regarding the situation." He stated that the strikers constituted a minority and that the majority of Disney artists were represented by the ACA, "apparently being convinced that the guild leadership is Communistic." He accused the Labor Relations Board of thwarting the ACA's attempts to certify "at every turn by stalling [and] meddling . . . which in my opinion almost warrants Congressional investigation."

But the company's refusal came in haste. At least one of the company's New York–based investors had just visited the Disney plant and reported to his investment agent back east that the strike was about to be settled. The company was guilty of a top-tier faux pas: Gunther Lessing had refused the arbitration services without the knowledge or approval of the shareholders.

Babbitt wouldn't have it. "The company's interest, in the eyes of Walt Disney, is evidently superior to the national interest," he announced. "The company has made it clear that it would prefer to deal with Willie Bioff, a discredited labor racketeer, than with its own Government. We don't fear the results of an impartial investigation of our dispute. If Walt Disney and Gunther Lessing are so certain of the justice of their cause, why are they unwilling to present the facts to the Federal Government?"

It appeared to Babbitt that Walt's stubbornness was leading the negotiations nowhere fast. Maybe if Walt could see the light from his most trusted artists, they could end this. Babbitt picked up the phone. He was going to attempt some unofficial business, without the consent or vote of his fellow committee members. If he were to succeed, he'd be a hero.

———————————

Late that morning of July 15, Fred Moore and Ward Kimball were working on *Dumbo* when Wilfred Jackson and Norm Ferguson approached them, asking if they would have lunch with Babbitt, Tytla, and some Disney Guilders.

Over lunch at Sardi's, Babbitt and the others told the four loyalists their aim: they hadn't dreamed the strike would go on for seven weeks. They said that both sides should unite before the whole studio collapsed—and that the non-strikers should get Walt to recognize the Guild.

Ward Kimball broke the sobering news to Babbitt's group, that the studio was finding out that it could do fine without the artists on strike. He added that the name-calling on the picket lines had made a lot of enemies. Babbitt acknowledged that he was as much to blame as anyone.

The meeting ended in a deadlock. As Kimball reflected that day, "They were there to guide us through the wilderness; we didn't want to be guided."

———————————

Around this time, a strike flyer appeared, called "Primer of the Disney Strike," with typical fervor and whimsy:

> A is for ARTIST, anonymous gent;
>> They said, "He's a comer!" the day that he went.
> B is for BIOFF the eminent thug,
>> Fresh from his sophomore year in the jug
> C is for CONTRACTS, illegal and phony,
>> Walt gets the gravy and we get baloney.
> D is for DISNEY, who lays down the law,
>> The only great artist who never could draw.
> E is for EVERYONE working for Walt,
>> Earning the sugar but getting the salt.

F is for FIELD OF ALFALFA, where dwells
  The Baron of Burbank asleep on his cels.
G is for GOONS sent to stymie the Guild;
  They all got away before any were killed.
H is for HUMORIST, topper of gags,
  He leaves us in stitches, and also in rags.
I is for INKERS, who ink with an "F",
  When passing the pickets they'd like to be deaf.
J is for JOB, some kind of a bizness
  To keep a guy up while he's working at Disney's.
K is for KNIFE that's slipped in the spine
  When the studio hands out a contract to sign.
L is for LOGGERHEADS; speaking of that
  That's where the Guild and the Disneys are at.
M is for MONEY the studio owes,
  For which it has shown us its thumb to its nose.
N is NEGOTIATE, isn't that silly?
  The Guild wanted Uncle [Sam] and Walt wanted Willie.
O is for OVERHEAD, soon to be put
  Out of the studio, under the foot.
P is for PANIC, the scabs who pass by
  Are jumpy as grandma the 4th of July.
Q is for QUOTA of pictures we made,
  For which we earned shekels which never were paid.
R is RELUCTANT, descriptive of Gunny
  When kindly requested to pay us our money.
S is for SCABBY; approach him on tip-toe,
  He's riding to glory asleep on his Scripto.
T is for TEMPUS which fugits away
  While artists are slaving for nothing a day.
U is the U.S.; the Studio feels
  They'd rather have Bioff to handle their deals.
V is for Victory; that's what we've got
  Whether the studio knows it or not.
W stands for the generous guy
  Who gives his men anything—up in the sky.

X is for Xtra the artists all do
　　for which they are fired when the picture is through.
Y is for YESWALT, the password to know
　　If you have any hopes for your salary to grow.
Z is for ZOMBIE, or Victory Scotch;
　　Drink 'em down double and let the scabs watch.

On Wednesday, July 16, the Screen Cartoonists Guild sent telegrams to the presidents of the AFL and of the Brotherhood of Painters and Decorators of America, asking them to fire Aubrey Blair.

On the evening of July 22, a large meeting was held to negotiate a settlement. Roy Disney was present with other Disney managers, along with representatives from the Guild, the Los Angeles Central Labor Council, and other Hollywood craft unions. There was debate about certain terms for a union contract, like whether the strikers should receive back pay and whether to reinstate the eighteen Guild artists fired in May.

Eager to settle, Roy relented and agreed on arbitration. He called Dr. Steelman's US Conciliation office and followed up with a telegram. Gunther Lessing and Bill Littlejohn each wired Dr. Steelman that they agreed to Steelman's proposal of a three-person arbitration board. The Los Angeles Central Labor Council lifted the Disney boycott, "trusting that we may have a pleasant and friendly relationship in the future," wrote J. W. Buzzell. (Nonetheless, the San Fernando Valley Central Labor Council maintained the boycott.)

On July 24 the US Conciliation commissioner, James F. Dewey, was assigned to arbitrate. In advance of arbitration, he would try to mediate a solution between Walt Disney Productions and the Guild. This infuriated the Disney loyalists of the ACA, who voted to strike if they weren't considered in negotiations. Dewey did not gratify them with a response; unsurprisingly, the ACA did not go on strike.

These non-strikers appeared to be more in agreement with the Guild than not. One of the ACA members wrote, "I have come to the conclusion that Walt is alright and is not trying to do us dirty, but that he is pig-headed and badly advised, and his head lawyer [Lessing] is . . . very dangerous when it comes

James F. Dewey, federal arbiter of the Disney strike, seen here in 1941.

to dealing with employees, most of whom . . . only want a fair deal with their employer. He is a dirty little so-and-so, I think, and really responsible for a lot of the trouble."

On Monday, July 28, commissioner Dewey held his first meetings with Disney executives and Guild leaders. Afterward, Roy Disney composed a memo for all Disney strikers that welcomed them back: "Effective at 8:30 am, Tuesday, 7-29-41 you are re-instated on the Walt Disney Productions payroll at your salary in effect as of May 28, 1941."

On Tuesday, July 29, the leaders of Disney management and the Disney strike sat in a government building for an arbitration hearing with US arbitrators Dewey and White. Roy Disney and Gunther Lessing were there, as well as Art Babbitt. Lessing complained that the Labor Relations Board favored the strikers, a position that Walt subsequently adopted.

On Wednesday, July 30, Gunther Lessing and Bill Littlejohn submitted a basic legal agreement to end the strike. Dewey and White amended the agreement later that day. On August 2, the Disney strikers received a union contract:

- Walt Disney Productions would be a closed shop. Union membership was required for all.
- Union heads could receive leaves of absence for union meetings.
- All low-level artists would receive a raise. Every employee earning less than fifty dollars a week would get a 25 percent increase in salary over twelve months. The wage scales were clearly stipulated, making them the highest salaries in the animation industry.
- The workweek would be 8:30–5:30 Monday through Friday. Overtime would pay time and a half for weekends and double for holidays.
- Men would get five sick days a year, women ten.
- Women would be rated in classifications equal to men.
- The union could protest termination of any employee through a grievance committee.
- Screen credit would be determined at a future hearing.
- The studio would be required to bear a union label.
- There would be no discrimination against the strikers, and the union could post flyers on the company bulletin board.
- Strikers were to receive one hundred hours of back pay.
- Babbitt (the only striker mentioned by name) would be protected from any discriminatory repercussion.

The strikers lit a bonfire of their picket signs. The Disney strike was finally over. It had spanned nine weeks to the day. It would also leave the studio forever changed.

30 | NOT THE DRAWING

AND SO THE UNION CELEBRATED. The ex-strikers entered the gates once again, alongside the loyalists. But the atmosphere was tense. One animator remembered it was "edgy—some people never spoke to each other again."

Roy attempted a diplomatic reunification. Like Abraham Lincoln to a restored nation, he addressed his employees, stressing that a change in attitude was essential to the survival of the studio.

Personnel director Hal Adelquist approached Babbitt as the artists entered the lot. Adelquist said he was sorry the strike had happened, and he was ready to put it all behind them; the studio was still suffering, and he only wanted to complete as much work as possible. The two shook hands and agreed to move on.

The strikers had heard a rumor that their offices had been taken by non-strikers. Now they saw it was true. The non-strikers had moved their furniture and occupied the more desirable rooms. A nonstriking, lesser animator was now sitting at Babbitt's desk. Babbitt was assigned a new room that only had an animation desk and a drawing cupboard on a linoleum floor. It did not have carpeting, additional furniture, a personal Moviola machine, or adjacent space for an assistant. It was a trainee's room.

Babbitt contacted Adelquist, demanding all the amenities of his old room. Adelquist promised to get him a Moviola as soon as possible. The process took days.

In the Personnel Department, a young secretary named Marge Gummerman worked under Hal Adelquist. She was given a very curious instruction.

Gummerman was to go through the pile of employee evaluations and separate the strikers from the non-strikers. Then, after each evaluation had STRIKER or NON-STRIKER written atop their photo, she was told to file the strikers separately. The STRIKER pile would be the first for layoffs.

Her task did not remain a secret for very long. Gummerman happened to be the girlfriend (and later wife) of one of the strikers.

Due to cost-cutting, the company still had to downsize by Friday, August 15. Management assembled a nine-person committee to decide who would be laid off. The committee was headed by Hal Adelquist, and it compiled a list of 256 employees, of whom 207 were ex-strikers, including Babbitt.

The list was submitted to the Screen Cartoonists Guild for approval. Naturally, the Guild was quick to reject it. Gunther Lessing protested, "We have a right to retain those employees of highest merit and ability. We have done that; we have not discriminated."

The Guild insisted that the conciliator get involved. US labor conciliator James F. Dewey was busy in Detroit. He informed Walt Disney Productions that he would need time to come up with a formula for accounting a new layoff list.

Walt Disney had other things to plan. With the strike settled, the US government gave the green light for his group's Latin America research trip. "I marvel at Disney's hypocrisy," wrote Babbitt in his journal. "After violating the wages and hours law—violating the Dept. of Labor arbitration decree and soaking the Government for the South American picture—he has the gall to advertise his patriotism while he lands a juicy defense pictures program."

Inside the studio there was still confusion. Many artists were waiting around, shooting craps or playing poker.

Columnist Westbrook Pegler had reached out to Walt during the strike, asking for details. Walt left Pegler's letter sitting until the morning of his flight, on August 11. Only then did Walt respond, writing out of exhaustion, resentment, and angst: "To me, the entire situation is a catastrophe. The spirit that played such an important part in the building of the cartoon medium has been destroyed." Walt felt that the Labor Relations Board was undemocratic and "lopsided" against him and that the press damaged his public image with "the lies, [and] the twisted half-truths." He considered quitting the business altogether "if it were not for the loyal guys who believe in me." In a fit of "disillusionment and discouragement," Walt left with his bags and boarded a plane for a ten-week production trip to South America. The government's Good Neighbor program awaited.

With Walt away, Roy Disney didn't take long to consider his options. He needed a new list requiring Guild approval. These layoffs would reorganize the studio. Roy took drastic action. Instead of laying off anyone on August 15, he shut down the studio and placed nearly its entire staff on unpaid leave.

"The closing of the Studio came as a great blow to our employees," wrote one of Roy's executives to him on August 17. The note, on behalf of many in studio management, bemoaned that the cries of "Communism" were an unfounded distraction and that Gunther Lessing was a poor advisor who should have not been involved. It called on Roy to rein in Hal Adelquist, who had allowed the Personnel Department to hunt ex-strikers. The note pleaded with Roy to lead "toward integration and reconstruction," to "take a stand against discrimination," and (referencing Walt's trip) "to take care of the Goodneighbor program here at home."

The letter partially worked. Adelquist would eventually be removed from the Personnel Department. Some strikers were embraced by the studio again, even earning high praise throughout their long tenure. Most, however, were spurned and quit within a few years. The studio never truly healed the divide between the strikers and non-strikers.

The Guild immediately hired a new business agent named William Pomerance, previously a field examiner for the Labor Relations Board. Pomerance began working to protect the jobs of Guild animators at Disney and across Hollywood.

Disney employees on furlough filed for government aid, nervous about the future and unsure when the studio would open again. The days turned into weeks. They were in a limbo, unable to work but unable to leave.

On September 9, Dewey handed down his "second arbitration settlement"—
a formula for a new and equitable layoff list. It had a specific ratio of strikers
to non-strikers in each department in production and how many of each the
management was permitted to lay off.

The Disney managers were at the mercy of the Labor Relations Board; they
were forced to add names of artists who hadn't gone on strike. They drew up
a new list that balanced strikers with non-strikers, and the Guild accepted it.
The studio reopened on Wednesday, September 17, minus 263 employees. This
time, Babbitt was designated to stay. It would not last long.

Things were very different around the studio. There were about seven
hundred total employees now, compared to twelve hundred a year before. The
artists now had to punch a time clock. Police officers directed everyone to
their buildings.

Babbitt sat at his desk, waiting for his first animation assignments. But
the assignments did not come, and Babbitt was left idle. He contacted Hal
Adelquist. Aside from being personnel director, Adelquist was also the "casting
director," distributing scenes to each animator as per that animator's ability.
The second week, Adelquist delivered three scenes to Babbitt for a new Goofy
cartoon, *How to Fish*. The scenes had been animated already (by John Sibley)
but were not satisfactory. Babbitt was tasked to redo those scenes.

Shortly thereafter, Babbitt again found himself idle. Again, he contacted Adelquist and waited several days before Adelquist delivered. Babbitt
received thirteen scenes of Ben Buzzard in a Donald Duck cartoon, *The Flying
Jalopy*.

Director Dick Lundy had handed those scenes over to Adelquist reluc-
tantly. All the loyalists had seen how deeply Babbitt had gotten under Walt's
skin, and many stayed as far away from Babbitt as possible. Old-timers like
Lundy may have done it out of self-preservation. Art-school graduates like Milt
Kahl may have considered the strike irreconcilable. Kahl encountered Babbitt
at the building's Coca-Cola dispensary, laughing and saying, "I'm not supposed
to talk to you," and nearly got into a fistfight. Gunther Lessing refused to sit
in a meeting with Babbitt, shouting, "I'll be god-damned if I will have that
son-of-a-bitch come up here!"

The non-strikers gathered at the Guild headquarters on September 29 to
pledge the oath of membership. Many did it begrudgingly. Fred Moore garbled
nonsense words with a random "son-of-a-bitch" thrown in.

They returned to the studio anxious to complete the next Disney feature. *Bambi* was moving to completion, so more animators were reassigned to the two other features in development—the "Mickey Feature" and *The Wind in the Willows.*

On October 9, Roy Disney returned from meeting with the company's distribution agents in New York with unhappy news. The studio, he said, would have to "drastically curtail its feature production" and shelve *The Wind in the Willows* and the "Mickey Feature." They would join the growing pile of discontinued projects, including *Peter Pan, Alice in Wonderland, The Little Mermaid,* new *Fantasia* segments, and what would be *Lady and the Tramp.* For now, the studio could only focus on short cartoons starring their staple characters.

When Walt returned from Latin America in late October, much had changed. The layoffs had put a dent in the studio. The amenities like the studio coffee shop and auto shop were nowhere to be seen. What's more, Walt no longer had final say in a lot of studio policy. The Guild's presence was tangible.

But the Guild had changed too. All the Disney artists were now Guild members. New elections were held for Guild stewards, and the Disney artists voted for nearly all non-strikers. Babbitt didn't even win a nomination. Animator Eric Larson became the new president, and animator Ward Kimball the new vice president.

The Personnel Department compiled another layoff list, this one with ninety-eight names, including Babbitt's. It was submitted to the Disney unit of the Screen Cartoonists Guild for approval. This time, under the auspices of Larson and Kimball, the Guild approved the list. On the afternoon of November 24, ninety-eight Disney artists received the memo for their immediate termination. All layoff grievances could be taken to Disney's director of labor relations, Anthony O'Rourke—still a member of Disney management.

Babbitt simply sat at his desk and penned a letter to the company. "I consider my status as an employee of your company unchanged," he wrote. "I shall expect payment of my regular weekly salary whether or not you wish to avail yourself of my services."

The move was bold, but ineffective. Babbitt unwillingly left the Disney lot yet again. The company had already tried to fire him in May and in August. Babbitt doubted the third time would be any more successful.

Babbitt filed two lawsuits against Disney. The first, for unpaid bonuses, officially called a "complaint for breach of contract and for accounting," was filed on December 19. The second, for wrongful termination, involved the Labor Relations Board and would need more time to prepare.

The United States had officially entered the Second World War. Over the next few days, Babbitt drove cross-country to New York, visited friends and family, and met up with Marge and her new partner. From Manhattan he sailed to Buenos Aries to meet Argentine cartoonist Dante Quinterno. Together they collaborated on a short cartoon and discussed possible employment in South America.

But deep anxiety festered within, for which he blamed the company. He journaled, "Little pangs of common sense keep pricking me—telling me that I should be home working—reestablishing myself and facing realities again." He lamented "the uncertainty of starting again in a profession that I love so much—but which (thanks to Disney and Lessing) has brought me so much unhappiness."

But below the surface, Babbitt blamed himself. On the steamship he wrote about a graphic nightmare in which he mistakenly and violently murdered a friend with his bare hands. Subconsciously, he feared his own inadvertent destructiveness.

When Babbitt returned from South America in April, he signed up for the US Marine Corps reserves. Without clear explanation, the Marine Corps canceled his enlistment. Babbitt called upon his colleagues for letters of recommendation. Bill Tytla wrote an attestation to Babbitt's industriousness and ambitiousness. Ex-production manager Herb Lamb did as well, adding, "I always found him to be a man of intelligence and high moral character." Babbitt's enlistment was accepted again.

On May 25, 1942, the Labor Relations Board filed Babbitt's unfair labor practice lawsuit against Disney. Both his trials would dovetail, the civil suit and the Labor Relations Board suit occurring back-to-back in October. Until then, Babbitt worked at the Warner Bros. animation studio under director Bob Clampett. He was offered a handsome salary, but he refused to work for anything more than scale minimum. The earnings would count against his Disney settlement, were he to win. And he wanted Disney to pay as much as possible.

He worked at Warner Bros. right up to his civil suit trial, held the week of October 5. In court Babbitt testified that he was owed between $2,000 and $17,000 in bonuses for *Pinocchio, Fantasia,* and several shorts. Gunther Lessing argued on behalf of Disney management that the bonus amounts were always at the behest of the company. The only clearly defined compensation was the salary stipulated in his contract. This argument was strikingly similar to Lessing's tactic in 1917 against Eugene Ives, a case Lessing had won. Lessing countered that Babbitt owed the company around $200 from unsettled loans he borrowed in 1939.

The civil suit trial adjourned on Wednesday, October 7, 1942. The labor suit trial began on Thursday, October 8. Babbitt set out to prove that he was a highly valued worker and that his termination was purely discriminatory.

Babbitt was composed and well-spoken as he sat in the witness stand. He testified continuously for the first two and a half days as his attorney questioned him. He recounted how he and Lessing built the Federation on company time and resources. He described his valued status within the studio. He argued that he was more valued than many of the animators who had not been fired. When Lessing objected to the lack of evidence, Babbitt laughed out loud.

Gunther Lessing countered, explaining that the strikers, including Babbitt, went on strike because they were subpar and sought job security.

Following Babbitt on the witness stand were Dave Hilberman and other Guild chairpersons. Warner Bros. cartoon directors Bob Clampett, Frank Tashlin, and Chuck Jones testified to Babbitt's skill. "Among animators and directors, there is a ranking," said Jones, "and we know who is at the top of the heap."

On the fourth day, the Disney company presented its case. Its chief witness was Hal Adelquist, who testified for nearly an entire day. Of Babbitt's termination, he said simply that there was a lack of work for him. During cross-examination, when Adelquist testified not knowing Babbitt's skill level, Babbitt nearly interrupted him, jumping out of his chair and emphatically shaking his head.

A slew of Disney directors testified against Babbitt, including Bill Roberts, Dick Lundy, Wilfred Jackson, Dave Hand, and Jack Kinney.

The company's final witness was Walt Disney himself. Walt was visibly shaken and out of his element. When he described how the drop in the foreign market caused the 1940 layoffs, he broke down in tears.

At last he collected himself and began to describe his experience working with Babbitt throughout the 1930s. "At the time, he was doing a good job," said Walt, "but the business progressed, moved up, and standards changed. . . . Other things crept into [his work]—little subtleties. It is not the drawing. It is not the drawing."

Walt said that Babbitt had lost his confidence. This made his animation stiffer, which made him even more self-conscious. "Mr. Babbitt had developed a terrific persecution complex," Walt testified. "For some reason he thought that everybody in the studio was against him. And I talked to Babbitt about it and I told him that he was carrying a chip on his shoulder, [that] the attitude that he had had always been argumentative with people that he worked with, and [that] he was 'building a fence around himself.'"

There appeared to be no bitterness in Walt that day. He had spent the past ten years seeing his studio transform. He had watched as the old guard animators who built the studio were slowly overshadowed by the newer ones. What Walt observed when he looked at Babbitt was accurate, whether Babbitt liked it or not.

After the day's closing arguments, Babbitt walked out of the courtroom. In less than a month he entered active duty in the US Marines. There was another war to fight.

31 | THE FINAL GOODBYE

ART BABBITT BEGAN HIS YEARS at war in Quantico, Virginia, working at the Marine Corps motion picture unit. He spent nine weeks learning about landfall recognition, rubber terrain model production, and photo surface terrain technology. He illustrated cartoons for Marine safety guides like they were out of a humor magazine, one about foot care, the other about flame thrower safety.

After a few months, Babbitt was transferred to Terrain Intelligence in the Pacific, specializing as a landfall technician. His base was on the dusty, tropical island of Guam, and he helped map the Japanese base of Pagan Island from above. Although his bad eyes kept him out of combat, he found himself on the airfields where squadrons of B-29s took off on bombing runs. When the marines captured Iwo Jima, Babbitt saw the planes celebrate their triumph overhead by "buzzing the island like a swarm of mosquitoes."

Babbitt's two lawsuits were settled while he was on active duty. On January 28, 1943, he lost his civil suit. The Disney company had presented the financial accounts of *Pinocchio* and *Fantasia* and publicly disclosed that the films each lost $1 million. The news surprised the press and did not bode well for stockholders. The judge ruled that it was not the studio's policy to pay bonuses on productions that lost money. Babbitt was also required to repay a balance of $222.10 that he had borrowed in 1939.

But that was small potatoes compared to the Labor Relations Board case, which was ruled in his favor in March 1943. In terminating Babbitt, Walt Disney Productions was officially held liable for breaking the National Labor Relations Act.

The company was granted an appeal, but on December 5, 1944, it was decreed in the Court of Appeals that the original order must be upheld. Disney had to:

- Cease and desist from discouraging membership in the Screen Cartoonists Guild.
- Rehire Babbitt at his former position.
- Reimburse Babbitt for any loss of pay he may have suffered from Disney's discrimination (about $9,000).
- Hang bulletins throughout the studio for sixty days stating that the company would not discriminate against the Screen Cartoonists Guild or any of its members.

Once again, the Disney company fought the verdict, this time petitioning for a Supreme Court review. On April 23, 1945, the chief justice of the US Supreme Court, Harlan Fiske Stone (one of Roosevelt's Nine Old Men), penned a letter of denial.

The Second World War ended in September 1945, and on October 29, Babbitt was honorably discharged as master technical sergeant first class. He was 38 years old.

He made his arrangements and arrived for work at Disney on Monday, December 3. The law guaranteed Babbitt's employment without discrimination, but human opinion was something else entirely.

Babbitt was warned to "sort of keep out of Walt's way." He was required to use a time clock—a requirement among junior animators who worked hourly. He wanted his seniority and full salary restored—not $170 per week, which was after the voluntary 15 percent cut, but his original $200-per-week salary. Most of all, he wanted a contract, like the senior animators always had.

By early April 1946, when the feature film department had begun production on *Fun and Fancy Free*, Babbitt was still relegated to short cartoons. He complained to his supervisor, and on mid-May he was assigned scenes on *Fun and Fancy Free* for Bongo the bear. All the while he was treated like a junior animator: given his scenes by a senior animator instead of the director and excluded from story conferences.

Additionally, most of the higher-level artists refused to have anything to do with Babbitt. They avoided him in the studio commissary. "Sit with Babbitt and get a black mark on your report card," they said. They joked that the "kiss of death" would be for Walt to see you with Babbitt's arm around you. Babbitt felt he was as being treated like a "leper."

In November Babbitt was given a minute of animation to complete in the "Pecos Bill" segment of the feature *Melody Time*. That minute was cut. In December Babbitt was put on a sequence called the "Flower Festival," and by January it too was cut. On Friday, January 10, the animation supervisor told Babbitt that since they had no work for him, the studio would be laying him off again, adding that Babbitt's animation just hadn't stood up since he returned from the Marines.

There was some truth to that. Babbitt's work had suffered. It can be seen in the opening to *Foul Hunting*. Goofy wiggles his fanny and fumbles his gun in a stilted, erratic way. It does not look smooth or graceful. It is the work of an animator trying to put more in than what is needed to get the point across—an animator who is overcompensating.

The Guild's grievance committee met on Tuesday, January 14, opposite Bonar Dyer and two other managers. The Disney company offered a large cash settlement if Babbitt was to resign. Babbitt accepted.

Almost immediately Babbitt received a notice on company stationery comprised of one sentence: "Dear Mr. Babbitt: We hereby accept your resignation from our employment, effective as of January 16, 1947, and our records have been adjusted accordingly." It was signed by the vice president, Gunther Lessing.

Babbitt packed his things and left the Disney studio again, this time for good. One wonders what Walt thought when Babbitt left that day. Maybe a sense of relief came over him as he stood in his corner office and looked out from his picture window. Maybe he recalled the first time Babbitt's live-action reference was used to bring his characters to life, or when they realized that the key to personality was Babbitt's character analysis. Maybe he recalled the first days of his studio's art school that Babbitt had initiated. And maybe for a moment, Walt remembered that day in the sweatbox watching Babbitt's skillful animation of the Mad Doctor, eager for Babbitt to raise the others up.

32 | AND THEY LIVED

ART BABBITT married Dina Gottliebova in 1948. He worked at a new animation studio called United Productions of America, or UPA, founded by ex-Disney strikers. There he animated on the first Mr. Magoo short, and it is rumored that the character's irascibility was at least partially based on Babbitt. He went on to work on commercials and co-ran a small studio called Quartet Films, winning a slew of awards for his commercials and industrial films.

He and Dina had two daughters, Michele in 1951 and Karin in 1954.

In 1959 Babbitt joined the faculty of University of Southern California, the first person to devise a curriculum and teach a course on animation. In 1960 a student named Carl Bell had moved from Ontario to take Babbitt's class. He sent notes to his friend Richard Williams, who had an obsession with golden-age animation.

Babbitt and Dina divorced in 1962. He was the co-owner of his own small production company, but Babbitt grew unhappy "having to direct and animate nights and week-ends in order to keep up with assignments." In 1964 he started a long tenure at Hanna-Barbera directing animated commercials. Some days, he got lost in his own regrets. Sitting on the couch with his daughter Michele, he sighed, "Don't be a hero. It's not worth it."

In 1966 he remarried a final time, to a professional dancer and actress named Barbara Perry. He told her seven-year-old daughter, Laurel, to address him as Bill Tytla had—as "Bones." The marriage evinced great mutual support and deep love.

By 1973 Richard Williams was running his own successful animation studio in London when he first made contact with Babbitt by phone and invited him over to teach. During the summers of 1973 and 1974, Babbitt gave daily lectures to the artists at the London studio. Williams gladly covered the expense. The lectures were transcribed, photocopied, and passed hand-to-hand across the industry. Animator Tom Sito wrote, "I don't know an animator from the '70s who doesn't have a copy somewhere."

In New York City in 1975, a young animator named John Canemaker was attempting a side career as an animation historian. He met Babbitt for an interview in a hotel, marking the first time he encountered an animation legend. Canemaker said, "Your notes from Dick Williams's seminars are being passed about here as if they were Galileo's."

Ever the victimized truth-teller, Babbitt replied, "Just so [long as] they won't burn me at the stake."

As an elder, Babbitt gladly stepped into the role of living legend, meeting with young journalists and historians, telling stories of his work at the Disney studio. It was a mission of sorts. He did not want his name to be erased from Disney history, and he feared that the company had attempted to do just that.

Bitterness bred bitterness. Veterans of the Disney strike called Walt an anti-Semite. This made Babbitt's martyrdom more personal and gave them justification to antagonize Walt Disney. It became a battle cry of the ex-strikers who wanted to punish Walt the way they felt they had been punished. However, the accusation had only emerged in the fury and aftermath of the labor dispute; at no time beforehand is it remotely alluded to. (Actually, Walt had a number of Jewish or half-Jewish people in his close orbit, like Lessing, Joe Rosenberg, Joe Grant, and Marc Davis.) The fact that Babbitt and some strikers were Jewish is more a statement about the propensity of Jewish activism in the twentieth century.

Babbitt periodically returned to the Richard Williams studio until the mid-1980s. In 1986, the studio was working on a big new project called *Who Framed Roger Rabbit*, and it would revive a global love for classic Hollywood cartoons. Many animators who had studied under Babbitt were now working on this film—including Richard Williams himself. Williams also sent animators to work directly with the seventy-eight-year-old Babbitt. He had become a catalyst for the animation renaissance of the late 1980s.

WILLIE BIOFF stood trial with George Browne on October 8, 1941. On November 6 the jury found Bioff and Browne guilty of extorting $1.2 million from movie producers. Browne was sentenced to eight years in prison; Bioff was sentenced to ten. In 1942 Bioff testified to federal investigators about his involvement with Frank

Nitti and the Capone gang. This led to a massive indictment of Chicago mobsters in 1943, the death of Frank Nitti, and the fall of the Capone crime syndicate.

Bioff was released in 1944 under the Witness Protection Program and moved with his wife to Phoenix. He didn't keep as low a profile as he should have, and he frequented casinos. On the morning of November 4, 1955, Bioff turned on his truck's ignition. The vehicle exploded in his driveway, throwing Bioff's body twenty-five feet into the air and scattering car wreckage over a hundred-foot radius. The mob had caught up with him. He was fifty-five.

WALT DISNEY never reinstated the studio art school, though the library of art books remained.

For a group of nine top animators who did not strike, Walt borrowed Franklin Roosevelt's term for the Supreme Court justices. Les Clark, Marc Davis, Milt Kahl, Ward Kimball, Eric Larson, John Lounsberry, Ollie Johnston, Frank Thomas, and Woolie Reitherman became known as Disney's Nine Old Men. The designation became a badge of honor, and their status remained forever secure, even legendary.

Fred Moore battled with alcoholism, and Walt fired and rehired him. Moore died in an auto accident (as a passenger) in 1952 at age forty-one.

Once Norm Ferguson segued into supervision, he butted heads with Walt for years and finally left Walt Disney Productions around 1953. He died in 1957.

Dick Lundy left the Disney studio in 1943 and remained in Hollywood as an animator and director. He died in 1990 at age eighty-two.

Gunther Lessing remained the company vice president and legal counsel until his retirement in 1964. He died in 1965 at age seventy-nine.

Bill Tytla had become persona non grata at Walt Disney Productions and left in 1943, returning to New York. He frequently reapplied to Disney but was consistently rejected. "He was the most displaced person I ever met," said a fellow animator. Tytla passed away in 1968 at age sixty-four.

Walt Disney would never again be the experimental filmmaker that he was before the strike. The period of explosive growth from 1933 to 1942, bookended with *Three Little Pigs* and *Bambi*, became known as the golden age of Disney animation. In 1966 Walt grew ill and checked into St. Joseph's Hospital, built atop the eucalyptus grove that the strikers had occupied years before. Walt Disney passed away the morning of December 15, 1966, from lung cancer. He was sixty-five years old.

The Walt Disney Company remains a union shop to this day.

EPILOGUE

FOR *SNOW WHITE*'S FIFTIETH ANNIVERSARY IN 1987, Walt's nephew Roy E. Disney invited Babbitt to an artists' reunion. It was the first time in fifty years that a Disney smiled beside Art Babbitt.

In 1992, when Babbitt was hospitalized for kidney failure, his wife Barbara delivered a package for him. It was a home video release of *Fantasia* with a handwritten note from Roy E. Disney, giving Babbitt the honor due to him "at last." Barely able to speak, Babbitt responded to his wife, "It's so nice to be part of the gang again."

Babbitt died on March 4, 1992, at age 85. His memorial service was attended by old and young animators alike, strikers and non-strikers. Frank Thomas, one of Walt's Nine Old Men, spoke at the service.

Babbitt's remains were interred at Forest Lawn Cemetery, overlooking Disney's Burbank headquarters. As a World War II veteran, he received a twenty-one-gun salute. One of the animators whispered to another, "If Art had his way, those guns would be pointed down at the studio!"

In 2007 Art Babbitt posthumously became a Disney Legend. Costumed Disney characters stood by at the ceremony, and Roy E. Disney presented the award with an anecdote. "Art kept a photo on his desk of the *Snow White* animation team," he said. "He had circled each face and written each of their names. By his own face he wrote, 'The Troublemaker'—not unrightfully." The audience erupted in laughter, and Babbitt's widow Barbara was escorted to the podium under Goofy's arm.

Art Babbitt at the Walt Disney studio on Hyperion Avenue, circa 1935.

ACKNOWLEDGMENTS

MORE THAN TEN YEARS have been spent on the project that became *The Disney Revolt*, and I couldn't have done it without the help of many. My apologies for anyone I missed.

I was given this assignment by my mentor and friend John Culhane, and I had complete cooperation over many wonderful visits with Barbara Perry Babbitt over the years. This book would not exist without them, and I wish they were still here to see it.

Huge thanks to the family of Art Babbitt: Michele Kane, Karin Babbitt, Laurel Lee James, Audrey James, Alan Babbitt, Susan B. Fine, Denise Silverman, and Steve Rabin.

Special thanks to Didier Ghez, who has been instrumental in every step of this long process, Lucas Seastrom for making multiple trips to scan the fifteen-hundred-page NLRB court case, Tom Sito for his help and blessing, and John Canemaker for his guidance from day one.

A special thanks to Marge Champion, Don Lusk, and my good friend Willis Pyle, all of whom passed before the completion of this book, and who generously shared their firsthand experiences of Disney's golden age.

For help with direction, support, and filling in some of the blanks along the way: Adam Abraham, Mindy Aloff, David Arnstein, the late Jacqueline Auguston, Nigel Austin, Michael Barrier, Joshua Bechtel-Lunior, Jerry Beck, Howard Beckerman, the late Carl Bell, David and Alice Bell, Debra Benjamin, Helge Bernhardt, Cameron Bossert, the late Tee Bosustow, Joe Campana, the late Charles L. Campbell, Kevin Carpenter, A. Scott Cauger, Gary Conrad, Bill Cotter, the late Sam Cornell, Bob Cowan, Lee Crowe, Andreas Deja, Harvey Deneroff, Ron Diamond, Michael Dolan, Renée Patin Farrington, the late June Foray, Levy Gansberg, Ghena Glijansky Korn, Eric Goldberg, Donald H. Graham, Deborah Grandinetti, Melissa Hecht, Jim Hollifield, Howard Green,

Linda Gramatky Smith, Linda B. Hall, Ann Hansen, Richard A. Harris, Josh Jacobs, Mindy Johnson, Charlie Judkins, Amy Bunin Kaiman, J. B. Kaufman, Kevin Kern, Gary Lassin, Jenny Lerew, Professor Jon Lewis, Tova Max, Uli Meyer, Carra Minkoff, Bill Moskin, Jeremy Oziel, Floyd Norman, Hans Perk, Elizabeth Peterson, Todd James Pierce, Janet Reid, Sam and Sharon Rosenfeld, Kim Schneiderman, Kevin Schreck, Paula Sigman-Lowery, Uwe Spiekermann, Emily Stern, Lawrence Stern, Jane Tear, Ted Thomas, Tim Walker, Maggie Wisdom, Laurie Wolko, and Stephen Worth.

For permissions and institutional research, thank you to Tricia Gesner at the Associated Press; Molly Haigh, Maxwell Zupke, and Estelle Yim from UCLA Special Collections; Jim Lentz at Heritage Auctions; Ashley Swinnerton at the MOMA Special Collections, Allison Chomet at the NYU Special Collections, Howard Prouty and Megan Harinski at the Academy of Motion Picture Arts and Sciences Margaret Herrick Library; Claude Zachary at USC; David Sigler and Ellen E. Jarosz at CSU, Northridge; Valerie Yaros at the Screen Actors Guild; and Raven Ramos and the Mercy College Faculty Development Grant.

Thanks to my teachers Shelly Brown, Shirley Kahn, Janet Wolf, and Susan Campbell Bartoletti. This book is a culmination of their skills in the classroom.

Thank you to my agent Eric Myers; my editors Jerry Pohlen, Joseph Webb, Devon Freeny, and Cathy Jones, and everyone at Chicago Review Press.

Thanks to my brother Aaron, who gave me notes on the draft. And to Joseph and Carol Friedman, who volunteered to be arrested and serve jail time during the 1972–1973 Philadelphia teachers' strike, then married, begat me, and filled my life with Disney.

Finally, thank you to my wife, Anya Revah-Politi, whose unyielding support has been crucial for the completion of this book.

IMAGE CREDITS

p. x: Bibliothèque nationale de France, courtesy of Wikimedia Commons

pp. xiii & 112: Illustration by the author

pp. 1, 65 (left), 189 (top) & 203: Courtesy of Los Angeles Daily News Negatives, Library Special Collections, Charles E. Young Research Library, UCLA

p. 8: *Appeal to Reason*, April 25, 1914

p. 10: Courtesy of Wikimedia Commons

p. 12: *Colton Daily Courier*, July 23, 1941

p. 16: *Exhibitor's Review*, February 27, 1926, 16, courtesy of Lantern Media History Digital Library

p. 24: *Universal Weekly*, May 11, 1929, 32, courtesy of Lantern Media History Digital Library

pp. 29, 37, 41, 46, 54 (top right), 75, 83, 103, 111, 189 (bottom) & 250: Courtesy of the Barbara Perry Babbitt Trust

p. 40: Courtesy of the Museum of Modern Art Department of Film Special Collections, New York

pp. 43, 58, 93, 126 & 233: Author's collection

pp. 54 (top left), 54 (bottom left) & 202: Courtesy of Jim Lentz, the Heritage Auctions Archive

p. 54 (bottom center): Courtesy of Hans Perk

p. 54 (bottom right): Courtesy of the Andreas Deja Collection

p. 65 (right): Associated Press

p. 113: Courtesy of the Gary Long Collection

p. 117: *Evansville (IN) Journal,* April 27, 1928

pp. 147 & 196: Courtesy of the Canemaker Collection, Fales Library and Special Collections, New York University

pp. 157 & 163: Ray Patin Archives, courtesy of Renée Patin Farrington

p. 179: Courtesy of Uwe Spiekermann

p. 184: Originally printed in the New York City liberal newspaper *PM,* June 6, 1941, 16

pp. 192, 200, 209, 220 & 223: Courtesy of MPSC Local 839, AFL-CIO Collection, Urban Archives Center, Oviatt Library, California State University, Northridge

pp. 222 & 226: Courtesy of the Cowan-Fouts Collection

p. 228: Courtesy of the Smith-Totten Collection

APPENDIX

THE STRIKERS

FOLLOWING IS A LIST of the Disney employees on strike, according to internal strike documents dated July 1941. Details have been corrected where necessary to the best of the author's ability. Those who remained at the studio past 1947 are italicized. Studio positions, strike roles, and aliases are included where known.

Abranz, Alfred, Assistant Animator

Alexander, Dick, Assistant

Amatuzio, Alexander "Alex," Junior Animator

Amatuzio (née Millot), Laura (camp cleanup and laundry)

Amos (née DeBeeson), Beryl (m. Beryl Pandit), Airbrush Artist

Amos, Homer, Animation Checker

Appleby, James "Jim," Assistant Animator (picket captain)

Armstrong, Jim (camp police)

Armstrong, Tom, Animator (treasurer of guild's Disney unit)

Atencio, Xavier, Assistant Animator

Ayers, Evelyn (m. Evelyn Grant), Inker

Babbitt, Art, Animator (negotiating committee; president of the Guild's Disney unit)

Baker, George, Assistant Animator

Baldwin, Barbara Wirth, Department Head—Airbrush/EFX (boycott committee)

Baldwin, James Howard, Animation Cleanup Supervisor (strike steering committee)

Barbour, Emily, Airbrush Artist and Painter

Barnes, Tom

Barron, John N., Assistant Animator (kitchen duty)

Baskerville, Lucille, Special Effects

Battaglia, Aurelius, Story Sketch Artist

Baur, Franz, Inbetweener (night duty)

Bedell, Nancy (m. Nancy Massie), Inker

Berman, Ted, Assistant Animator

Bertino, Albert, Assistant

Biggs, Gene R., Trainee

Blair, Preston, Animator

Blake, John Hudson, Assistant Animator

Blotter, Ernest "Ernie," Color Model Artist

Bock, Miriam, Airbrush Artist and Painter

Bonnicksen, Ted, Animator (picket captain)

Bosustow, Stephen "Steve," Animator (picket captain)

Bradbury, Jack, Animator (kitchen duty)

Bream (née DeForest), Eleanor (m. Eleanor Bream-Peck), Painter

Bronson, Vonda Lee (m. Vonda Lee Wise), Inker

Brown, Eileen, Inker

Brown, Jerome "Jerry," Assistant Animator

Buckley, Jack, Assistant Animator (kitchen duty)

Busch, Paul, Animator

Cannata, George, Assistant Animator

Carmichael, Jim, Layout Artist (picket captain)

Case, Brad, Junior Animator

Caspary, Gretchen (m. Gretchen DeStefano), Ink & Paint

Christensen, Don, Story Artist (strike photographer)

Cika, George, Trainee (picket captain)

Clabby, Jim, Assistant

Clapp, Dorothy, Painter

Cleworth, Eric, Assistant Animator (mimeograph)

Clinton, Walt, Animator (sign committee)

Cobean, Sam, Story Sketch Artist (strike leaflet office)

Coe, Al, Assistant

Coleman, Kathryne, Painting and Color Models (leaflet checking)

Coles, Helen (leaflets)

Collins, Jack McClain, Trainee

Couch, Glen, Assistant Animator (picket captain)

Cox, Rex, Story Artist (steering committee)

Coyle, Kathleen (m. Kathleen Klune), Inker

Davis, George, Assistant Animator

De Beeson, George, Animator

De Grasse, Robert "Zeke," Assistant Animator

De La Torre, Bill, Assistant

De Pew, Mary Ann, Airbrush Artist

De Mattia, Edward "Ed," Assistant Animator

Devirian, Cliff, Story Sketch Artist

Dempster, Albert "Al," Background Artist

Ditullio, Robert "Bob," Trainee

Doe, Bart (a.k.a. Peter Jay; real name Pete Alvarado), Assistant Animator

D'Orsi, Ugo, Effects Animator

Douglas (née Hanna), Evelyn (m. Evelyn Mehring), Inker (leaflet checking)

Drake, George, Assistant

Duncan, Phil, Animator (camp chairman)

Dunn, Ed, Animator

Dyson, Russ, Assistant Animator (picket captain)

Eastland, Henry, Trainee

Eastman (née Whitham), Mary Louise "Mary Lou," Color Model Supervisor (strike office)

Eastman, Phillip "P. D.," Story Sketch Artist

Edgington, Bill, Trainee

Elstad, Rudolph "Rudy," Inbetweener
(kitchen duty)
Elton, Leslie "Les," Assistant Animator
(mimeograph, publicity)
Engel, Julius "Jules," Inbetweener
(kitchen duty)
Erwin, Martha Jean "Jean," Painter
Escalante, Jim, Effects
Evans, Genevieve, Painter
Fagin, Maurice "Maurie," Assistant
Animator (camp kitchen: lunch)
Fernandez, Juanita, Inker (cooking and
service)
Fitzpatrick, Paul, Effects Animator
(strike photographer)
Fourcher, Betty (purchasing)
Fourcher, Edwin, Assistant Layout Artist
(camp kitchen)
Freeman, Earl, Assistant Layout
Garbutt, Bernard, Animator (strike
transport)
Gardner, Viola, Inbetweener
Gayek, Joseph "Joe," Assistant Animator
Gesteland, Robert "Bob," Assistant
Animator (kitchen duty)
*Gibson, Blaine, Assistant (camp kitchen
duty)*
Giroux, George, Assistant (picket
captain)
Glas, Sherman, Animation Checker (in
charge of carnival)
Gleeson, Catherine, Inbetweener
Gollub, Morris "Mo," Assistant
Gorham, Barbara A. (m. Barbara A.
Chaddock), Paint Laboratory
Gould, Jay, Inbetweener
Grable, Fred, Assistant Animator
Graham, Margaret, Paint Laboratory

Grant, Bob, Comic Strip Artist
Gray, William "Bill," Assistant Animator
(leaflets; recreation & education)
Griffin, Betty, Transparent Shading Artist
Griffin, Murray, Assistant Animator
(strike photographer)
Griffith, Don, Layout Assistant
Griswald, Marie/Mary, Inker
Grundeen, J. Franklin "Frank,"
Junior Animator (leaflets; sign
committee)
Gunther, Bob, Assistant Animator
*Gurney, Eric "John," Junior Animator
(picket captain)*
Hammer, Betty, Transparent Shading
Artist (leaflet checking)
Hamsel, Harry, Effects Animator
Hansen, Eric, Background Artist
Hanson, Helen, Inker
Harbough, John, Assistant Animator
Hartman, C. L., Inbetweener
Hawkins, Emery, Animator
Haupt, Khent, Paint Laboratory
Hazelton, Gene, Story Sketch Artist
Heimdahl, Ralph, Animation Training
Supervisor (camp kitchen duty)
Herwig, William "Bill," Layout Artist
(picket captain)
Hilberman, David, Layout (secretary of
Guild's Disney unit)
Hiser, Gifford "Giff," Inbetweener
Holahan, Jean, Inbetweener
Holt, Benjamin "Ben," Inbetweener
(picket captain)
*Holt, Harry, Animation Cleanup
Supervisor*
Hubbard, Allen "Al," Assistant Animator
(picket captain; camp sanitation)

McDermott, John Richard "Dick" (a.k.a. J. M. Ryan), Junior Animator (picket captain)

McElmurry, Charles O., Inbetweener

McGugin, John, Animation Checker

McIntyre, William "Bill," Assistant

McLeish, John, Story Artist (leaflets)

McSavage, Frank, Junior Animator (mimeograph)

Melchione, Hugo, Trainee

Melendez, Bill, Assistant (camp sanitation)

Menges, Charles, Assistant Animator (picket captain, publicity)

McQuaide, Jack, Animation Checker (picket captain)

Miller, George, Assistant (leaflets)

Moore, Art, Assistant

Moore, Paul, Inbetweener

Moorehouse, Marjorie, Shadow Painter (strike office)

Moran, Marjorie, Inbetweener

Morgan, Roger, Inbetweener (picket captain)

Morley, Richard "Dick," Trainee (camp kitchen: dinner)

Morrison, L. Dean, Animation Checker

Murray, Margaret, Assistant

Muse, Kenneth "Ken," Animator (sign committee)

Nevius, Gerald "Jerry," Background

Nicholas, George, Animator

Noble, Maurice, Background

Nolan, Edward, Assistant

Noonan, Daniel "Dan," Junior Animator

Okamoto, Tom, Trainee

Onaitis, Franklin, Effects Animator

Orcutt, Alice (m. Alice Rinaldi), Shading Painter

Otterstrom, Charles "Chic," Junior Animator

Page, Janet (m. Janet Keller), Inbetweener

Parmelee, Ted, Assistant (picket captain)

Parr, Jack, Assistant

Partch, Virgil "Vip," Assistant (camp sanitation)

Patin, Ray, Animator (strike documentarian)

Patterson, Don, Animator Level #8

Patterson, Ray, Animator

Patton, Earl, Assistant

Peed, William "Bill Peet," Story Sketch Artist

Perkins, Curtiss "Curt," Story Sketch Artist

Peterson, Kenneth, Animator (steering committee; negotiating committee)

Pignataro, Joseph "Joe"

Pike, Miles E., Effects Animator (strike leaflet office)

Porter, Henry "Hank," Publicity and Comics (camp kitchen duty)

Pratt, Hawley, Assistant (camp kitchen duty)

Price, Daniel, Animation Checker

Prosk, Gerald, Assistant (strike playwright; performer of "Walt")

Pursel (née Downs), Ruberna, Airbrush Artist

Pyle, Willis, Assistant Level #5 (strike leaflet office)

Quon, Milt, Assistant (sign committee)

Reden, Morey, Junior Animator

Reese, Bill, Animation Checker (leaflets)

Rice, Fred, Assistant

Rickert, Douglas "Bud," Background

Rinaldi, Joe, Story Sketch Artist (mimeograph)

Riswold, Art, Trainee

Ritchie, Jean "Jeanne," Inbetweener

Rivera, Tony, Story Sketch Artist

Robin, Archie, Junior Animator

Robinson, C. K. "Ed," Assistant (camp kitchen duty)

Roemer, Robert, Assistant Checker

Roether, George, Assistant

Roman, Dunbar "Dun," Story Artist

Rosene, Russell D. "Russ," Jar Washer

Rossi, Mildred "Milicent Patrick," Assistant Animator

Ruohomaa, Kosti, Assistant (strike photographer)

Ruse, Per "Pete Hansen," Assistant

Ruse, Tota, Painter (strike office)

Ryan, Vivian K., Inker

Sabo, Joseph L., Story Sketch Artist

Salkin, Leo, Animator (strike photographer)

Sarbry, Jay S., Assistant

Schloat, G. Warren Jr., Animator

Schmitt, Louis "Louie," Animator (camp kitchen duty)

Schnerk, Jack P., Assistant

Scott, W. Arthur Jr., Assistant (picket captain)

Scott, Walt, Layout Artist (picket captain)

Selby, Margaret (m. Selby Kelly), Paint Laboratory

Sewall, John "Jack," Animator (picket captain)

Shaffer, Armin R., Animator Level #7

Shaw, Charles "Chuck," Assistant (sign committee)

Shaw, Dick, Trainee

Shaw, Molly, Inbetweener

Shrimpton, Gloria (m. Gloria Van Doren), Inker

Shrimpton, Joan E. (m. Joan E. Wilson), Inker

Shull, William M., Animator

Siegal, Jack, Story Layout Artist

Silva, Freeman, Assistant

Simmons, Grant, Animator

Smith, Betty Louise (m. Betty Smith Totten), Inbetweener

Smith, Claude Jr., Animator (picket captain)

Snyder, John Vincent "Jack," Assistant

Standiford, Edward Vance*

Starbuck, Joe Jr., Junior Animator

Stark, Dwight V., Assistant

Stetter, Al, Assistant (camp kitchen duty)

Stevens, Arthur C. "Art," Assistant

Stevens, George, Assistant

Stimson, Marie, Inbetweener

Stirrett, Marion Wylie, Background Artist

Sturm, William A. "Bill," Junior Animator

Svendsen, Julius, Assistant

Swift, Howard, Animator

Tanaka, James "Jim," Assistant (mimeograph)

Tanous, Henry, Assistant

---

* Identified solely from strike footage

Tate, Norman "Norm," Animation
(leaflets)

Taylor, Happy, Paint Laboratory

Terrazas, Ernest "Ernie," Story Sketch
Artist

Terri, Louis "Lou," Junior Animator
(picket captain)

Thorne, Sidney H. "Sid," Assistant

Timmins, Reuben, Effects Animator
(picket captain)

Tobin, Don, Effects Animator

Toles, Helen M., Painter

Totten, Robert "Bob," Assistant

Tucker, J. Noel, Effects Animator

Tytla, William, Animator

Van Benthem, Richard "Dick," Assistant

Van Horn, Ivy Carol (m. Ivy Carol
Christiansen), Inker

Van Pelt, Viola, Inker

Wallett, William "Bill," Story Sketch
Artist (art sale co-organizer)

Walsh, Stanley L. "Stan," Assistant

Waltz, John, Effects Animator

Weaver, William T. "Bill," Assistant
(picket captain)

Webster, Barbara, Inbetweener

*Weeks, Clair, Assistant (camp kitchen
duty)*

Wells, Art, Inbetweener (sign
committee)

*Whitaker, Wetzel Orson "Judge,"
Animator*

White, Lew, Trainee

Wiggenhorn, Bard, Assistant

Will, James, Effects Animator

Williams, Alfred "Bill," Assistant

Wilson, Fred, Paint Laboratory (camp
maintenance)

Wilson, William W. "Bill," Assistant
(strike transport)

Witt, Vernon G., Effects Animator

Wright, Karran Eccles "Kay E.," Assistant

Wood, Cornett, Effects Animator
(leaflets)

Woolery, Ade Daniel, Animation
Checker

Young, Bob (camp health)

Young, Cyrus, Animator

Zima, John, Inbetweener (camp
maintenance)

NOTES

Epigraph

"If a person leads": Don Hahn and Tracy Miller-Zarneke, *Before Ever After: The Lost Lectures of Walt Disney's Animation Studio* (White Plains, NY: Disney Editions, 2015), 54. The quote is from an undated lecture by Art Babbitt and Dr. Morkovin.

Prologue

"Two periods in my": *Walt and El Grupo*, dir. by Theodore Thomas (Los Angeles: Theodore Thomas Productions, 2008).

"Walt Disney, you ought": Thomas Brady, "Whimsy on Strike," *New York Times*, June 29, 1941.

1. My Father Was a Socialist

"Upon which side": This became known as Bryan's "Cross of Gold speech."

a man chased after him: Walt Disney, interview by Pete Martin, 1961, author's collection.

"My father was a Socialist": Disney, interview by Martin.

1.9 million: Sidney Redner, "Population History of Chicago from 1840–1990," Boston University, accessed December 8, 2021, http://physics.bu.edu/~redner/projects /population/cities/chicago.html.

Crime was rampant: Michael Barrier, *The Animated Man: A Life of Walt Disney* (Berkeley: University of California Press, 2007), 11.

his Dreaming Tree: "Walt's Tree," Walt Disney Hometown Museum, accessed December 8, 2021, https://waltdisneymuseum.org/marceling/walts-dreaming-tree-and-barn.

"Those were the happiest": Kathy Merlock Jackson, *Walt Disney: Conversations* (Jackson: University Press of Mississippi, 2006), 11.

There was the bliss of receiving: Jackson, 137.

"Don't be afraid to": Neal Gabler, *Walt Disney: The Triumph of the American Imagination* (New York: Knopf, 2006), 15.

"bawling out": Barrier, *Animated Man*, 16.

"Churchy": Walt Pfeiffer, quoted in Gabler, *Walt Disney*, 26.

"Dad was always meeting up": Disney, interview by Martin.

"myriad schemes": Robert H. Bahmer, "The American Society of Equity," *Agricultural History* 14, no. 1 (1940): 40, 42.

"He believed people": Disney, interview by Martin.

Without the eldest brothers' help: Barrier, *Animated Man*, 17; Gabler, *Walt Disney*, 17.

In May 1911: Barrier, *Animated Man*, 17.

Meanwhile, Elias: Barrier, *Animated Man*, 19–20.

He would sneak: Gabler, *Walt Disney*, 26–27.

Walter continued drawing: Spring Art Association, Spring 1933; *Liberty Magazine*, January 1933.

"The Appeal to Reason": Disney, interview by Martin.

He landed a seat: Gabler, *Walt Disney*, 216. The five screenings drew sixty-seven thousand newsboys in all, outnumbering the twelve thousand seats per screening each day.

touring the country, protesting: Erick Trickey, "When America's Most Prominent Socialist Was Jailed for Speaking Out Against World War I," *Smithsonian Magazine*, June 15, 2018, https://www.smithsonianmag.com/history/fiery-socialist-challenged-nations-role-wwi-180969386/.

The IWW protested: "Testimony in I.W.W. Trials Reveals Plots," *Quincy Daily Whig*, May 3, 1918; "Giant Conspiracy to Obstruct Draft," *Quincy Daily Whig*, May 4, 1918; "I.W.W. Chiefs Asked Private to Spread Plot," *Quincy Daily Whig*, May 31, 1918; "Burned Threshers in Harvest Fields," *Quincy Daily Whig*, June 1, 1918; "I.W.W. Conspiracy," *Quincy Daily Herald*, June 1, 1918.

During the 1917–18 school year: S. J. Woolf, "Walt Disney Tells Us What Makes Him Happy," *New York Times Magazine*, July 10, 1938, 5.

"He never understood": Bob Thomas, *Building a Company: Roy O. Disney and the Creation of an Entertainment Empire* (New York: Hyperion, 1998), 4. The quote is from a 1957 speech.

IWW members were tried: "I.W.W. Workers Are Found Guilty," *Quincy Daily Herald*, August 20, 1981; "Haywood Gets 20 Year Term in US Prison," *Quincy Daily Whig*, August 31, 1918; "Haywood Is Given Limit," *Quincy Daily Herald*, August 31, 1918.

"I missed that darn": Walt Disney, 1956 interview, quoted in Jon Seidel, "100 Years Ago: The Bombing of Chicago's Federal Building," *Chicago Sun-Times*, September 2, 2018, https://chicago.suntimes.com/2018/9/2/18430034/100-years-ago-the-bombing-of-chicago-s-federal-building.

occupant of a passing car: Seidel, "100 Years Ago," https://chicago.suntimes.com/2018/9/2/18430034/100-years-ago-the-bombing-of-chicago-s-federal-building; "Chicago Bombs," Smithsonian National Postal Museum, accessed December 8,

2021, https://postalmuseum.si.edu/exhibition/behind-the-badge-case-histories-dangerous-mail-bombs/chicago-bombs.

On September 16: Gabler, *Walt Disney*, 36–37.

By the time Walter arrived: Gabler, 36–37.

He illustrated: Gabler, 40. One such drawing was printed in the *Colton Daily Courier*, July 12, 1941, p. 4.

Elias never drank: Jim Korkis, *Even More Unofficial Disney Stories Never Told*, vol. 3 of *The Vault of Walt*, ed. by Bob McLain (Orlando, FL: Theme Park Press, 2014), 19.

2. Poor and Starving

Walt moved back into: Gabler, *Walt Disney*, 61. The home was at 3028 Bellefontaine Street. Herb's wife was Louise, and the daughter was Dorothy.

He secured an illustration: Barrier, *Animated Man*, 24. The job paid ten dollars a week. Jackson, *Walt Disney*, 24.

happy cows and enthusiastic chickens: Harry Carr, "The Only Unpaid Movie Star," *American Magazine,* March 1931, 55–57.

programs for the town's grand new cinema: Gabler, *Walt Disney*, 56.

during breaks from work: Gabler, 46.

the words TURMOIL, STRIKES, REDS: Gabler, 45.

both quit: Gabler, 50. Walt quit in February, with Iwwerks following in March.

Cauger's operation: The original name was the Kansas City Slide Company; it produced slides for advertisements before a show that predated motion pictures. It wouldn't officially change its name to Kansas City Film Ad Company until summer 1920.

cutout animation was prevalent: This included the work of Germany's Lotte Reiniger and Argentina's Quirino Cristiani, and most animation in Japan.

convinced his father to rent it: Richard H. Syring, "One of the Great Geniuses!," *Silver Screen*, November 1932, 47.

Elias never collected: Gabler, *Walt Disney*, 51.

Walt conceived of some shorts: Barrier, *Animated Man*, 28.

"He has the courage": Syring, "One of the Great Geniuses!," 48.

"I told him that": Douglas W. Churchill, "Disney's 'Philosophy,'" *New York Times Magazine*, March 6, 1938. The interview doesn't specify which employer provoked Walt's response; that it referred to his job at Film Ad is inferred.

Elias and Flora sold the family home: Gabler, *Walt Disney*, 59.

reflected upon the animation art form: Walt Disney, "Growing Pains," *Journal of Society of Motion Picture Engineers* 36 (January 1941): 32.

moved to an office building: The McConahay Building at 1127 East Thirty-First Street.

Laugh-O-Gram team operated: Gabler, *Walt Disney*, 66.

The interiors of the inked lines: In the days of black-white-gray paint, the act was called *opaquing*. Tommy Morrison, interview by Harvey Deneroff, June 15, 1970, Canemaker Collection, Fales Library and Special Collections, New York University. Animator Morrison worked for Paul Terry as of 1933.

promoting the Laugh-O-Gram company: Barrier, *Animated Man*, 141.

at local schools: Liberty Magazine, January 1933.

clubs, and church benefits: National Board of Review Magazine, October 1931.

kept up a written correspondence: Gabler, *Walt Disney*, 79.

headed for Los Angeles: Carr, "Only Unpaid Movie Star," 56.

3. The Value of Loyalty

quality of his films was "lacking": Gabler, *Walt Disney*, 89, 101.

sixty-by-forty-foot: According to one account, the plot was about sixteen hundred square feet. Gabler, 98.

Walt and Roy had agreed on a name change: Thomas, *Building a Company*, 52. According to different accounts, the name change was Roy's (Thomas, 53), or Walt's (Gabler, *Walt Disney*, 98) idea.

"snooping": Roy Disney, quoted in Thomas, 53.

"den of strife": Gabler, *Walt Disney*, 101.

"couldn't bear the abuse": Ham Hamilton, as remembered by Isadore Freleng, quoted in Gabler, 100.

"They seem to think": Barrier, *Animated Man*, 51; Gabler, *Walt Disney*, 102.

Walt hired a teenage artist: John Canemaker, *Walt Disney's Nine Old Men & the Art of Animation*. (Los Angeles: Disney Editions, 2001), 9. Les Clark was hired on February 23, 1927.

"I want characters": As remembered by Isadore Freleng, quoted in Canemaker, 12, and Gabler, *Walt Disney,* 103.

musicians who played in the orchestra pit: Bill Rohdin, "The History of Local 802," Local802afm.org, accessed December 8, 2021, https://www.local802afm.org/history/.

"iron-clad" two-year contracts: Barrier, *Animated Man*, 56.

"We are still hanging": Gabler, *Walt Disney*, 109.

Mintz was under no obligation: Gabler, 106–10.

kept to the back room: The Hand Behind the Mouse: The Ub Iwerks Story, dir. by Leslie Iwerks (Santa Monica, CA: Leslie Iwerks Productions, 1999).

inked and opaqued: Inking was also called *tracing* or *blackening*. Kathleen Dollard Smith was also hired to prepare the cels. Mindy Johnson, *Ink & Paint: The Women of Walt Disney's Animation* (Los Angeles: Disney Editions, 2017), 52, 54.

It cost $3,528.50: Roy's ledger, reprinted in Thomas, *Building a Company*, 65. Steamboat Willie" would cost $5,121.65, excluding Cinephone expenses.

Walt peddled Plane Crazy: Carr, "Only Unpaid Movie Star," 57.

no distributor picked up: "The Evolution of Mickey Mouse," *Motion Picture Daily*, June 20, 1931, 7.

sound in films was a new invention: "Evolution of Mickey Mouse," 7.

Iwerks conceived of a bouncing ball: Roy Disney, Method of and Means for Scoring Film Production, US Patent 1,913,048, filed October 16, 1928.

"Boy, the unions": Leslie Iwerks and John Kenworthy, *The Hand Behind the Mouse: An Intimate Biography of Ub Iwerks* (Los Angeles: Disney Editions, 2001), 67.

On October 1: Walt Disney, "Mickey Mouse Is 5 Years Old," *Film Pictoral*, September 30, 1933, 36.

promoter for the Colony Theater: Gabler, *Walt Disney*, 123–26. The promoter of the Colony was Harry Reichenbach. According to Thomas, Reichenbach offered $1,000, and Walt took it. See Thomas, *Building a Company*, 62.

"Almost overnight the Disney outfit": "How Mickey Mouse Came About," *National Board of Review Magazine*, October 1931, 5.

"far and away": Henry F. Pringle, "Mickey Mouse's Father," *McCall's*, August 1932, 7, 23.

4. Arthur Babbitt: Hell-Raiser

In 1906 she emigrated: Ship manifests, via Ancestry.com; Fanny Rabin, interview by John Canemaker, March 22, 1992, reprinted in *Walt's People: Talking Disney with the Artists Who Knew Him*, vol. 9, ed. Didier Ghez (self-pub., 2010), 32. Rabin mentions two children who died in Russia.

"This was my first": Art Babbitt, unpublished memoir, 1974, Barbara Perry Babbitt Trust.

Arthur remembered having: Art Babbitt, interview by Michael Barrier, December 13, 1986, reprinted in *Walt's People: Talking Disney with the Artists Who Knew Him*, vol. 3, ed. Didier Ghez (self-pub., 2006), 110.

"ever an optimist": Babbitt, unpublished memoir.

peddled rags or fish: Babbitt, 108.

"Zelda really was": Fanny Rabin and Susan B. Fine, interview by John Canemaker, October 14, 1993, Canemaker Collection.

also provided little Arthur: Art Babbitt, interview by Bill Hurtz, International Animated Film Society, n.d., Barbara Perry Babbitt Trust.

Arthur's home: "1913 Easter Tornado: Storm Ripped Scar Across Omaha," *Sunday World-Herald*, March 17, 2013; Dennis Hihelich, *Ribbon of Destruction: The 1913 Douglas County Tornado* (Omaha, NE: Douglas County Historical Society and Nebraska Jewish Historical Society, 2013). The Babitzkys' address was 2216 Charles Street.

"the metropolis of the northwest": *Sioux City Directory 1924* (Sioux City, IA: R. L. Polk, 1924), 1.

In February 1915: Irving "Ike" Babbitt, interview by Alan Babbitt, n.d., collection of Alan Babbitt. The new address was 705 West Sixth Street.

"formerly homes of non-Jewish": Ike Babbitt, interview by Alan Babbitt.

name-calling: Elsie Babbitt, interview by John Canemaker, October 14, 1993, Canemaker Collection.

KKK marches: Fanny Rabin, interview by John Canemaker, March 22, 1992, Canemaker Collection.

Meatpacking was one of the cornerstones: Susan Berman, *Easy Street: The True Story of a Mob Family* (New York: Dial Press, 1981), 111.

barn for the family's horse: Ike Babbitt, interview by Alan Babbitt.

The end of winter: Ike Babbitt, interview by Alan Babbitt.

"anyone else who": Elsie Babbitt, letters to John Canemaker, 1992, Canemaker Collection.

Jewish war relief fund: "Jews Set $12,000 as Goal," *Sioux City Journal*, February 6, 1917.

Zelda dressed up: Susan Fine, interview by the author, 2013.

"down south": Ike Babbitt, interview by Alan Babbitt.

"was very much the leader": Ike Babbitt, interview by Alan Babbitt.

"I was this strange": Babbitt, interview by Barrier, December 13, 1986, 109.

Arthur led the boys: Babbitt, 110.

they sneaked into the shed: Ike Babbitt, interview by Alan Babbitt.

"We weren't vandals": Babbitt, interview by Barrier, December 13, 1986, 110.

Arthur drew a waterfall: Babbitt, interview by Hurtz.

Arthur refused to sing: Art Babbitt, interview by Hurtz. He identified the teacher as Ms. Wolsky.

By high school: Art Babbitt, interview by Hurtz.

"[Emperor Claudius] expelled": *Maroon and White*, yearbook (Sioux City, IA: Central High School, 1924), 73.

meatpacking plant: Art Babbitt, interview by John Culhane, 1973, and Art Babbitt, interview by John Canemaker, June 4, 1975, Canemaker Collection.

as a stock boy: Art Babbitt, interview by Canemaker.

the psychological science of hypnosis: Babbitt, interview by Canemaker. He names Viennese psychiatrist Dr. Paul Schilder (erroneously calling him "Schild") and Dr. Kauders. The English edition of Schilder's book *The Nature of Hypnosis* was printed in 1922. Schilder and Dr. Otto Kauders collaborated on *Hypnosis*, first published in English in 1927.

"perpetually tired": Babbitt, unpublished memoir.

There had been an accident: Babbitt, unpublished memoir; Babbitt, interview by Barrier, December 13, 1986, 108; Elsie Babbitt, interview by Canemaker.

decided to move to Brooklyn: Elsie Babbitt, interview by Canemaker.

Arthur rushed to earn: Sioux City High School diploma, January 24, 1924, Barbara
   Perry Babbitt Trust.

5. Fighting for His Salary

Arthur remembered surviving: Art Babbitt, interview by Harvey Deneroff, July 21, 1980,
   collection of Harvey Deneroff; Art Babbitt, interview by Canemaker, June 4, 1975.
In May: Babbitt, interview by Deneroff.
He found a business card: Art Babbitt, interview by Canemaker, June 4, 1975.
an unpaid apprenticeship: The 1924 phone book locates Pitts & Kitts Manufacturing
   & Supply Company at 342 Madison Avenue, across the street from the newly
   constructed Roosevelt Hotel.
For each six-day workweek: Babbitt, interview by Deneroff; Art Babbitt, interview by
   John Culhane, 1971, collection of the Culhane family; Babbitt, interview by Hurtz.
work on an art portfolio: Babbitt, interview by Culhane, 1973.
his supervisor chastised him: Babbitt, interview by Hurtz.
Next, Arthur found work: Babbitt, interview by Deneroff. Art said that after Pitts &
   Kitts he worked at "Stern and Hirsch, or Hirsch and Stern; it was an advertising
   agency on 5th Avenue and 28th Street." In his 1942 testimony, he mentioned
   working only for "Sterns and I can't think of the partner's name" and Simmonds,
   for about four months each.
each Friday it was his job: Art Babbitt, interview by Canemaker, June 4, 1975; Babbitt,
   interview by Deneroff.
After about four months: Babbitt's testimony, National Labor Rel. Board v. Walt Disney
   Productions, 146 F.2d 44 (9th Cir. 1944), 33.
the Babitzkys moved closer: Elsie Babbitt, interview by Canemaker. Elsie remembered
   that these relatives were medical professionals.
tried in vain to freelance: Art Babbitt, interview by Canemaker, June 4, 1975; Babbitt,
   interview by Deneroff.
one of the school's top instructors: Babbitt, unpublished memoir.
Late in 1925: Babbitt, interview by Culhane, 1973.
"the boy from Babbitt's": Babbitt, interview by Culhane.
brought in a business partner: Babbitt's testimony, *NLRB v. Disney*, 33–34. The partner's
   name was Anthony Palozzo.
Babbitt painted butterflies: Babbitt, unpublished memoir. He identifies them as "Earl
   Carroll girls."
He began a photo collection: Art Babbitt, *Earl Carroll Girls*, photographs, collection of
   the Babbitt estate.
He had peers: According to autobiographical notes in the Barbara Perry Babbitt Trust.

a poster-sized letter: Art Babbitt, interview by Michael Barrier, June 2, 1971, Canemaker Collection.

an ornate die-cut business card: Business card, Barbara Perry Babbitt Trust.

"Death—she's anot": Art Babbitt, diary, January 15, 1942, Barbara Perry Babbitt Trust.

Rose Cohen: "Babbitt-Cohen Betrothal Told," *Passaic Daily Herald*, January 10, 1929; obituary for "Mrs. Isadore Cohen," *Passaic Herald-News*, March 20, 1956.

he landed an illustration assignment: Babbitt, interview by Hurtz.

Arthur and Rose were married: "Miss Rose Cohen United in Marriage to Arthur Babbitt in Brooklyn," *Passaic Daily News*, September 30, 1929; ship manifest for the SS *Port Victoria*, October 14, 1929, via Ancestry.com. The address in Passaic was 88 Paulison Avenue.

His business partner mentioned: Babbitt, interview by Culhane, 1973.

Babbitt closed his business: Babbitt, interview by Hurtz.

Paul Terry had opened his studio: The original location was in New Rochelle, but Babbitt spent the majority of his Terrytoons employment at the Bronx location at 2826 Decatur Avenue.

finally to the editor: The Terrytoons editor at the time was George MacAvoy.

referred to his product as "merchandise": Paul Terry, interview by Harvey Deneroff, December 20, 1969, Canemaker Collection.

Babbitt graduated to trainee animator: Babbitt, interview by Barrier, June 2, 1971. His first short was *Swiss Cheese*, the studio's seventh short, according to Terrytoon animation notebooks, Museum of Modern Art Department of Film Special Collections, New York.

That's like being: Art Babbitt, interview by John Canemaker, 1975, Canemaker Collection.

"Every day is gravy": Babbitt, interview by Canemaker.

His first scene: Babbitt, interview by Barrier, June 2, 1971. According to the original 1930 work drafts, his memory was accurate.

Terry's "good animator": Terry, interview by Deneroff.

"little sparks of electricity": Art Babbitt, interview by Canemaker, 1975.

his circle of commercial artists: Tytla's friends included artists Oscar Barshak, Hank Berger, and Maurice "Mooch" Rawson.

Babbitt credited Tytla: Art Babbitt, interview by Canemaker, 1975.

"Go in and tell Paul": Art Babbitt, interview by Canemaker, 1975.

he drew Mickey Mouse: *Merry-Go-Round*, August 1932.

a job designing hats: "Miss Rose Babbitt with Maxine's Shop," *Passaic Herald-News*, May 12, 1937.

"didn't give him": Elsie Babbitt, interview by Canemaker.

The two separated: Babbitt, interview by Deneroff.

a strategy that he had picked up: Babbitt, interview by Hurtz.

an enormous piece of paper: Babbitt, interview by Hurtz.

He addressed it: Babbitt, interview by Deneroff. Said Babbitt, "It was fully six weeks after I left Terry before I came on out here." He told John Canemaker on June 4, 1975, "I did a commercial film, Buster Brown shoes for Frank Goldman who was with Audio-Cinema at the time, and this was sort of an interim step before I went to California." This was likely a short animated ad called *Sole Mates*. In 1929 F. Lyle Goldman had produced the famous *Finding His Voice* short animated film advertising motion picture soundtracks. Art Babbitt's cousin Elsie Babbitt wrote to Canemaker in a 1992 letter, "On his way to Hollywood he stopped in Sioux City to visit for a few days. I remember he had with him one of his own films called 'Squeaky'—about a little mouse with oversized shoes that squeaked. It was quite witty because we all laughed."

6. You Can't Draw Your Ass

an enormous strike: *Chicago Daily Tribune*, August 23, 1932, 9; "Iowa Farmers on Strike," *Barrier Miner* (Wales), August 23, 1932, http://trove.nla.gov.au/ndp/del /article/46663087.

everything was dazzlingly painted: Shamus Culhane, *Talking Animals and Other People* (Boston: De Capo Press, 1986), 113.

"You had a feeling": Don Peri, *Working with Walt: Interviews with Disney Artists* (Jackson: University Press of Mississippi, 2008), 183. Quote from Jack Cutting, who was hired in 1929.

"[Walt] said, well": Babbitt, interview by Hurtz.

"Mr. Babbitt came into": Walt Disney's testimony, *NLRB v. Disney*, 953.

Babbitt rented a house: The house was located at 2320 North Highland Avenue.

started at the Disney studio: Respondent exhibit #8, *NLRB v. Disney*.

8:30 AM to 5:30 PM: Ward Kimball, interview by Gary Conrad, 1976, collection of Gary Conrad.

began as an inbetweener: Art Babbitt, interview by Canemaker, 1975. In his 1942 testimony, he said forty dollars.

the inbetweeners' room: Christopher Finch, *The Art of Walt Disney: From Mickey Mouse to the Magic Kingdom*, concise ed. (New York: Portland House, 1995), 96.

"The only difficulty": Peri, *Working with Walt*, 56. The quote is by Dave Hand.

a strip or a loop: Phil Klein, interview by Harvey Deneroff, collection of Harvey Deneroff.

"like eggs frying": Jack Kinney, *Walt Disney and Assorted Other Characters: An Unauthorized Account of the Early Years at Disney's* (New York: Harmony Books, 1988), 44.

These tests cost more: Frank Thomas and Ollie Johnston, *The Illusion of Life: Disney Animation* (Los Angeles: Disney Editions, 1981), 83. The pencil-testing process is described in detail in this source. Because the film was undeveloped, the image in the aperture was a negative—white lines against black.

to work under Chuck Couch: Art Babbitt, interview by Canemaker, 1975.

To his shock: Art Babbitt, interview by Canemaker, 1975.

"a hard but fair taskmaster": Kinney, *Walt Disney*, 28.

"They had to go": Peri, *Working with Walt*, 8.

"the handout": Thomas and Johnston, *Illusion of Life*, 223.

assigned challenging or important scenes: Original animation drafts, collection of Hans Perk.

Babbitt tackled their scenes: Art Babbitt, interview by Canemaker, 1975.

"dipping your pen": Kinney, *Walt Disney*, 37.

"had a conglomeration": Peri, *Working with Walt*, 70. The quote is by Jack Kinney.

"You can't draw": Kinney, *Walt Disney*, 36, 47.

"He would get you": Ken Peterson, quoted in Canemaker, *Nine Old Men*, 17.

7. The Disney Art School

"Walt seemed to know": Thomas and Johnston, *Illusion of Life*, 84.

"We're going to have": Babbitt, interview by Barrier, June 2, 1971.

"Where no class": Kimon Nicolaides, *The Natural Way to Draw* (Boston: Houghton Mifflin, 1941), 3.

One of the other trainees: Art Babbitt, interview by Canemaker, 1975. The school recommended a model named Marie Coleman. See Art Babbitt, letter to John Canemaker, 1979, Canemaker Collection.

That night, every animator: Babbitt, interview by Hurtz; Art Babbitt, interview by Canemaker, 1975. The fee was sixty cents an hour.

This time, twenty animators: Art Babbitt, ASIFA talk with John Canemaker, July 12, 1979, Canemaker Collection. A potential model lived near the studio. Art arrived at her home one Saturday afternoon to meet her. Kids were playing outside, and a young man was leaving the house. She welcomed Art in, wearing a dressing gown. As they talked about fees, she asked, "Don't you want to see my body?" and dropped her gown to her ankles. As Babbitt later said, "I couldn't get out of there fast enough. I just about damn near sank through the floor."

"$1.25 an hour": Babbitt, interview by Hurtz.

On Babbitt's invitation: Art Babbitt and Don Graham, interview by John Culhane, 1973, collection of the Culhane family.

"On November 15th 1932": Finch, Art of Walt Disney, 98.

The classes were held: Finch, 98.

"Only if the drawings": Don Graham, Composing Pictures (Los Angeles: Silman-James Press, 2010), 375.

Jackson on "Horrible Harmonica": Disney company bulletin, vol. 1, no. 20 (March 14, 1939), author's collection.

"corn-fed hick": John Canemaker, Paper Dreams: The Art & Artists of Disney Storyboards (New York: Hyperion, 1999), 79.

working with a merchandising executive: The merchandising exec was Kay Kamen.

"It is the rhythm": New York Sunday News, December 1, 1929, quoted in Jackson, Walt Disney, 4.

"was especially noisy": Kinney, Walt Disney, 84.

"Frank Churchill over at": Thomas and Johnston, Illusion of Life, 223.

"Without a definite personality": John Culhane, Aladdin: The Making of an Animated Film (New York: Hyperion, 1992), 7. Disney told John Culhane this in 1953.

8. Three Little Pigs

When he drew: Frank and Ollie, dir. by Theodore Thomas (Los Angeles: Theodore Thomas Productions, 1995).

Moore who had redesigned: Don Graham, interview by John Culhane, 1973, collection of the Culhane family.

"Freddie Moore girls": Thomas and Johnston, Illusion of Life, 121.

Dick Lundy: Dick Lundy to Mark Mayerson, quoted in "Dick Lundy," 50 Most Influential Disney Animators (blog), May 11, 2011, https://50mostinfluentialdisneyanimators. wordpress.com/2011/05/11/44-dick-lundy/.

nervous New York energy: Thomas and Johnston, Illusion of Life, 105.

called the Charlie Chaplin of the studio: Culhane, Talking Animals, 152. Grim Natwick gave Ferguson this appellation in 1936.

"I don't mean they": San Francisco Chronicle, December 31, 1933, quoted in Jim Korkis, Unofficial Disney Stories Never Told, vol. 1 of Vault of Walt, ed. Bob McLain, (Orlando, FL: Theme Park Press, 2012), 77.

"to develop quite": Korkis, 77.

three-page outline: Devon Baxter, "Walt Disney's 'Three Little Pigs,' (1933)," Cartoon Research (blog), May 18, 2016, http://cartoonresearch.com/index.php/walt-disneys -three-little-pigs-1933/.

twenty-five-dollar bonus: William Peet, Bill Peet: An Autobiography (Boston: Houghton Mifflin, 1989), 94.

Walt practically lived in Gillett's music room: Ben Sharpsteen interview by Don Peri, 1975, referenced in Gabler, *Walt Disney*, 182.

assigned on Monday, February 20: Baxter, "Walt Disney's 'Three Little Pigs.'" The due date was Friday, April 7.

passing them along to an assistant: In a 1973 interview with John Culhane, Babbitt identified some of his early assistants: Murray Griffith, Larry Clemmons, and Norman Schaefer.

"I don't like it": This became one of Babbitt's oft-told stories, including in Babbitt, interview by Barrier, June 2, 1971.

the illusion of appearing soft: Animator Jack King singled out "the Disney style of distortion in the characters, the looser treatment on the pigs." Barrier, *Hollywood Cartoons: American Animation in Its Golden Age*, (Oxford, UK: Oxford University Press, 1999), 90. King's scenes were of Practical Pig playing piano.

loved how the pigs' houses: Thomas and Johnston, *Illusion of Life*, 78. The artist responsible is identified as Albert Hurter; Finch, *Art of Walt Disney*, 66.

notes to see which gags: Kinney, *Walt Disney*, 46.

"hit the country like wildfire": Peri, *Working with Walt*, 50. The quote is from Marc Davis, who was hired in 1935.

"the tune by which 1933": Jerry Beck, ed., *The 50 Greatest Cartoons: As Selected by 1,000 Animation Professionals* (Atlanta: Turner Publishing, 1994), 73.

couldn't stop humming: Peri, *Working with Walt*, 168. Herb Ryman made the assertion.

"with absolute awe": Maureen Furniss, *Chuck Jones: Conversations* (Jackson: University Press of Mississippi, 2005), 26.

displayed in local theater lobbies: Art Babbitt's memorial, March 28, 1992, home video, Barbara Perry Babbitt Trust.

"Three Little Pigs is proving": Korkis, *Unofficial Disney Stories*, 75.

he wrote to Tytla: Series 6B, box 5, folder 229, Canemaker Collection.

eager journalists estimated.: *New York Herald Tribune*, March 12, 1934, referenced in Gabler, *Walt Disney*, 184. According to the *Herald Tribune*, the short cost $29,600 and grossed $125,000.

"I've heard estimates": "M. Mouse Poorly Paid," *New York Times*, March 12, 1934.

reinvest everything back into the company: "The Big Bad Wolf," *Fortune*, November 1934, 88–95, 142–148.

never command the same price: Ghez, *Walt's People*, 3:26. That's according to Ben Sharpsteen, who was production manager at the time.

luxurious, Spanish-style home: Adrienne Tytla, *Disney's Giant and the Artist's Model* (self-pub., 2004), 119. The address was 5600 Tuxedo Terrace.

a Japanese fellow: Adrienne Tytla recalls the tenant being Japanese, while Ward Kimball calls him Filipino.

"I'm not going to": Series 6B, box 5, folder 229, Canemaker Collection.

"You know what I'd like": Babbitt, interview by Barrier, June 2, 1971; Bill Hurtz, Babbitt's memorial, home video.

9. Enter Bioffsky

There was plenty to fear: "The First 100 Days," Digital History, accessed December 9, 2021, http://www.digitalhistory.uh.edu/disp_textbook.cfm?smtid=2&psid=3439.

the Emergency Banking Act: The act was enacted with the aid of Frances Perkins, Roosevelt's Secretary of Labor and the first female presidential cabinet member.

International Alliance of Theatrical Stage Employees: *Official IATSE Bulletin* 660 (2Q 2018), https://iatse.net/the-official-bulletin-2018-q2-no-660/.

sitting IATSE president: The president was William Elliot.

IATSE membership dropped: Eric Hart, "A Brief History of IATSE," *Prop Agenda* (blog), September 6, 2010, http://www.props.eric-hart.com/features/a-brief-history-of-iatse/.

Zuta was gunned down: David Witwer, *Shadow of the Racketeer: Scandal in Organized Labor* (Champaign: University of Illinois Press, 2009) 63.

listed him as a public enemy: "Stage Union Linked to 'Public Enemy,'" *New York Times*, August 2, 1939.

Balaban and Katz: Witwer, *Shadow of the Racketeer*, 63–67.

He suggested that the gang: Witwer, 67. That's according to the testimony of George Browne.

the perfect front man: Witwer, 67. This is according to the testimony of Willie Bioff.

at the IATSE convention: "Past Executive Boards: 1932–1950," IATSE official website, accessed August 8, 2020, http://www.iatse.net/past-executive-boards-1932-1950 (page discontinued).

Browne immediately installed Bioff: Witwer, *Shadow of the Racketeer*, 73.

10. The Cult of Personality

Tytla's salary: Art Babbitt to Bill Tytla, November 27, 1933, series I, subseries B, box 3, folder 11, Canemaker Collection.

"When I hire a man": From a 1936 lecture by Tytla, quoted in Thomas and Johnston, *Illusion of Life*, 135.

"Remember this one thing": Art Babbitt to Bill Tytla, December 6, 1933, box 5, series 6, subseries B, folder 229, Canemaker Collection.

January 29, 1934: Art Babbitt to Bill Tytla, November 8, 1934, Barbara Perry Babbitt Trust.

$125 a week: Babbitt's testimony, *NLRB v. Disney*, 240. Babbitt's salaries were as follows: $50/week (September 19, 1932); $60/week (February 6, 1933); $54/week (March 20,

1933, in connection with the Depression's bank holiday); $67.50/week (June 5, 1933); $100/week (October 2, 1933); $125/week (January 29, 1934); $150/week (February 2, 1935); $200/week (December 7, 1936); $170/week (March 24, 1941, because of the studio's financial hardship).

Babbitt was overjoyed: Art Babbitt to Bill Tytla, February 12, 1934, series 6, subseries B, box 5, folder 229, Canemaker Collection.

"Ben [Sharpsteen] told me": Babbitt to Tytla, February 12, 1934.

"seemed to me like": Babbitt to Tytla. The short was *Burlesque*.

director, Burt Gillett: Barrier, *Hollywood Cartoons*, 131.

scenes of Peter Pig: Original animation drafts, Disney Animation Research Library, Glendale, CA.

"I think he used": Frank Thomas, Babbitt's memorial, home video.

Babbitt was mocked for it: Thomas and Johnston, *Illusion of Life*, 73. Thomas says the scene continued to be shown as a counterexample for years.

eagerly bought two books: Babbitt, interview by Culhane, 1973.

His artists sat spellbound: The story of Walt's pitch is retold, among elsewhere, in J. B. Kaufman, *The Fairest One of All* (San Rafael, CA: Weldon Owen, 2012). It was likely right before the June 3 announcement in the *New York Times*, related in Barrier, *Hollywood Cartoons*, 125.

The art classes would have to: Finch, *Art of Walt Disney*, 98. Finch relates an account by Don Graham. The two instructors were Eugene Fleury and Palmer Schoppe.

"There is a chance": Disney Animation Research Library.

left on vacation August 11: "Society in Filmland," *Hollywood Evening Citizen-News*, August 8, 1934.

boarded a steamship: *Santa Elena* ship manifest, via Ancestry.com. They arrived September 3, 1934.

1934 publicity shoot: *Peculiar Penguins* was released September 1, 1934. Babbitt worked on it as well.

Babbitt was now privy to: Babbitt, interview by Culhane, 1973.

On Babbitt's exposure sheet: Babbitt stated it was "seven feet" of film, approximately 4.16 seconds; Babbitt, interview by Culhane, 1973.

Babbitt attempted to identify: Babbitt, interview by Barrier, June 2, 1971.

made him rather unpopular: Babbitt, interview by Barrier.

"as a composite of": See Hahn and Miller-Zarneke, *Before Ever After*, 36. for a reprint of "Character Analysis of the Goof." Babbitt credits actor Stepin Fetchit for inspiring the piece. Babbitt, ASIFA talk with Canemaker.

11. A Feature-Length Cartoon

Additional young artists: Canemaker, *Nine Old Men*, 93, 136, 174. Milt Kahl had been inbetweening there for three months when Thomas arrived, and Kahl would soon begin assisting an animator named Bill Roberts.

"like a drawing robot": Peet, *Bill Peet*, 85, 89. Peet's salary account is accurate as per the salary plan of the time.

cantankerous department supervisor: Canemaker, *Nine Old Men*, 136, 174–75. The supervisor was George Drake.

last animator Walt hired: Respondent exhibit 9, *NLRB v. Disney*. Bill Tytla's first day was November 15, 1934.

Walt was very protective: Marge Champion, interview by the author, 2014.

The model, Marjorie Belcher: Champion, interview by the author.

soirees at the home that he shared: Ward Kimball, interview by John Canemaker, 1975, Canemaker Collection.

The press made him: Roamin' Around in Hollywood, *Hollywood Citizen-News*, May 3 & 20, 1935; Society in Filmland, *Hollywood Citizen-News*, August 8 and September 12, 1934, and April 24, 1935; photos and notes about Cagney and Buhlig, Barbara Perry Babbitt Trust.

Doris Harmon: Tytla, *Disney's Giant*, 65.

Above Babbitt's bed: Photos and home movies, Barbara Perry Babbitt Trust.

he was the only man: Barbara Babbitt, interview by the author, 2012..

Babbitt and a paramour necking: Ward Kimball, interview by John Culhane, August 24, 1978, author's collection.

fundraiser parties: Tytla, *Disney's Giant*, 42.

he knew a young single mother: Dickie's story was related by Barbara Babbitt and Richard Harris. In one version of the story, Dickie Harris, who was born to Esther Belle Keller on June 10, 1932, arrived at Babbitt's house before Tytla moved in and stayed for eight months. Babbitt's memorial, home video.

Oscar-winning film editor: Harris won an Oscar for *Titanic* and was nominated for *Terminator II*.

management experimented with profit-sharing: Board exhibit 13, *NLRB v. Disney*, 240.

believable human animation: Barrier, *Hollywood Cartoons*, 129.

Walt saw it becoming: Disney, "Growing Pains," 37.

character was also being animated: *Mickey's Fire Brigade* was released on August 3, 1935. According to the original drafts, Disney Animation Research Library, Woolie shared Goof duties with animator Leonard Sebring.

not have its own commissary: Babbitt's testimony, *NLRB v. Disney*, 37.

"Mouse Trap Café": Willis Pyle, interview by the author, 2013. The "Mouse Trap" makes a cameo in Bill Peet's illustrated autobiography. Peet, *Bill Peet*, 82.

suing the owner of a local hardware store: Babbitt v. Broadway Department Store Inc. (case no. C387814), Los Angeles Superior Court.

"If Babbitt's contention": "Test of Legality of Collection of Sales Tax Begun," *Whittier News*, May 15, 1935.

peers at the studio thought: Thomas, Babbitt's memorial.

"I fight for the things": Thomas, Babbitt's memorial.

Babbitt sought Lessing out: Lessing's testimony, *NLRB v. Disney*, 851.

"Occasionally, one [animator]": "Meet Hollywood's Men of Action," *Californian*, May 11, 1935.

Other times he took: Photographs, Barbara Perry Babbitt Trust.

invited to Rogers' ranch: Korkis, *Unofficial Disney Stories*, 30. The date was April 21, 1935. Grim Natwick also joined them. Rogers died during production of the short, so his caricature was eliminated from the cartoon.

Forty-five percent: Walt gave this figure in a 1960 interview, included on the *Snow White and the Seven Dwarfs* Blu-ray. Walt Disney, interview, 1960, on *Snow White and the Seven Dwarfs*, dir. by David Hand (1937; Los Angeles: Walt Disney Productions, 2016), Blu-ray.

A European visit: For more on this trip, see Didier Ghez, *Disney's Grand Tour: Walt and Roy's European Vacation, Summer 1935* (Orlando, FL: Theme Park Press, 2014).

director Dave Hand: David Hand, interview by Michael Barrier, 1973, via MichaelBarrier .com, http://www.michaelbarrier.com/Interviews/Hand/interview_david_hand.htm.

tough but fair: Kinney, *Walt Disney*, 29.

"a boy scout": Babbitt, interview by Culhane, 1973.

complete about five seconds: That's according to an interview with Chuck Jones, who, at Warner Bros., had to complete forty feet a week, compared to Disney's eight. Furniss, *Chuck Jones*, 67.

precise planning: Hand, interview by Barrier.

Scene 17: According to the animation drafts, Babbitt's scenes included 17–17b, 18a–18b, 19–19b, 20–20b.

asked the Bank of America: Gabler, *Walt Disney*, 165; Walt Disney, interview, 1960.

Roy and Walt made it known: Culhane, *Talking Animals*, 185.

Walt demanded the hiring: Richard Holliss and Brian Sibley, *The Disney Studio Story* (New York: Crown, 1988), 28.

Dr. Boris V. Morkovin: Tom Sito, "Walt and the Professor," *Animation Magazine*, August/September 2014, 16–17.

Moving Day: The short was released on June 20, 1936.

first live-action reference: Testimony, *NLRB v. Disney*, 981.

Studying Colvig's action: Art Babbitt, Disney training course lecture, September 23, 1936, 13, Canemaker Collection.

"Action Analysis": Memorandum, October 17, 1935, Walt Disney Archives, in Barrier, *Hollywood Cartoons*, 145.

the animators' favorite action: Disney, interview by Martin.

"Animation is based on": Charles Solomon, "Training Disney Artists: Don Graham and the Chouinard Institute," in *Once Upon a Time: Walt Disney: The Sources of Inspiration for the Disney Studios*, ed. by Bruno Girveau (New York: Prestel, 2007), 92. The quote is from a Don Graham lecture dated July 26, 1937.

Adelquist was among the guests: Adelquist's testimony, *NLRB v. Disney*, 461, 498, 584.

walking together with Marge: Art Babbitt, interview by John Culhane, April 18, 1971, *Walt's People*, 9:37; Adelquist's testimony, *NLRB v. Disney*, 499.

Babbitt visited her on the soundstage: *Animating Art*, dir. by Imogen Sutton (Imogen Sutton Productions, 1988).

to a Main Street burlesque house: Sara Hamilton, "The Dramatic Life and Death of Dopey," *Movie Mirror*, May 1938, 62; John Canemaker, notes retained after interview with Babbitt, 1975, series I, subseries B, box 5, folder 3, Canemaker Collection. Sound effects engineer Jimmy McDonald provided the vocal effects for Dopey, according to *Disney Family Album*, season 1, episode 4, "Jimmy MacDonald," dir. by Mike Bonifer, written by Jim Fanning, Disney Channel, first aired September 4, 1984.

12. Bioff Stakes His Claim

"film union czar": "Maloy Killers Elude Police," *Chicago Tribune*, February 5, 1935.

Maloy was driving to work: "Maloy Killers Elude Police," *Chicago Tribune*.

Browne took over Local 110: Mike Nielsen and Gene Mailes, *Hollywood's Other Blacklist: Union Struggles in the Studio System* (London: British Film Institute, 1995), 17.

"Start a new union": "Bioff's Boss," *Chicago Tribune*, April 24, 1940.

on the night of May 13: "Osterberg, Foe of Maloy, Shot Four Times," *Chicago Tribune*, May 14, 1935.

"It looks mighty good": "Kill Alterie in Labor Feud," *Chicago Tribune*, July 19, 1935.

Willie Bioff was questioned: Witwer, *Shadow of the Racketeer*, 118.

William Randolph Hearst: Witwer, 152.

American Liberty League: Witwer, 179. The organization started in 1934.

IATSE controlled projectionist: Nielsen and Mailes, *Hollywood's Other Blacklist*, 17.

increasing the fees for IATSE: Witwer, *Shadow of the Racketeer*, 109–110, 103.

some twelve thousand workers: Nielsen and Mailes, *Hollywood's Other Blacklist*, 20–21.

Basic Studio Agreement: Witwer, *Shadow of the Racketeer*, 94.

13. A Drunken Mouse

Starting in September: Barrier, *Hollywood Cartoons*, 140.

Don Graham Memorial Institute: Home movies, Barbara Perry Babbitt Trust.

"Always Your Ass": Art Babbitt interview by John Culhane, 1971, collection of the Culhane family.

"Now that you have": Walt Disney, address to artists on *The Country Cousin*, November 27, 1935, Walt Disney Animation Research Library.

Beside Walt stood: Disney, address. Other attendees included animator Milt Kahl and story artist Bianca Majolie.

He rented theater space: Marc Davis, as read by John Canemaker, "Commentaries," *Snow White and the Seven Dwarfs*, Blu-ray.

underwater nature documentary: Culhane, *Talking Animals*, 142.

The two were lovestruck: Tytla, *Disney's Giant*, 65, 71, 122.

they arrived at the house: Tytla, 51, 121.

the death of his father: New Montefiore Cemetery records, West Babylon, Suffolk County, New York. (Mae Questel, the actress who voiced Betty Boop and Olive Oyl, is also buried in this cemetery.)

never joined Bill and Adrienne: Tytla, *Disney's Giant*, 122.

The first animation: Barrier, *Hollywood Cartoons*, 143. The princess was animated by two supervising animators, Ham Luske and Grim Natwick. Natwick had previously created Betty Boop for the Fleischer studio.

Fred Moore and Bill Tytla: John Canemaker, *Bill Tytla: Master Animator* (Katonah, NY: Katonah Museum of Art, 1994), 14. Tytla is one of four supervising animators credited.

"Roy, we'll make": Hand, interview by Barrier.

completed much of his Goofy: The animation work draft is dated February 4, 1936.

When Babbitt previewed: An undated lecture with Dr. Morkovin, ca. 1936, 16, referenced in Hahn and Miller-Zarneke, *Before Ever After*, 57. Specifically, Babbitt refers to the gag that sends Goofy into the refrigerator eating a watermelon, versus his reactions to the piano.

he preached the benefits: Champion, interview by the author.

he wouldn't stop expounding: Culhane, *Talking Animals*, 146–147; Kinney, *Walt Disney*, 39, illustration.

"In the opening": Story meeting notes, Walt Disney Animation Research Library.

"We see him drinking": Story meeting notes. Other attendees included Les Clark and Don Graham.

Ads for Disney jobs: Ads in *Daily Variety*, referenced in Barrier, *Hollywood Cartoons*, 145.

a two-month hiring spree: Ad in *Daily Variety*, March 19, 1936, referenced in Barrier, 145.

end of March: *Country Cousin* files, Walt Disney Animation Research Library. Clark's assignment was given on April 3, 1936.

he hoped Babbitt would do: Babbitt's testimony, *NLRB v. Disney*, 262, 982.

"If I'm going to": This story is told several times, including in Babbitt, interview by Barrier, June 2, 1971.

he struggled with himself: Babbitt, training course lecture, 12.

"The important thing": Babbitt, 12.

14. Disney's Folly

Babbitt would sometimes hypnotize: Champion, interview by the author.

A generous new policy: Bill Roberts's testimony, *NLRB v. Disney*, 698.

earned him $958.00: Interoffice memo, April 7, 1936, author's collection.

negotiated with the Bank of America: Gabler, *Walt Disney*: 165.

The bank was reluctant: Disney, interview by Martin. In this interview, Walt referred specifically to Joe Rosenberg of Bank of America.

Gramatky left Disney: Hardie Gramatky, diary, collection of the Gramatky family. He left L.A. on May 1, 1936.

promoted to assistant director of: *NLRB v. Disney*, 462. Adelquist states on p. 587 that this role entailed working on sound synch, assisting the director, making exposure sheets, working with animators on changes in their scenes, maintaining production records on a sequence, and working directly on editing with the cutting department.

directors got hold of a copy: Warner Bros. director Frank Tashlin's testimony, 1942, *NLRB v. Disney*, 456

a whopping $1,204: Interoffice memo, July 1, 1936, author's collection.

"The animator must have": Babbitt, interview by Barrier, June 2, 1971.

"This business has been": Babbitt, Disney training course lecture, 12.

preview of The Country Cousin: The short was released on October 31, 1936.

"Hey, Art": Babbitt, interview by Culhane, 1971.

just like with Moving Day: Tashlin's testimony, 1942, *NLRB v. Disney*, 456.

"the Studio's tour de force": Robert D. Feild, *The Art of Walt Disney* (New York: Macmillan Publishers, 1942), 47.

his animators could now tackle: Culhane, *Talking Animals*, 138.

a bonus check for $1,201.00: Babbitt's testimony, *NLRB v. Disney*, 240.

An additional clause: Board exhibit 19a (contract of employment), exhibit 19 (bonuses), *NLRB v. Disney*.

"have his badge": Home videos, Barbara Perry Babbitt Trust. Babbitt tells the story of the cop in *Animating Art*, dir. by Imogen Sutton. The club Barney Oldfield's, identified on his film canister, was located on 14200 Ventura Boulevard until 1942.

scrapped two complicated sequences: Story man Dick Creedon made this suggestion in November. Gabler, *Walt Disney*, 163.

first completed animation was delivered: Gabler, 260.

Each inker was expected: Martin Krause and Linda Witkowski, *Walt Disney's Snow White and the Seven Dwarfs: An Art in Its Making* (New York: Hyperion, 1994), 41.

The first completed cels: Gabler, *Walt Disney*, 260.

required 250,000 drawings: Krause and Witkowski, *Walt Disney's Snow White*, 41. An animator had to complete ten feet of film a day, equaling 160 frames. Most drawings are held for two frames, but for fast action, they're held for one.

"trying to find an hour": Pinto Colvig, interoffice memo, February 3, 1937, accretions 2000, section I, subsection B, box 1, folder 30, Canemaker Collection.

She observed the rules: Champion, interview by the author.

one of 32 Disney animators: Krause and Witkowski, *Walt Disney's Snow White*, 43.

assigned to someone other than Babbitt: *Hawaiian Holiday* animation drafts, Disney Animation Research Library. It would not be the last time someone other than Babbitt animated Goofy. Reitherman and Bill Roberts shared Goofy in *Clock Cleaners* (released October 15, 1937), and Dick Huemer animated Goofy in *Lonesome Ghosts* (released December 24, 1937). Gerry Geronomi animated Goofy in *Boat Builders* (released February 25, 1938) and *Mickey's Trailer* (released May 6, 1938).

"Here is what I think": Respondent exhibit 22, *NLRB v. Disney*. The transcript of this conversation is dated March 3, 1937.

Walt's guest to the Academy Awards: Babbitt's testimony, *NLRB v. Disney*, 261.

his new house: According to records, courtesy of Joe Campana, Babbitt moved from Tuxedo Terrace to 5600 Hill Oak Drive between August 1936 and March 1937.

dropped from ninety-one: Krause and Witkowski, *Walt Disney's Snow White*, 47.

felt his animation of the Queen: Babbitt's testimony, *NLRB v. Disney*, 262.

"depths of passion": Culhane, *Talking Animals*, 175–176.

$886 bonus check: Adelquist's testimony, *NLRB v. Disney*, 499.

Babbitt and Marjorie Belcher were wed: Marriage license, Barbara Perry Babbitt Trust. The marriage was filed on August 15.

in Santa Barbara: "Cartoonist Weds Girl Met at Studio," *Los Angeles Times*, August 11, 1937.

one of the groomsmen: Adelquist's testimony, *NLRB v. Disney*, 499.

a ballet at the Redlands Bowl: "Mary Lee Glass Sparkles in Ballet Group," *San Bernardino County Sun*, August 12, 1937.

"This crying attitude": Interoffice memo, August 14, 1937, quoted in John Canemaker, *Paper Dreams: The Art & Artists of Disney Storyboards* (Los Angeles: Disney Editions, 2006), 84.

Colvig was gone: Goofy's lines were given to the studio's casting director (and the voice of Snow White's Huntsman), Stuart Buchanan. J. B. Kaufman, *Pinocchio: The Making of the Disney Epic* (San Rafael, CA: Weldon Owen, 2015), 270.

15. Defense Against the Enemy

the Supreme Court ruled on April 12: Nielsen and Mailes, *Hollywood's Other Blacklist*, 25.

dormant group of unions: *Variety*, April 21, 1937, 1, referenced in Nielsen and Mailes, 26.

RKO and Loew's saved $3 million: Witwer, *Shadow of the Racketeer*, 93.

On April 30, 1937: Nielsen and Mailes, *Hollywood's Other Blacklist*, 27.

Studio Utilities Employees caved: *Variety*, June 9, 1937, 2, referenced in Nielsen and Mailes, 28–29. The vote was held on June 7.

the studios surrendered: Babbitt's assistant in 1937 mentioned this strike in a speech several years later. Bill McCorkle, speech, February 19, 1941, oversize various A, 23, MPSC Local 839, AFL-CIO Collection, Urban Archives Center, Oviatt Library, California State University, Northridge.

nearly a hundred animation artists: Culhane, *Talking Animals*, 199.

"the only bona fide organization": Guild paper, January 1938, collection of Tom Sito, reprinted in Tom Sito, *Drawing the Line: The Untold Story of the Animation Unions from Bosko to Bart Simpson* (Lexington: University Press of Kentucky, 2006), 105.

ask the Bank of America: Month and amount via Gabler, *Walt Disney*, 266. Walt later pointed out that six months later the studio had reaped the sales of the film. Walt Disney, interview, 1960.

recount the events years later: Disney, interview by Martin.

"There would be all kinds": Peet, *Bill Peet*, 85.

their 8:30 AM–5:30 PM weekday: Memorandum by Dave Hand, interoffice memo, CC'd to junior animator Clair Weeks, October 15, 1937, collection of Stephen Worth. Saturday work hours remained 8:00–1:00.

extending their Saturday hours: Culhane, *Talking Animals*, 179.

"night and day": RKO newsreel footage, on *Snow White and the Seven Dwarfs*, Blu-ray.

"Please God, send me": Norman M. Klein, *7 Minutes: The Life and Death of the American Animated Cartoon* (London: Verso, 1998), 96–97. Klein witnessed the sketch.

IT WAS FUNNY: Krause and Witkowski, *Walt Disney's Snow White*, 44. The sign was described by Frank Thomas.

animators swapped doodles: Culhane, *Talking Animals*, 180–182.

raced against the December 1 deadline: Photography ended on December 1. Gabler, *Walt Disney*, 268.

"You've no more chance": "Cinema: I.A.T.S.E." *Time*, December 6, 1937, http://content .time.com/time/subscriber/article/0,33009,758548,00.html.

"cook up something": Babbitt's testimony, *NLRB v. Disney*, 65.

"I knew nothing about": Babbitt's testimony, *NLRB v. Disney*, 60–61

"A very important meeting": Board exhibit 2, *NLRB v. Disney*.

"solid, compact group": Babbitt's testimony, *NLRB v. Disney*, 82.

called President Roosevelt's government corrupt: "The Press: Mister Pegler," *Time*, October 10, 1938, http://content.time.com/time/subscriber/article/0,33009,883713,00.html.

"It was decided that": Board exhibit 3, *NLRB v. Disney*.

Babbitt led five more meetings: The meetings that included Babbitt and Lessing are recounted by both Babbitt and Lessing. *NLRB v. Disney*, 63–94, 858–860.

"Aaaah, that's nobody!": Culhane, *Talking Animals*, 183.

MY SINCERE APPRECIATION: *Snow White and the Seven Dwarfs*, dir. by Dave Hand (Los Angeles: Walt Disney Productions, 1937).

16. A Growing Divide

happiest event since the armistice: Westbrook Pegler, January 1938, quoted in The Screen in Review, *New York Times*, February 8, 1940.

Waco, Texas: Michael Barrier, "On Gunther Lessing," MichaelBarrier.com, March 2, 2015, http://www.michaelbarrier.com/WhatsNewArchives/2015/WhatsNew ArchivesMarch15.html#onguntherlessing.

graduated from Yale Law: Yale Law Journal 18 (1909): 442.

"high-priced lawyer": Mona D. Sizer, *Texas Bandits: Real to Reel* (Plano, TX: Republic of Texas Press, 2004), 5.

Lessing began working: Dominique Brégent-Heald, *Borderland Films: American Cinema, Mexico, and Canada During the Progressive Era* (Lincoln: University of Nebraska Press, 2015), 242n72. Lessing's January 5, 1914, contract is available at the Centro de Estudios de Historia de Mexico, Fundación Carlos Slim.

after he opened a law firm: Yale Alumni Weekly 26, no. 1 (1917): 847. The firm Jackson, Isaacks & Lessing was located in suite 605 of the newly constructed Martin Building at 217 N Stanton Street.

handle a case in Arizona: Ives v. Lessing, civ. no. 1558, *Reports of Cases Argued and Determined in the Supreme Court of the Territory of Arizona*, vol. 19 (San Francisco: Bancroft-Whitney, 1919), 209–10; Ives v. Lessing, civ. no. 1558, filed November 8, 1917, *Pacific Reporter* 168: 506.

He witnessed actress Dolores del Río: Linda B. Hall, *Dolores del Río: Beauty in Light and Shade* (Stanford, CA: Stanford University Press, 2013), 130.

a four-year, $35,000 contract: Lessing v. Gibbons, civ. no 9320 (1st App. Distr., Div. 2, May 6, 1935), 1.

Lessing and del Río had an amiable: Hall, *Dolores del Río*, 133.

Lessing began working for Walt: NLRB v. Disney, 857.

helped Walt protect the copyright: "Lessing, Gunther," D23 (The Official Disney Fan Club), accessed December 10, 2021, https://d23.com/a-to-z/lessing-gunther/.

continued to work for del Río: Hall, *Dolores del Río*, 143.

Jaime's sudden death: "Jaime del Rio: Biography," Internet Movie Database, accessed December 10, 2021, http://www.imdb.com/name/nm0215825/bio.

"lack of gratitude": Hall, *Dolores del Río*, 131.

full time on January 1, 1930: Employee card 7726, Walt Disney Archives.

trapped in a miserable marriage: "Wife Wins Divorce from 'Poor Loser,'" *Oakland Tribune*, April 19, 1932. Here, her name is mistakenly rendered as "Lolla."

foisted a second lawsuit: Hall, *Dolores del Río*, 133.

argued that he protected her: Hall, 141

"home wrecker": "Calls Actress Home Wrecker," *San Bernardino Sun*, July 24, 1930.

"Lessing's legal action": Hall, *Dolores del Río*, 130, 133.

won a $16,000 settlement: "Hollywood Lawyer Is Awarded $16,000 in Judgment Against Dolores Del Rio for Services." *San Bernardino Sun*, December 16, 1931.

granted her divorce: "Wife Wins Divorce," *Oakland Tribune*.

jumped into the next big project: Kaufman, *Pinocchio*, 29.

working on the Geppetto character: Thomas and Johnston, *Illusion of Life*, 203. The original design and personality were inspired by the original voice actor, Spencer Charters.

working script was progressing: Kaufman, *Pinocchio*, 29–45.

Polar Trappers: The cartoon was released on June 17, 1938.

Under Reitherman's pencil: This is according to the original animation drafts, dated January 1, 1938, collection of Hans Perk. On the original model sheet (titled "Arctic Trappers"), Reitherman is assigned as the Goof's animator.

One of the NLRB's: The other NLRB regional director present at Babbitt's initial meeting was Dr. Towne Nylander.

the temporary executive board: Also included was story man Hugh Hennesy and animator Ed Dunn.

Fourteen Disney employees: Attendees included director Ham Luske, story man Hugh Hennesy, animator Norm Ferguson, story man Dick Huemer, front office workers A. G. Keener and Paul Scanlon, assistants Ed Dunn and Murray McClellan,

Ink & Paint employees Joan Orbison and Rae Medby, and cameraman Mickey Batchelder. Babbitt's testimony, *NLRB v. Disney*, 93–104.

Gunther Lessing was also: *NLRB v. Disney*, 93–116, 861.

"A mass meeting": The flyer comes from Stephen Worth and is in the author's collection. The address was 2036 North Highland Avenue.

"To bargain collectively": Federation of Screen Cartoonists newsletter, vol. 1, no. 1 (March 7, 1938), oversize various A, 7, MPSC Local 839, AFL-CIO Collection.

executive officers were chosen: Story man Dick Huemer was vice president. Paul Scanlon and A. G. Keener, two front-office employees, were secretary and treasurer, respectively.

Members of the executive board: Evelyn Coats (inker), Tom Conneally, Merle Cox (animator), Ed Dunn (animator), Murray McClellan, Joan Orbison (painter), Bill Roberts (animator), and George Rowley (effects).

"Higher pay": Federation of Screen Cartoonists newsletter, vol. 1, no. 1.

earned $22.50 a week: Culhane, *Talking Animals*, 200. The Fleischer Studio salary is according to veteran Fleischer animator Nick Tafuri.

started at $35 a week: Canemaker, *Nine Old Men*, 212. This amount was Ollie Johnston's salary for painting at Paramount.

"tryout period": Peet, *Bill Peet*, 82, 84.

"Everyone was so scared": Betty Ann Guenther, quoted in Thomas and Johnston, *Illusion of Life*, 150.

"The purposes of your": Federation of Screen Cartoonists newsletter, vol. 1, no. 1.

"One fear is constantly": Churchill, "Disney's 'Philosophy.'"

More than sixty seconds: Thomas and Johnston, *Illusion of Life*, 204.

chose to keep Babbitt on: *NLRB v. Disney*, 278–279

"open to all cartoonists": SCG newsletter, January 3, 1938, reprinted in Sito, *Drawing the Line*, 105.

The Guild went so far: Matter of Walt Disney Productions Ltd. (case nos. 1102 & 1103), 13 N.L.R.B. 865 (1939), 866.

"We have one common": Federation of Screen Cartoonists newsletter, vol. 1, no. 1.

It was March 12: Federation of Screen Cartoonists newsletter, vol. 1, no. 1.

17. The Norconian

The Whalers: Disney released the short on August 19, 1938.

Norm Ferguson, the Pluto specialist: Shamus Culhane, *Animation from Script to Screen* (New York: St. Martin's Press, 1988), 23.

Fred Moore, the Mickey Mouse specialist: Thomas and Johnston, *Illusion of Life*, 123.

"a week, maybe two": Thomas and Johnston, 137.

Ferdinand the Bull: The short was released on November 25, 1938.

Kimball handled the bullfighter: The other caricatures are Ham Luske and Jack Campbell; some argue the matador was Walt. Original animation work drafts, via A. Film L.A. blog, accessed January 12, 2022, https://ftp.afilm.com/blog/RS9-FtB-05.jpg.

Tytlas began making plans: Tytla, *Disney's Giant*, 247.

the studio was out of debt: Gabler, *Walt Disney*, 284. The exact date was May 20, 1938.

"Characters: Entire studio": From the collection of Clair Weeks, courtesy of Stephen Worth.

He announced the winners: Kinney, *Walt Disney*, 114.

Walt began by outlining: Homer Brightman, *Life in the Mouse House: Memoir of a Disney Story Artist* (Orlando, FL: Theme Park Press, 2014), 46. Brightman completed his book in 1986.

"For two years": Bill Justice, quoted in Ghez, *Walt's People*, 3:123.

rode one of the horses: Todd James Pierce, "Walt's Field Day—1938," *Disney History Institute* (blog), September 16, 2013, http://www.disneyhistoryinstitute.com/2013/09/walts-field-day-1938.html.

"there were naked swim": Bill Justice, quoted in Ghez, *Walt's People*, 3:123.

couples swapping partners: Pierce, "Walt's Field Day." The artist in question was Ken Anderson.

Fred Moore drunkenly: Kinney, *Walt Disney*, 114.

now the chief assistant: Adelquist's new title per Kaufman, *Pinocchio*, 25.

lead a meeting on Geppetto's redesign: Adelquist's testimony, *NLRB v. Disney*, 613–14. Bill Schull was another animator whose designs were spurned.

including muralist Diego Rivera: Undated placard in the Walt Disney Family Museum, San Francisco, CA.

Development Board would be formed: Interoffice memo, July 11, 1938, respondent exhibit 19, *NLRB v. Disney*.

offered Babbitt a promotion: *NLRB v. Disney*, 825.

Babbitt passed on the offer: *NLRB v. Disney*, 45. Babbitt added the excuse that being a supervisor would make him ineligible for running the federation.

On June 28: Brightman, *Life in the Mouse House*, 47.

grossed $2 million: Holliss and Sibley, *Disney Studio Story*, 24.

"That was a tactical": Culhane, *Talking Animals*, 185.

Word spread that the bonuses: Brightman, *Life in Mouse House*, 47.

"There was more confusion": Culhane, *Talking Animals*, 185.

poorly managed: Thomas and Johnston, *Illusion of Life*, 153.

Babbitt earned no bonus: The evidence of this is in Babbitt's superior court case, Arthur Babbitt v. Walt Disney Productions, Superior Court, Los Angeles County, no. 471865, filed January 7, 1942, 8.1, in which Babbitt requests bonuses paid for *Snow White*; and in the company document found in respondent exhibit 14, *NLRB v. Disney*, listing the bonuses Babbitt earned, which omits *Snow White*.

The Whalers: The short was released on August 19, 1938.

no bonus for that either: Babbitt v. Walt Disney Productions, 8.1.

By early September 1938: Kaufman, *Pinocchio*, 29.

By the end of September: Gabler, *Walt Disney*, 308. Gabler dates this to September 30, 1938.

rich with visual opportunity: John Culhane, *Walt Disney's Fantasia* (New York: Abrams, 1987), 46, 50. The mushrooms earned their own model sheet on November 4, 1938.

"too slick, too facile": Culhane, *Talking Animals*, 186–187, 224. Culhane dates these seminars near the end of story sessions on *Pinocchio*.

The charge opened up: The charge was made on September 7, 1938. Jeff Kibre made the allegations on behalf of the Motion Picture Technicians. "Bribery Is Alleged in Film Labor Pact," *New York Times*, September 8, 1938; "NLRB Calls Hearing on Film Union Charge," *New York Times*, September 9, 1938.

Notices for the hearing: The notice was issued September 27 and amended on October 11. The regional director was William Walsh. On October 17, the NLRB consolidated the federation's claims with those of the Society of Motion Picture Film Editors, a union that would represent fifteen Disney employees.

took place on October 24: Board exhibit 21, *NLRB v. Disney*, 13.

Seven separate attorneys: Clore Warne, Milton Black, Harold V. Smith, Elmer L. Smith, Herbert Aller, Thomas C. Ryan, and Lewis Blix represented IATSE. Disney was also represented by T. N. Butterworth. William Walsh represented the NLRB. The trial examiner was William R. Ringer. Matter of Walt Disney Productions Ltd., N.L.R.B. (1939), 866.

588 union membership cards: Matter of Walt Disney Productions Ltd., 865–875. During the trial, the federation relinquished jurisdiction over editors, assistant editors, film librarians (to be assigned to the Society of Motion Picture Film Editors), musicians (to be assigned to the American Federation of Musicians of the United States and Canada), and the studio technicians, photographers, film technicians, sound technicians, and makeup artists (claimed to be under the jurisdiction of IATSE).

it would hold classes: Dave Hand counted himself among the instructors, along with Ham Luske and six other specialists. Special guest lecturers taught every seven weeks. Group A also included Shamus Culhane. Group B had twelve names, including Ward Kimball and Les Clark. Group C had fifteen names, including Babbitt's earlier assistant, Larry Clemmons, and newbie Walt Kelly. Respondent exhibit 21,

NLRB v. Disney. Teachers were Dave Hand (Story Construction), Ham Luske (Timing), Tom Codrick (Scene Cutting), Perce Pearce (Acting and Pantomime), Charlie Philippi (Composition), T. Hee (Caricaturing of Characters), Ken Anderson (Character Handling), and Sam Armstrong (Color Reproduction).

renewed at $200 a week: Babbitt v. *Walt Disney Productions*, 7.

In November: NLRB v. Disney, 968.

for $25 a week: "Classification Salary Plan," respondent exhibit 14, *NLRB v. Disney*; Bill Hurtz, Babbitt's memorial, home video.

Hurtz was terrified: Hurtz, Babbitt's memorial.

18. A Wooden Boy and a World War

"Dear Art": Babbitt, interview by Culhane, 1973.

"Why, I'm so proud": This film clip is widely available, including on *Snow White and the Seven Dwarfs*, Blu-ray.

"trapped in": Bill Hurtz, interview by Milt Gray, January 15, 1977, quoted in Barrier, *Hollywood Cartoons*, 261.

considered too "cartoony.": Picture Plays and Players, *New York Sun*, February 6, 1940, quoted in Kaufman, *Pinocchio*, 32.

"an irascible, nasty": Kinney, *Walt Disney*, 112.

"Fine": This story is retold several times, including in Babbitt, interview by Culhane, 1973.

design was proportionately human: Kaufman, *Pinocchio*, 78.

"I was just trying": Thomas and Johnston, *Illusion of Life*, 152–153; *Frank and Ollie*, dir. by Thomas.

"My only regret is": S. J. Woolf, "Disney Talks About His Work," *New York Times*, July 10, 1938.

"Walt was excited": Peet, *Bill Peet*, 110.

a mural of Snow White: "Whose Paintings Are They?" *People Magazine*, February 19, 2007, 107–108; "Artist Sought to Reclaim Her Auschwitz Portraits" *Los Angeles Times*, August 1, 2009.

interest in the federation waned: Federation of Screen Cartoonists memo, circa July 1939, box 1, folder 26, MPSC Local 839, AFL-CIO Collection.

one Warner Bros. cartoon director: Furniss, *Chuck Jones*, 90.

Goofy and Wilbur premiered: Disney released the short on March 17, 1939.

animated three sections: This is according to the *Goofy and Wilbur* animation drafts. via A. Film L.A. blog, accessed January 12, 2022, http://afilmla.blogspot.com/2011/01/prod-2218-goofy-and-wilbur.html.

no bonus for his work: Babbitt v. *Walt Disney Productions*, 8.1.

The Autograph Hound was revised: Babbitt's testimony, *NLRB v. Disney*, 279; Lundy's testimony, *NLRB v. Disney*, 826. Jack King directed the short, which premiered on September 9, 1939.

earning $6.7 million: Gabler, *Walt Disney*, 277.

granting a charter: "Union Bargaining," *Motion Picture Herald*, July 29, 1939, 8.

could not provide evidence: Matter of Walt Disney Productions Ltd., N.L.R.B. (1939), 871.

rallying Disney artists: Federation of Screen Cartoonists memo, circa July 1939, box 1, folder 26, MPSC Local 839, AFL-CIO Collection.

new Burbank studio: "$4,000,000 Is Spent on Studio Expansion; Disney Biggest Contributor," *Daily Variety*, October 22, 1940.

cost him $3 million: *Motion Picture Herald*, March 2, 1940, 9.

"War scare, you know": Ward Kimball, diary, September 3 and September 12, 1939, courtesy of John and Virginia Kimball.

Babbitt stepped down: Norm Ferguson was also elected to the board. According to Ward Kimball, the Federation meeting was around September 17. Kimball, diary, September 18, 1938.

"No demands were": Bill McCorkle, speech.

Janofsky presented Roy: Babbitt's testimony, *NLRB v. Disney*, 121.

Roy agreed to meet: Babbitt's testimony, 115–116. Other attendees were Disney's secretary-treasurer George Morris, production control manager Herb Lamb, and executive board members Norm Ferguson, Hugh Hennessy, and Baumister. The second meeting place was Willard's Restaurant.

met to vote on their next move: Board exhibit 21, *NLRB v. Disney*.

he borrowed $200: *Babbitt v. Walt Disney Productions*, 10.

"girls are getting": Kimball, diary, December 6, 1939.

19. Dreams Shattered

boxed up their belongings: Kimball, diary, January 4–5, 1940.

The interior of the new studio: Floyd Norman, interview by the author, 2016. Kem Weber was the architect and designer.

"You can't imagine": "Letters to the Times: Disney Dirge." *Los Angeles Times*, September 11, 1941. The letter was signed by "S. C." in Glendale.

"beloved benefactor": Kinney, *Walt Disney*, 157.

"As soon as you make": Babbitt, interview by Culhane, 1973.

helped revise a contract: Board exhibit 21, *NLRB v. Disney*, 12.

retreated to his personal workspace: Champion, interview by the author.

a touring vaudeville show: Gary Lassin, interview by the author, 2013.

bombarded with messages from Art: Champion, interview by the author. The dancer she shared a room with was Evelyn Farney.

Gulliver's Travels: The film premiered on December 18, 1939.

several of his former artists: Other ex-Disney artists were animators James "Shamus" Culhane, Al Eugster, Grim Natwick, and Tom Palmer.

grossed $8 million: "Disney Dollars," *Motion Picture Herald*, March 2, 1940, 9.

"Walter Elias Disney is": "Disney Dollars," 9. The piece concludes, "The holding company for Walt Disney Productions is Consolidated Corporation, formed in 1938, with an authorized capital stock of $2,000,000 in the form of 200,000 shares of $10 par value certificates."

top animators worked on Fantasia: Culhane, *Fantasia*, 51.

"It was the story": Culhane, *Fantasia*, 53. According to Babbitt's testimony, *NLRB v. Disney*, 984, Babbitt had hired a dance model but ignored the live-action reference, and instead took dance classes for two months, four to five nights a week, under teacher William Moffa.

Babbitt ignored Plummer's model: In a video interview, artist Jules Engel, newly hired at the time, remembers that he was brought in midway to add storyboard drawings that might inspire the mushrooms' choreography. Later, when Babbitt became a persona non grata, Engel's credit on the mushroom dance would be vastly overexaggerated, which misled early historians and infuriated Babbitt.

"These old-timers are": Hurtz, Babbitt's memorial.

Walt only gave one note: Babbitt, interview by Culhane, 1973.

"He deserves it": Kimball, diary, March 18–19, 1940.

Pinocchio cost $2.6 million: Joel H. Amernic and Russell J. Craig, "Accountability and Rhetoric During a Crisis: Walt Disney's 1940 Letter to Stockholders," *Accounting Historians Journal* 27, no. 2 (2000): 78–81. The article reprints Disney's 1940 and 1941 letters to stockholders in full.

Dumbo would cost less: *Daily Variety*, May 8, 1941, 9. Per Walt Disney's testimony, *NLRB v. Disney*, 944, the first two movies each cost $2 million, and *Dumbo* cost $700,000.

he yelled and drank: Kimball, diary, March 5, 1940, September 7 & 11, 1941.

"What the hell": Kimball, diary, March 25, 1940.

"I found that it": Board exhibit 21, *NLRB v. Disney*, 2. The event happened on December 16, 1940, and the cameraman's representative was Mickey Batchelder.

never had to answer to stockholders: "Talk by Walt to Studio Personnel," February 11, 1941, respondent exhibit 29, *Disney v. NLRB*.

755,000 shares of Disney stock: Amernic and Craig, "Accountability and Rhetoric," 81. The date of sale varies among sources between April 1 and April 2.

"Christ, that bastard": Kimball, diary, May 14, 1940.

"'Pinocchio' I hear": Walter Winchel, On Broadway, *Waterloo (IA) Daily Courier*, April 16, 1940.

talked about bad story ideas: Kimball, diary, April 17, 1940.

Cannon's contract was not: Kimball, diary, April 23, 1940.

"The main idea": Transcript of story meeting, May 14, 1940, via Barrier, *Animated Man*, 180.

by 40 to 45 percent: According to Kimball, diary, May 15, 1940, the amount was 35 percent. The NLRB case put it at 40 to 45 percent. Board exhibit 21, *NLRB v. Disney*, 12.

"I felt responsible": Walt Disney's testimony, *NLRB v. Disney*, 942.

"It was obvious": Disney's testimony, 943–945. The numbers agree with the 1940 letter to stockholders.

"Our personnel is": Sylvia Holland to her brother-in-law Glen Holland, May 26, 1940, collection of Theo and Laura Halladay.

"We are all fighting": Kimball, diary, June 4, 1940.

studio was still over budget: Kimball, diary, June 13, 1940.

nearly impossible for the average employee: Kimball, diary, June 21, 1940.

He filed for divorce: Final Judgement of Divorce, Arthur Harold Babbitt v. Marjorie Celeste Babbitt, June 21, 1940, Barbara Perry Babbitt Trust.

animated sky-bound Goofy: The sweatbox notes are dated between June 20 and August 22. Board exhibit 27, *NLRB v. Disney*.

20. Hilberman, Sorrell, and Bioff

"Have you at any time": Jackson, *Walt Disney*, 37.

Walt named four people: Jackson, 34–41. Jackson reprints the entire testimony of Walt Disney before the committee on October 24, 1947.

Cleveland School of Art: "Exhibitions and Among Artists," *Cleveland Plain Dealer*, November 3, 1935.

"leftwing artists": David Hilberman, interviews by John Canemaker, June 16 and July 12, 1979, Canemaker Collection.

club trip to Communist Russia: William F. McDermott, "Play House Actor Gets a Job in Russian Theater, Finds It Exciting," *Cleveland Plain Dealer*, January 29, 1933.

"Between scenes": William F. McDermott, "Play House Mime Writes from Russia," *Cleveland Plain Dealer*, December 4, 1932.

"he finds America": McDermott, "Play House Actor Gets a Job."

he was recruited: Hilberman, interviews by Canemaker.

the pay was: Hilberman, interviews by Canemaker.

Hilberman who picked up the issue: Hilberman's testimony, *NLRB v. Disney*, 355.

"You were about": Bob Givens, quoted in Adam Abraham, *When Magoo Flew: The Rise and Fall of Animation Studio UPA* (Middletown, CT: Weslyan University Press, 2012), 10.

"The powers that": Hilberman, interviews by Canemaker.

only a top inbetweener's salary: Salary plan, December 1940, respondent exhibit 14, *NLRB v. Disney*.

penned a vitriolic note: This story is related by Bill Hurtz in Babbitt's 1992 memorial and by Babbitt himself in his July 21, 1980, interview with Harvey Deneroff. Ward Kimball noted the date in his diary (August 17, 1940) but miswrote the job position and the salary. According to Babbitt in the 1942 NLRB case, the assistant was Chuck Shaw, and the event was in April 1941 (Babbitt's testimony, *NLRB v. Disney*, 153, but the situation could have transpired with both Shaw and Hurtz.

lost $1.25 million: Amernic and Craig, "Accountability and Rhetoric," 82.

Called The Reluctant Dragon: "Disney Fixes Lineup for His Benchley Dragon Feature," *Daily Variety*, September 23, 1940, 10.

put on the cartoon Baggage Buster: Babbitt's testimony, *NLRB v. Disney*, 983.

"Suddenly I had": Babbitt, interview by Culhane, 1971.

"Mr. Babbitt required": Kinney's testimony, *NLRB v. Disney*, 798; Walt Disney's testimony, *NLRB v. Disney*, 957.

learned that the IATSE had signed up: The *NLRB v. Disney* testimony from 1942 incorrectly dates this meeting as October 1940, but the board's exhibit 21, a transcript of a federation meeting from December 16, 1940, dates this meeting before mid-September. According to *NLRB v. Disney*, 119–123, the other members of the committee included Norm Ferguson, Jim Baumeister, and Hugh Hennessy.

"We can't do anything": Babbitt's testimony, *NLRB v. Disney*, 119.

"didn't want it to look": Babbitt's testimony, 119.

"let it die": Board exhibit 21, *NLRB v. Disney*.

one out of every five: Gerald Horne, *Class Struggle in Hollywood, 1930–1950: Moguls, Mobsters, Stars, Reds, & Trade Unionists* (Austin: University of Texas Press, 2001), 50. This statistic comes from Becky Marianna Nicolaides's PhD dissertation from Columbia University, "In Search of the Good Life: Community and Politics in Working-Class Los Angeles 1920–1955."

"The burning questions": E. Scott Cracraft, "Show Me Socialists: Missouri's Early Radical Heritage, 1861–1920," Southeast Missouri State University Press, http://www.semopress.com/show-me-socialists-missouris-early-radical-heritage-1861-1920/. The pastor was Frank G. Tyrrell.

"I heard him say": Herbert K. Sorrell, testimony before the House Committee on Education and Labor, 80th Cong., 2nd sess. (1948), in *Jurisdictional Disputes in the Motion-Picture Industry*, vol. 3 (Washington, DC: US Government Printing Office, 1948), 1838.

"I hold no prejudice": Sorrell, testimony, 1841.

"because I could see": Sorrell, testimony, 1843.

"As soon as we": Sorrell, testimony, 1847.

"I am not pulling": Sorrell, testimony, 1850.

Sorrell confronted Willie Bioff: Sorrell, testimony, 1858. The final agreement was for a 15 percent raise, with a promise for an additional 5 percent the next time any other craft received a raise.

"studio labor's No. 1": *Variety*, January 6, 1941, referenced in Horne, *Class Struggle*, 58. By late 1941 Sorrell would form, and be president of, the Conference of Studio Unions, a twelve-union organization.

won a 10 percent raise: "Cameramen Win Increases" and "Laboratory Strikes Over," *Motion Picture Herald*, October 14, 1939, 48; "Sorrell Quits as Painters Rep," *Daily Variety*, March 3, 1940, 8.

Bioff received a letter: Sorrell, testimony, 2001. The general manager was MGM's Eddie Mannix.

the legal representative for cartoonists: Matter of Walter Lantz Productions Universal Pictures Co. Inc. (case nos. R-1449–R-1452), 19 N.L.R.B. 423 (1940), 423–425.

Warner Bros. was the home: Leon Schlesinger Productions and Raymond Katz Studio produced the cartoons for Warner Bros.; Bugs Bunny came in full form in *A Wild Hare* (July 27, 1940) and was named in *Elmer's Pet Rabbit* (January 4, 1941).

MGM was working on: Loew's Inc. was MGM's financier; Tom & Jerry debuted in *Puss Gets the Boot* (February 10, 1940) and would be named in *The Midnight Snack* (July 19, 1941).

Universal produced cartoons: Walter Lantz Productions produced the cartoons for Universal; Woody Woodpecker debuted in *Knock Knock* (November 25, 1940).

"Willie Bioff, the labor": Witwer, *Shadow of the Racketeer*, 156.

"It looks like": "Court Orders Bioff Seized in 1922 Case," *New York Times*, November 23, 1939. Bioff was a chairman of the American Federation of Labor, host to those twenty local unions.

"I would call my": "Bioff in Chicago; Is Jailed, Bailed," *New York Times*, February 21, 1940.

This gave George Browne: *Variety*, February 14 & 28, 1940, quoted in Nielsen and Mailes, *Hollywood's Other Blacklist*, 65. The senator was Martin Dies of Texas.

stated publicly that this senator: "Dies' Red-Hunting," *Motion Picture Herald*, March 2, 1940, 9.

"Since he left here": "Ranching's Healthy, Willie," *Daily Variety*, September 20, 1940, 2.

"I hope those who": "Bioff Quits Prison; Hollywood Is Goal," *New York Times*, September 21, 1940.

21. The Federation Versus the Guild

"The cartoonists throughout": Sorrell, testimony, 1905.

"is to most people": Feild, *Art of Walt Disney,* xiv

"the usual opposition": Sorrell, testimony, 1875.

made front-page headlines: "Strike Threatened at Metro," *Daily Variety,* September 19, 1940, 1.

Hilberman needed proof: Hilberman, interviews by Canemaker.

also front-page news: "Cartoonists Given 100% Closed Shop at Metro," *Daily Variety,* September 23, 1940, 1, 12.

Suddenly, Guild membership cards: NLRB v. Disney, 121.

"will add a further burden": Brightman, *Life in the Mouse House,* 58.

"For the first time": Brightman, 57–58.

the studio assigned the last: Kimball, diary, November 11, 1940.

To animate him: Babbitt, interview by Culhane, 1973.

Walt was clearly agitated: Board exhibit 4, December 4, 1940, *NLRB v. Disney.*

was an accurate count: Board exhibit 21, *NLRB v. Disney,* 17.

everything he can to resist: Bill Roberts confirms this in a December 16 meeting (Board exhibit 21, *NLRB v. Disney,* 15). Roberts said of Walt, "Not seriously for the record, but just talking like he does—but he said if the unions got in there and tried to control the business and make him pay bigger wages even if he could afford it, he'd cut the business down to the size that he'd like to have it."

instructed Babbitt to call: Board exhibit 21, December 16, 1940, *NLRB v. Disney,* 14. "Lessing told Hal [Adelquist] and Hal told [supervisor] Johnny Bond," said Babbitt.

"a dirty trick": Babbitt's testimony, *NLRB v. Disney,* 132.

scheduled a federation meeting: Attendees included Roberts, Babbitt, Jack Kinney, Eloise Tobelman, Truman Woodworth, Rae Medby, Joan Orbison, Jim Baumeister, Russel Dyson, George Goepper, Harry Reeves, Nick Hays, Harry Hamsel, Brice Mack, Jean Ritchie, and Norm Ferguson. The lawyer was Leo Ward. Roberts's testimony, *NLRB v. Disney,* 683.

"I had no intention": Board exhibit 21, *NLRB v. Disney.*

"Then you're for": Camera operator Truman Woodworth asked the question.

"If this other thing": The speaker was Harry Reeves.

22. The Guild and Babbitt

supervisors soon appeared: Babbitt's testimony, *NLRB v. Disney*, 138, 143.

Roberts had a secret meeting: Kimball, diary, January 4, 1941. The meeting was at Eric Larson's house, with Ollie Johnston, Jim Algar, Frank Thomas, Woolie Reitherman, and Ward Kimball.

guild began its campaign: "Cartoonists in Drive at Walt Disney Studio," *Daily Variety*, January 10, 1941, 1–4; Sorrell, testimony, 1936.

"How can I show": "What Is the Guild? What Is the Federation?" (flyer), box 1, folder 18, MPSC Local 839, AFL-CIO Collection.

"What a bunch": Kimball, diary, January 15, 1941.

"big majority": "Cartoonists Drive Ended at Disney," *Daily Variety*, January 17, 1941, 4.

"I explained to them": Jackson, *Walt Disney*, 37.

preparing for the general release: "Disney Engineer Goes to Boston; Erects 'Fantasia Stuff,'" *Daily Variety*, January 24, 1941, 6.

"He doesn't mind": Kimball, diary, January 24, 1941.

costing the studio $480,000: *Daily Variety*, October 24, 1940, 4.

around three-quarters the cost: "Disney's 'Dumbo' Will Be Ready for RKO Release Aug. 15," *Daily Variety*, May 8, 1941, 10. Dumbo cost less than $650,000.

At the editor's bay: Respondent exhibit 13, *NLRB v. Disney*; Babbitt's testimony, *NLRB v. Disney*, 986.

"I told Mr. Walt": O'Rourke's testimony, *NLRB v. Disney*, 635, 636.

"guest speaker Anthony G. O'Rourke": "Open Meetings," n.d., box 1, oversize various A, 11, MPSC Local 839, AFL-CIO Collection. All meetings were at the Abraham Lincoln School, three blocks north of the Disney studio on Buena Vista Street.

"It insures just": "The Following Is a Brief Explanation of the Impartial Chairmanship Plan," box 1, folder 26, MPSC Local 839, AFL-CIO Collection.

Screen Gems, began negotiations: "Cartoonists Guild Recognized as Screen Gems Rep," *Daily Variety*, January 29, 1941.

"interfered with, restrained": "RKO-Radio," *Film Bulletin*, February 22, 1941, 11.

opened an investigation: "Labor Charges Strike Disney," *Daily Variety*, February 4, 1941, 1, 8.

"I know that the head": "Luncheon Meeting" (interoffice meeting transcript), February 12, 1941, collection of Didier Ghez.

the "Control System": Babbitt, interview by Culhane.

a $140,000 profit: "Disney Shows 140G Quarterly Profit; Officers Elected," *Daily Variety*, February 5, 1941, 8.

"Statistics prove that": "Inter-Office Communication from Walt to All Employees," February 6, 1941, box 1, folder 24, MPSC Local 839, AFL-CIO Collection.

"This appeal to our": Brightman, *Life in Mouse House*, 59.

"The Federation of Screen Cartoonists": "Labor Row: Disney Studio Claims It Obeys NLRB Law," *Bakersfield Californian*, February 6, 1941.

"I think the two words": "Life, Liberty, and the Pursuit of Bread," *Graffiti*, October 1984, 6–7, Canemaker Collection.

"IMPORTANT MEETING TODAY!": "Inter-Office Communication from Walt to Those Concerned," February 10, 1941, box 1, folder 24, MPSC Local 839, AFL-CIO Collection.

"In the twenty years": Respondent exhibit 29, *NLRB v. Disney*.

There was a huge turnout: "Walt Disney Cartoonist Guild Unit Completed," *Daily Variety*, February 11, 1941, 8.

"We had a drink": Lessing's testimony, *NLRB v. Disney*, 867.

Lessing told him: Babbitt's testimony, *NLRB v. Disney*, 151–152; Lessing's testimony, *NLRB v. Disney*, 866–867.

Walter Lantz, the animation producer: "SCG Screen Gems Mull Basic Pact," *Daily Variety*, February 10, 1941, 4.

On Tuesday, February 18: "Art Babbitt Heads New Disney SCG Unit," *Daily Variety*, February 18, 1941, 7.

a new pay scale: "Classification Salary Plan," February 20, 1941, box 1, folder 26, MPSC Local 839, AFL-CIO Collection.

Is DISNEY BOYCOTT IN HANDS: "Is Disney Boycott in Hands of MGM Guild?," circa March 1, 1941, box 1, oversize various A, MPSC Local 839, AFL-CIO Collection.

ARE THESE 25 TO JEOPARDIZE: "Disney Boycott Demanded by Guild!," circa February 25, 1941, box 1, oversize various B, MPSC Local 839, AFL-CIO Collection.

"CALM DOWN BOYS!!": "Calm Down Boys!!," circa March 1, 1941, box 1, folder 18, MPSC Local 839, AFL-CIO Collection.

"Benedict Arnold": Kimball, diary, February 6, 1941.

23. Disney Versus the Labor Board

At the Academy Awards: "Walt Disney Pulls Out of Academy Awards Lineup," *Daily Variety*, January 22, 1941, 7.

"Fred is so used to": Kimball, diary, February 14, 1941.

Moore struggled with animating: Bill Hurtz's testimony, *NLRB v. Disney*, 975.

Babbitt recalled in 1942: Babbitt's testimony, *NLRB v. Disney*, 161–165.

Bill Roberts, Wilfred Jackson, Ben Sharpsteen: According to the Roberts's testimony, *NLRB v. Disney*, 691, Roberts was Babbitt's supervisor on *Dumbo*.

given a Dumbo sequence: Babbitt's & Roberts's testimony, *NLRB v. Disney*, 275, 692–698. The other animators were Berny Wolf and Walt Kelly. In Canemaker's 1975 interview, Babbitt said he thought the scene assignment held no significance.

Three such sequences: The others were animated by Berny Wolf and Walt Kelly.

"The artists in the": Animator: Bulletin of the Screen Cartoon Guild, March 1941, box 1, folder 18, MPSC Local 839, AFL-CIO Collection.

At the following general-membership: Animator, March 1941.

"The NLRB has its": Animator: Bulletin of the Screen Cartoon Guild, April 1941, box 1, folder 18, MPSC Local 839, AFL-CIO Collection.

designating "efficiency experts": "Luncheon Meeting," February 12, 1941.

suspicion of animators: "The bonus system had an inherent weakness: the largest rewards went to the swiftest rather than the best. Certain men took a very pragmatic view of this opportunity and spent most of their time looking for shortcuts, often giving their lesser-paid assistant much of the work to do." Thomas and Johnston, *Illusion of Life*, 153.

"on a scouting expedition": Brightman, *Life in the Mouse House*, 60. Brightman identifies the experts as Hal Adelquist and Harry Teitel. Other details from "Disney Strike Leader Tells of New Kind of 'Animation,'" *Daily Worker*, June 7, 1941.

"A few complaints regarding": Respondent exhibit 12, *NLRB v. Disney*.

Do Not Disturb: "Disney Strike Spread Threat," *Daily Variety*, May 28, 1941, 1, 11.

more than 400 attendees: "150 New SCG Members Initiated; Bodle Talking to Pal," *Daily Variety*, March 12, 1941, 6.

twice-weekly sketch classes: Animator, April 1941.

deputy labor commissioner: The deputy labor commissioner was Samuel Kalish.

Burbank police charged Babbitt: Respondent exhibit 24a–e, *NLRB v. Disney*; "Sentence Suspended in Gun Permit Case," *Hollywood Citizen-News*, March 22, 1941; Babbitt, interview by Culhane, 1973.

accepted the standard 15 percent: Babbitt's testimony, *NLRB v. Disney*, 240.

"God damn": Kimball, diary, March 24 & 25, 1941.

Wages and Hours Act hearing: Animator, April 1941.

On March 27 the union: Exposure Sheet: Publication of the Disney Unit of the Screen Cartoon Guild, March 28, 1941, collection of Didier Ghez.

AFL prepared to lead hundreds: "Strike Call at Disney Mapped," *Daily Variety*, April 2, 1941, 1, 6.

"there has been no evidence": "Inter-Office Memo from Gunther Lessing to Entire Studio Personnel," April 4, 1941, box 1, folder 24, MPSC Local 839, AFL-CIO Collection.

security guards were deputized: "Demands for Labor Check at Disney Studio Today," *Daily Variety*, April 9, 1941, 3.

"He would say he": Sorrell, testimony, 2115.

"I told Mr. Sorrell": Jackson, *Walt Disney*, 37.

"a hospital filled with workers": "Walsh Will Ask NLRB for Disney Complaint," *Daily Variety*, April 30, 1941, 1, 8.

"This could be turned into": "Mickey Mouse Studio Center of Union Battle," *Chicago Tribune,* May 20, 1941.

"and much of the responsibility": "Walsh Will Ask," *Daily Variety,* 8.

"white-livered cowards": *Animator: Bulletin of the Screen Cartoon Guild,* May 1941, box 1, folder 19, MPSC Local 839, AFL-CIO Collection; "The Following Is a Report by Howard Painter, Legal Counsel for the Federation . . .," May 2, 1941, box 1, oversize various A, MPSC Local 839, AFL-CIO Collection.

waved the latest edition of Variety: Kimball, diary, April 30 and May 2, 1941.

In his office, Walt wired: "To All Employees," circa May 5, 1951, box 1, folder 25, MPSC Local 839, AFL-CIO Collection.

BUT MR. BABBITT: "But Mr. Babbitt . . .," circa May 10, 1941, box 1, folder 25, MPSC Local 839, AFL-CIO Collection.

"THE VERY OFFICER": "The Following Is a Report," May 2, 1941.

"any violence occurs": "Speedy Hearing for Disney," *Daily Variety,* May 5, 1941, 8.

"right the hell out": Babbitt's testimony, *NLRB v. Disney,* 159–160.

24. The Final Strike Vote

"If the Board finds": Walter Spreckels, internal bulletin, May 5, 1941, collection of Didier Ghez.

a lot of work to be done: "Disney's 'Dumbo' Will Be Ready for RKO Release Aug.15," *Daily Variety,* May 8, 1941, 10.

Hyperion Avenue studio for $75,000: "Walt Disney Productions . . . ," *Daily Variety,* May 9, 1941, 2.

On Friday, May 9: "Threat of Disney Strike Offed," *Daily Variety,* May 12, 1941, 7.

"The certification from": "The Federation Disbands," May 15, 1941, oversize various A, 12.

Disney management reneged: "Disney Turns Down SCG Grievance Arrangement," *Daily Variety,* May 16, 1941, 8.

"Today marks the introduction": *Cartoonist: Bulletin of the American Society of Screen Cartoonists,* May 16, 1941, box 1, oversize various B, MPSC Local 839, AFL-CIO Collection.

"Put a lot of jokes": Chuck Jones, interview by Michael Barrier, 1969, in Furniss, *Chuck Jones,* 26.

"We tried very hard": Sorrell, testimony, 1905.

the Guild's Warner Bros. unit: "Schlesinger Closes Studio," *Daily Variety,* May 19, 1941, 1, 10; "Schlesinger Lensers Ankle," *Daily Variety,* May 20, 1941, 1, 4. Other committee members included Gerry Chinoquy and John Carey.

"Raise the price": Sorrell, testimony, 1906.

took place as scheduled on May 19: "Tentative Deal Arranged for Disney Consent Decree," *Daily Variety*, May 20, 1941, 1, 6.

"circumstances beyond the control": Respondent exhibit 2, *NLRB v. Disney*. It is inferred that the spoken statement was to the group at once.

seventeen were Guild members: The total of seventeen (including Babbitt, eighteen) comes from multiple strike documents in MPSC Local 839, AFL-CIO Collection.

mass firing a "Blitzkrieg": "Instructions for Speakers," box 1, folder 30, MPSC Local 839, AFL-CIO Collection; Kimball, diary, May 20, 1941.

inched below half: Respondent exhibit 23a–h, August 22, 1941, *NLRB v. Disney*.

"Babbitt and his Guild": Kimball, diary, May 21, 1941.

"My employees . . . are free": "AFL Tops Meet Tonight on Disney," *Daily Variety*, May 23, 1941, 1–6.

meeting at the Roosevelt Hotel: "Strike at Disney Awaits Word on Guild Report," *Daily Variety*, May 26, 1941, 1, 4.

"Art got me to one side": Hurtz, Babbitt's memorial.

"The union committee": "Strike at Disney Awaits Word," *Daily Variety*, 4.

Walt was coordinating: Untitled document, circa June 1, 1941, box 1, folder 28, MPSC Local 839, AFL-CIO Collection.

"I believe it only fair": Respondent exhibit 30, May 27, 1941, *NLRB v. Disney*.

a tremendous ovation: Kimball, diary, May 27, 1941.

As he exited the studio restaurant: Babbitt, interview by Culhane, 1973.

"disturbed the morale": Board exhibit 5a, *NLRB v. Disney*.

"Walt Disney Productions": Board exhibit 5b, *NLRB v. Disney*.

permission to pack his things: Babbitt's testimony, *NLRB v. Disney*, 174–178.

Tytla paced the building's steps: Kimball, diary, May 27, 1941.

25. Strike!

picket signs, many painted: "Further Information on Disney Strike," circa June 7, 1941, box 1, folder 28, MPSC Local 839, AFL-CIO Collection.

Traffic entering the studio: Kimball, diary, June 9, 1941.

AN APPEAL TO REASON: "An Appeal to Reason," box 1, folder 19, MPSC Local 839, AFL-CIO Collection.

"The salaries of the Disney": Untitled document, circa June 1, 1941.

The Disney carpenters: "Disney Strike Hits Theatres," *Daily Variety*, May 29, 1941, 1–4.

One striker photographed: "Walt Disney Cartoonists Strike in Bargaining Dispute," *Los Angeles Times*, May 29, 1941.

a striker in a beret: Kimball, diary.

"*guys pouring their individual*": Kimball, diary, May 28, 1941.

"*The average age*": Sorrell, testimony, 1908.

leaped onto car bumpers: Brightman, *Life in the Mouse House*, 62.

others rocked cars: Don Lusk, interview by the author, 2017.

greeted with cheers and claps: "Walt Disney Cartoonists Strike," *Los Angeles Times*.

"*I felt terrible*": Kimball, diary, May 28, 1941.

"*How the hell can*": Kimball, diary.

strikers warned them: Kimball, diary.

"*Any agreement made*": Kimball, diary.

Babbitt was also dating: As represented in gag drawings by Disney artist Jesse Marsh, lot nos. #97019–97022, Heritage Auctions, Animation Art Auction 7207, June 15–16, 2019, Dallas, TX.

"*For years I have*": Walt Kelly, *Dreamin' of a Wide Catfish*, vol. 4 of *Walt Kelly's Pogo and Albert* (Columbia, MO: Eclipse Books, 1990), 12.

"*from 10 to 11*": Sorrell, testimony, 1907.

"*I'm going to see*": Kimball, diary, May 29, 1941.

309 absences out of 1,214: "Walt Disney Cartoonists Strike," *Los Angeles Times*.

Bill Littlejohn figured: "Central Labor Council Enters Disney Strike," *Daily Variety*, June 5, 1941, 1, 12.

while Babbitt counted: "Walt Disney Cartoonists Strike," *Los Angeles Times*.

spouses and friends: "Walt Disney Cartoonists Strike," *Los Angeles Times*.

The evenness: William Pomerance, interview by John Canemaker, April 17, 1979, Canemaker Collection.

"*The request of the*": "Walt Disney Cartoonists Strike," *Los Angeles Times*.

Walt called a few trusted artists: Kinney, *Walt Disney*, 137.

"*Unless the Screen Cartoonists*": "Disney Studio Picket Line May Include All Houses Showing Cartoons," *San Bernardino County Sun*, May 29, 1941.

the sound wagon announced: "Disney Strike Hits Theaters," *Daily Variety*, 1, 4.

loyalists held an emergency meeting: "Disney Strike Hits Theaters," 1, 4.

"*back to work*" *effort*: "Disney Scab Move Fizzles; Strike Grows," *Daily Worker*, June 1, 1941.

"*wrong crowd*": Willis Pyle, interview by the author, 2014; Tytla, *Disney's Giant*, 173a.

Babbitt's days were packed: Babbitt's testimony, *NLRB v. Disney*, 181.

During the day: Ray Patin's home movies, courtesy of Renée Patin Farrington and the Patin Collection.

"*Chalk-talk pickets*": "Strike at Disney," *Screen Actor*, June 1941, 17.

"*Disney has long paid*": "Dear Sirs and Brothers," May 31, 1941, box 1, folder 19, MPSC Local 839, AFL-CIO Collection.

"*The workers tried*": "Disney Strike Hits Theaters," *Daily Variety*.

Technicolor film-processing plant: "Unions in Disney Fite After RKO," *Daily Variety,* June 2, 1941, 1, 5.

"flying squadrons": Untitled document, circa June 1, 1941.

One of these employees called: "Unions in Disney Fite," *Daily Variety,* 5.

conciliator came on Monday: The conciliator was Lyman Sisely.

non-strikers wrote a petition: Board exhibit 24, *NLRB v. Disney.*

"to drive Fantasia": "U.S. Labor Conciliator Steps into Disney-Cartoonists Strike Impasse," *Weekly Variety,* June 4, 1941, 23.

ticket-holders had to navigate: "'Fantasia' Held Two More Carthay Weeks Despite Picketing," *Daily Variety,* June 3, 1941, 5.

"once in a lifetime": "Disney Panned in Det. for Quick Return of 'Exclusive' Roadshowing," *Weekly Variety,* June 4, 1941, 23.

Reluctant Dragon's release was postponed: "Central Labor Council Enters Disney Strike," *Daily Variety,* June 5, 1941, 1, 12; *Film Daily* notes the release postponement in its issue of May 29, 1941.

26. The Big Stick

"Camp Cartoonist": "Strike at Disney," *Screen Actor,* June 1941, 17; Archery film courtesy of Renée Patin Farrington and the Patin Collection.

"Skunk Hollow": Sorrell, testimony, 1908. Sorrell also said that the strikers called the grove "pleasure island."

"We served dinner": Sorrell, 1908.

When musicians weren't available: Untitled document, circa June 1, 1941.

"Hollywood's favorite strike": "Further Information on the Disney Strike," circa June 7, 1941, box 1, folder 28, MPSC Local 839, AFL-CIO Collection.

Littlejohn flew overhead: Tom Sito, "Bill Littlejohn: Off We Go . . . Taking Our Pencils Yonder," Animation World Network, August 24, 2007, https://www.awn.com /animationworld/bill-littlejohn-we-go-taking-our-pencils-yonder.

"Be sure and give": "Disney Strike Leader Tells of New Kind of 'Animation,'" *Daily Worker,* June 7, 1941.

A handmade effigy: On the Line, June 6, 1941, box 1, folder 28, MPSC Local 839, AFL-CIO Collection.

"As serious as the issues": Hank Ketcham, *The Merchant of Dennis the Menace: The Autobiography of Hank Ketcham,* repr. ed. (Seattle, WA: Fantagraphics Books, 2005; orig. publ. 1990), 54. Al Bertino is a listed striker.

"If she had it in": Rabin and Fine, interview by Canemaker.

"Heard that this morning": Kimball, diary, June 3, 1941.

always stayed around 330: Gunther Lessing wrote on August 22, 1941, that thirty-seven strikers went back in, not including five who went in after the first day. Respondent exhibits 23a–h, *NLRB v. Disney*. This is a conservative number; Brady, "Whimsy on Strike," reports sixty.

"Well here comes": Kimball, diary, June 10, 1941.

wives of loyalists joined: *On the Line*, June 9, 1941, box 1, folder 28, MPSC Local 839, AFL-CIO Collection.

"There were phone calls": Tytla, *Disney's Giant*, 167, 169.

"Those who have remained": *On the Line*, June 9, 1941.

second meeting with the council: Respondent exhibit 31, *NLRB v. Disney*.

loyalists ditched work early: Kimball, diary, June 12, 1941.

SEVERANCE PAY OR: Courtesy of Reneé Patin Farrington and the Patin Collection; *On the Line*, June 17, 1941, box 1, folder 29, MPSC Local 839, AFL-CIO Collection.

"sewer rats": Brady, "Whimsy on Strike."

feelings about Walt: Brady, "Whimsy on Strike."

"Another appeal to": *On the Line*, June 13, 1941, box 1, folder 29, MPSC Local 839, AFL-CIO Collection.

"Walt Disney, you ought": Brady, "Whimsy on Strike."

"Why you dirty sonofabitch!": Brady, "Whimsy on Strike"; Kimball, diary, June 13, 1941.

27. The 21 Club

"A bankroll can": *On the Line*, June 16, 1941, box 1, folder 29, MPSC Local 839, AFL-CIO Collection.

"Committee of 21": *On the Line*, June 17, 1941, box 1, folder 29, MPSC Local 839, AFL-CIO Collection.

"to pull the RED HERRING": Untitled letter, circa July 1941, box 1, folder 32, MPSC Local 839, AFL-CIO Collection.

"The Committee of 21 meets": *On the Line*, June 17, 1941.

seeking a solution: "Strike News Service: Screen Cartoon Guild," circa June 18, 1941, box 1, folder 29, MPSC Local 839, AFL-CIO Collection.

"The strikers feel": "Strike News Service," ca. June 18, 1941.

Roy traveled back to New York: Broadway, *Weekly Variety*, June 18, 1941, 53.

shared a new development: "New Disney Strike Peace Efforts Made," *Hollywood Citizen-News*, June 18, 1941.

an industry-wide art sale: *On the Line*, June 23, 1941, box 1, folder 30, MPSC Local 839, AFL-CIO Collection.

"I'm the Kansas City Kid": "My Little Red Axe," n.d., box 1, folder 35, MPSC Local 839, AFL-CIO Collection.

went rogue and tried: Tytla, *Disney's Giant*, 466e.

"peace proposal": Kimball, diary, June 17, 1941.

meeting confirmed the disbanding: "Screen Cartoonists" memo, circa June 20, box 1, folder 29, MPSC Local 839, AFL-CIO Collection.

"Good meeting": Kimball, diary, June 19, 1941. The artists were Bill Peet and Riley Thompson.

Both the director of film distribution: On the Line, June 26, 1941, box 1, folder 30, MPSC Local 839, AFL-CIO Collection. Hal Horne, director of distribution of Disney films, and Dick Condon, head of eastern publicity, were the two who resigned.

Lamb quit as well: Resignation dated June 20, 1941, per employee card 7426, Disney Archives.

"YOU ARE LOST": Untitled letter, circa July 1941.

Roy returned from New York: "Pix Cartoonists' Strike," Weekly Variety, 6.

strike had delayed the film: "Release 'Reluctant Dragon' June 27 Instead of June 6," Film Daily, May 29, 1941, 2.

premiered that Friday: "What's Heat to 'Dragon?'" Film Daily, June 30, 1941, 2.

street dance fundraiser: Brady, "Whimsy on Strike."

had raised $570: On the Line, June 30, 1941, box 1, folder 30, MPSC Local 839, AFL-CIO Collection.

"egocentric paternalist": Brady, "Whimsy on Strike."

28. Willie Bioff and Walt Disney

Bioff held considerable power: "FBI Presses Extortion Inquiry," Film Daily, May 26, 1941.

arrested for tax evasion: "Gov't Files Tax Evasion Suit Against Wm. Bioff," Film Daily, April 30, 1941.

charged Bioff with tax fraud: "Bioff Tax Evasion Trial Set Despite Schenck Appeal," Weekly Variety, April 30, 1941, 4; "Browne Names Bioff to Watch Defense," Motion Picture Herald, May 24, 1941, 16; "FBI Presses Extortion Inquiry," Film Daily.

"You can say for me": "Bioff and Browne Indicted Here for $550,000 Film Union Racket," New York Times, May 24, 1941.

"I never committed": "Union Head Surrenders," New York Times, May 28, 1941.

"I want it clearly understood": "Bioff Trial Starts in New York Aug. 18," Film Daily, June 13, 1941.

"members of the Communist party": "Bioff Denies Guilt in Extortion Case," New York Times, June 13, 1941.

"Is that all you": "Bioff Denies Any Extortion," New York Times, May 24, 1941.

Immediately following Walt's: "Walt Cannot Bioff Us!," circa July 9, 1941, box 1, folder 31, MPSC Local 839, AFL-CIO Collection.

SWEEPING VICTORY FOR: "Sweeping Victory for Cartoonists in Strike Settlement with Disney," Weekly Variety, July 2, 1941, 1, 6.

"application for reinstatement": "Cartoonists Repudiate Undercover Deal," circa July 8, 1941, box 1, folder 31, MPSC Local 839, AFL-CIO Collection.

June 30, nine guests arrived: "Bioff Blocks Strike Washup," *Daily Variety*, July 2, 1941, 1, 4.

vice president of the AFL: "Unions Looks for a New 'Shuffle' in Negotiations with Producers," *Motion Picture Herald*, May 31, 1941, 31-32. Browne was reelected as AFL VP in Nov 1940; "Bioff and Browne Indicted," *New York Times*.

Bioff's home suggested: John William Tuohy, "Gone Hollywood: How the Mob Extorted the Hollywood Studio System," AmericanMafia.com, May 2002, http://www.american mafia.com/Feature_Articles_208.html.

"Female employees shall receive": Board exhibit 6, *NLRB v. Disney*.

received thunderous applause: "Sweeping Victory for Cartoonists in Strike Settlement," *Weekly Variety*, July 2, 1941, 6.

AFL leaders arrived: "Bioff Blocks Strike Washup," *Daily Variety*, July 2, 1941, 1, 4.

"If the IATSE had": Sorrell, testimony, 1908.

Babbitt alone voiced: Babbitt's testimony, *NLRB v. Disney*, 189.

leaped from the vehicle: Guild committee member Howard Baldwin, quoted in Sorrell, testimony, 1909, 1916.

two guild members: Sorrell, testimony, 1908.

Babbitt rejected the offer: Babbitt, interview by Culhane, 1973.

"take over": "To All Disney Artists," circa July 9, 1941, box 1, folder 31, MPSC Local 839, AFL-CIO Collection.

"I did not show up": Sorrell, testimony, 1909.

"not to enter into": "To the Rank and File of Local 683," circa July 10, box 1, folder 31, MPSC Local 839, AFL-CIO Collection.

drafted an open letter: "Willie Bioff Entrance Balks Strike Washup," *Daily Variety*, July 2, 1941.

"To My Employees": Advertisement, *Daily Variety*, July 1, 1941.

"Dear Walt": "Walt Disney . . ." advertisement, *Daily Variety*, July 2, 1941

"Every time we think": "Disney Workers Told Why Strike Parlay Broke Down," *Los Angeles Times*, July 3, 1941.

traveled to Herb Sorrell's home: Sorrell, testimony, 1909.

"Do you know about": "Walt Cannot Bioff Us!" circa July 9, 1941.

"The strikers were never": "A F of L Quits Disney Strikers," *Daily Variety*, July 9, 1941, 1, 5.

"We're going ahead": "Studio Strike Continues," *Ottawa Citizen*, July 5, 1941.

"If Bioff reestablishes": "To the Rank and File of Local 683," circa July 10.

support began pouring in: On the Line, July 3, 1941, box 1, folder 31, MPSC Local 839, AFL-CIO Collection.

wrote letters in protest: "Back to Work," *Screen Actor*, August 1941, 17.

"indispensable man": "Bioff Botches," *Screen Actor*, July 1941, 11.

Friday, July 4: "U.S. Labor Conciliator Steps In to Hasten Disney-Cartoon Peace," *Weekly Variety*, July 9, 1941, 22.

Picket signs with familiar: "Artists Repudiate Undercover Deal," circa July 8, box 1, folder 31, MPSC Local 839, AFL-CIO Collection.

"Walt is still the": "Before Seeing the Reluctant Dragon Read About the Reluctant Disney," n.d., box 1, folder 33, MPSC Local 839, AFL-CIO Collection.

"to sell the stockholders": "'The Reluctant Dragon' Okay as a Novelty," *Box Office Digest*, June 19, 1941, 11.

"A curious coincidence": Review of *The Reluctant Dragon*, *Weekly Variety*, June 11, 1941, 14.

"I would say that": "Published by and for the Women's Auxilliary . . .," circa July 7, 1941, box 1, folder 31, MPSC Local 839, AFL-CIO Collection.

"Keep their lines busy: "Published by and for the Women's Auxilliary . . .," circa July 7, 1941.

"Mr. Disney, when he": Sorrell, testimony, 1908.

Sorrell had the private officers: Sorrell, testimony, 1908.

"that anyone who tries": Sylvia Holland to her brother-in-law Glen Holland, July 24, 1941, collection of Theo and Laura Halladay.

"Walt is helpless": Sylvia Holland to Glen Holland.

"Believe me, he honestly": Walt Disney to Westbrook Pegler, August 11, 1941, collection of Didier Ghez.

Herb Sorrell politely: "Labor Conciliator Steps In," *Weekly Variety*, 22.

Bioff was spotted entering: "A F of L Quits," *Daily Variety*, 1, 5. The AFL western director was Meyer Lewis, with his office at 511 Hill Street. The attendees at the meeting were international representative of the IATSE Carl Cooper, Teamsters rep Joseph Tuohy, Soundmen rep Harold V. Smith, International Brotherhood of Electrical Workers rep Al Speede, Plasterers rep Ben Martinez, Laboratory Workers rep Norvall Crutcher, Utility Workers rep Lou C. Helm, Projectionists rep John Swartz, Cameramen rep Herbert Aller, and AFL rep Aubrey Blair.

ninety-eight souls: "Another Union Ends Strike at Disney," *San Francisco Examiner*, July 10, 1941.

Guild counted twenty-one: On the Line, July 10, 1941, box 1, folder 31, MPSC Local 839, AFL-CIO Collection.

"cleaning out Commies": "Labor Conciliator Steps In," *Weekly Variety*, 22.

additional Technicolor prints: "Film Editors Back on Jobs," *Santa Ana Register*, July 10, 1941. Seventy-five prints of *Dragon* had been processed before the strike was called.

the AFL called off: "A F of L Quits," *Daily Variety*, 1, 5.

Guild meeting that evening: "A F of L Quits," *Daily Variety*, 1, 5.

IATSE ordered the film editors: "Smith Heads Film Eds," *Weekly Variety*, July 16, 1941, 6.

"The defection of certain": "Unions Deserting Strike at Disney," *San Bernardino County Sun*, July 10, 1941.

"The demands of the union": "Another Union Ends Strike at Disney," *San Francisco Examiner*, July 10, 1941.

Bodle charged the company: On the Line, July 10, 1941.

arbitrator Stanley White: "Labor Conciliator Steps In," *Weekly Variety*, 22.

"The government wanted me": Walt Disney's testimony, *NLRB v. Disney*, 946.

29. The Guild and the CIO

"Still with chip-munk": Untitled document, n.d., box 1, folder 32, MPSC Local 839, AFL-CIO Collection.

"We don't know": "We Received Our Third Letter . . .," n.d., box 1, folder 32, MPSC Local 839, AFL-CIO Collection.

"extend full support": "Resolution in Support of the Screen Cartoonists Guild," July 11, 1941, box 1, folder 32, MPSC Local 839, AFL-CIO Collection.

they had long been eager: Douglas W. Churchill, "Dogfights Roar over Hollywood," *New York Times*, July 20, 1941.

all CIO projectionists: "Published by and for the Women's Auxilliary . . .," circa July 14, 1941, box 1, folder 32, MPSC Local 839, AFL-CIO Collection.

between one hundred thousand: "Gov't Holds Off Action in Disney Strike; Studio Alone in Balking Arbitration," *Weekly Variety*, July 16, 1941, 23; *On the Line*, July 22, box 1, folder 34, MPSC Local 839, AFL-CIO Collection.

Machinists Union had unanimously: On the Line, July 11, 1941, box 1, folder 32, MPSC Local 839, AFL-CIO Collection.

Technicolor once again: "Technicolor Will Not Process Disney Film!," circa July 11, 1941, box 1, folder 32, MPSC Local 839, AFL-CIO Collection.

Laboratory Technicians Union: On the Line, July 14, 1941, box 1, folder 32, MPSC Local 839, AFL-CIO Collection.

turned into a "riot": On the Line, July 11, 1941.

"We, as patriotic": "Disney Strike Deadlock Grows Tighter," *Hollywood Citizen-News*, July 15, 1941.

"possess full information": "Disney Rejects Federal Mediation Offer with Blast at Labor Board," *Hollywood Citizen-News*, July 14, 1941.

"apparently being convinced": "Disney Strike Tangle Told," *Los Angeles Times*, July 15, 1941.

refusal came in haste: "Whitney's Angle," *Weekly Variety*, July 16, 1941, 23.

"The company's interest": "Gov't Holds Off Action," *Weekly Variety*.

"They were there": Kimball, diary, July 15, 1941. Additional Disney loyalist Eric Larson attended, as did Disney strikers Murray McClellan, Ken Peterson, and Howard Baldwin.

a strike flyer appeared: "Primer of the Disney Strike," n.d., box 1, folder 34, MPSC Local 839, AFL-CIO Collection.

"They said, 'He's a comer!'": "Comer" is a mispronunciation of "Commie."

"F is for FIELD OF ALFALFA": Bioff supposedly bought an alfalfa farm.

"The Baron of Burbank": Refers to Walt.

"who ink with an 'F'": Refers to a "fink," slang for picket-crosser.

"asleep on his Scripto": A Scripto is a typical pencil animators used for cleanup drawings.

"TEMPUS which fugits away": "*Tempus fugit*," means "time flies" in Latin.

"W stands for the generous guy": This is Walt.

"Z is for ZOMBIE, or Victory Scotch": A zombie is a cocktail invented in Hollywood.

sent telegrams to the presidents: *On the Line*, July 17, 1941, box 1, folder 33, MPSC Local 839, AFL-CIO Collection. The telegrams were sent to William Green and Lawrence P. Lindelof.

held to negotiate a settlement: "U.S. Assigns Mediator to Disney Studio Strike," *Film Daily*, July 25, 1941, 1, 8.

Roy relented and agreed: "Toss Disney Strike to U.S. Arbitration," *Hollywood Reporter*, July 23, 1941.

each wired Dr. Steelman: "Toss Disney Strike," *Hollywood Reporter*.

"trusting that we may": "U.S. Ready to Order Cartoon Strike Halt," *Daily Variety*, July 24, 1941, 1, 6.

Nonetheless, the San Fernando Valley: "U.S. Mediator Due Monday for Disney Parley," *Los Angeles Daily News*, July 25, 1941.

Dewey, was assigned: "Mediation Planned in Disney Strike," *Los Angeles Times*, July 25, 1941.

infuriated the Disney loyalists: "Union Demands Part in Disney Labor Parley," *Long Beach Press-Telegram*, July 25, 1941.

"I have come to": Sylvia Holland to her brother-in-law Glen Holland, collection of Theo and Laura Halladay.

"Effective at 8:30 AM": Board exhibit 10, *NLRB v. Disney*.

an arbitration hearing: Respondent exhibits 24a–24e, *NLRB v. Disney*.

highest salaries in the animation industry: Home movies of the strike, courtesy of the Barbara Perry Babbitt Trust.

protected from any discriminatory: Board exhibits 7, A, 8, *NLRB v. Disney*.

bonfire of their picket signs: Film footage, collection of Barbara Perry Babbitt Trust.

30. Not the Drawing

"edgy—some people": Ward Kimball to Gary Conrad, December 1, 1976, 3, collection of Gary Conrad.

Roy attempted a diplomatic: Oliver B. Johnston, memo to Roy Disney, August 17, 1941, collection of Didier Ghez. Roy's address took place around August 3.

Adelquist approached Babbitt: Babbitt's testimony, *NLRB v. Disney*, 122.

they saw it was true: Babbitt's testimony, *NLRB v. Disney*, 195–96. The artist in his old room was Milt Neil.

Marge Gummerman: Lusk, interview by the author; employee evaluations, accretions 2000, series I, subseries B, box 1, folder 40, Canemaker Collection.

headed by Hal Adelquist: Adelquist's testimony, *NLRB v. Disney*, 504.

a list of 256 employees: "U.S. to Act in New Disney Row," *Los Angeles Daily News*, August, 13, 1941.

"We have a right": "U.S. to Act," *Daily News*.

"I marvel at Disney's": Babbitt, diary, January 4, 1942.

Many artists were waiting: Respondent exhibits 23a–h, August 15, 1941, *NLRB v. Disney*.

"To me, the entire": Disney to Pegler.

"The closing of the Studio": Johnston, memo to Roy Disney. Johnston was assistant secretary-treasurer of the board of directors; "Disney Shows 140G Quarterly Profit," *Daily Variety*.

agent named William Pomerance: Pomerance, interview by Canemaker.

The studio reopened: Adelquist's testimony, *NLRB v. Disney*, 506–507. According to Gabler, *Walt Disney*, 374, 694 total employees remained at the studio. The reopening date matches that in Kimball's diary.

about seven hundred: The total comes from Walt's letter to Pegler.

twelve hundred a year before: This figure comes from Disney's 1940 letter to stockholders; Amernic and Craig, "Accountability and Rhetoric," 78.

had to punch a time-clock: Kimball, diary, September 17, 1941.

Director Dick Lundy: Lundy's testimony, *NLRB v. Disney*, 828.

"I'm not supposed": Kimball, diary, October 14, 1941.

"I'll be god-damned": Babbitt's testimony, *NLRB v. Disney*, 233.

"son-of-a-bitch": Kimball, diary, September 30, 1941.

"drastically curtail its feature": Adelquist's testimony, *NLRB v. Disney*, 508–510.

late October: *Santa Clara* ship manifest, via Ancestry.com. The vessel departed Chile on October 4, 1941, arriving in New Orleans October 20, 1941. Walt was at *Dumbo*'s premiere in New York City on October 23, 1941.

Guild had changed too: Kimball, diary, October 21, 1941.

"I consider my status": Board exhibit 12, *NLRB v. Disney*.

"complaint for breach": *Babbitt v. Walt Disney Productions*, 1.

Babbitt drove cross-country: Babbitt, diary, January 14, 1942, and April 25, 1942.

"Little pangs of common sense": Babbitt, diary, March 18, 1942.

a graphic nightmare: Babbitt, diary, January 29, 1942.

Tytla wrote an attestation: Board exhibit 18, *NLRB v. Disney*.

"I always found him": Board exhibit 22, *NLRB v. Disney*; Pat Casey (chairman of the Producers' Committee of the AFL) also later provided a letter of recommendation, dated October 21, 1941.

Both his trials would dovetail: Babbitt, interview by Culhane, 1973.

between $2,000 and $17,000: "Disney Victor in Bonus Fight," *Los Angeles Times*, January 28, 1943.

"Among animators and directors": Chuck Jones's testimony, *NLRB v. Disney*, 431.

"At the time, he was": Walt Disney's testimony, *NLRB v. Disney*, 936–959.

31. The Final Goodbye

"buzzing the island": Records and accounts of Babbitt's time at war, Barbara Perry Babbitt Trust.

presented the financial accounts: "Pinocchio, Fantasia Costly to Disney, Court Case Shows," *Whittier News*, January 30, 1943.

company was granted an appeal: "Court Directs Disney Obey NLRB Order," *Los Angeles Daily News*, December 6, 1944.

Cease and desist from discouraging: Decree 10603, December 5, 1944, *NLRB v. Disney*, 1–3.

petitioning for a Supreme Court review: "Labor Case Review Denied to Disney," *Los Angeles Times*, April 24, 1945; letter from Harlan F. Stone, November 1, 1943; Petition of Walt Disney Productions for Rehearing, December 26, 1944, *NLRB v. Disney*. A writ of certiorari was issued by a clerk in the US Supreme Court on March 5, 1945.

arrived for work at Disney: Art Babbitt, typed memo, ca. January 1947, Barbara Perry Babbitt Trust. The memo detailed Babbit's brief return to the Disney studio from November 1945 to January 1947.

"sort of keep out": Babbitt, typed memo.

"Sit with Babbitt": Babbitt, typed memo.

The Guild's grievance committee: For the union, Maurice Howard, Howard Baldwin, Phil Eastman, Bill Melendez, Les Clark, and Volus Jones attended. The studio was represented by Bonar Dyer, Ken Peterson, and Andy Engman.

"Dear Mr. Babbitt": Letter of resignation acceptance, Barbara Perry Babbitt Trust.

32. And They Lived

Babbitt married Dina Gottliebova: Marriage license, April 17, 1948, Barbara Perry Babbitt Trust.

his commercials and industrial films: One was *Doctor* for Ford (winner of the Los Angeles Art Director's Medal); another was *Fluff* for Heinz (winner of Los Angeles and New York Art Director's Medals). He also worked on Western Airlines's *The Only Way to Fly*. This partial list is according to records of the Barbara Perry Babbitt Trust.

a student named Carl Bell: *Animation Program and Department of Cinema Progress Report*, 1961, Doheny Memorial Library, box 220, University of Southern California.

He sent notes: Carl Bell, interview by the author, 2010. In 1963 at Chuck Jones's studio, Hal Ambro generously shared information with Bell, as Frank Thomas had done with Ambro.

"having to direct": Babbitt, unpublished memoir. According to his brief 1974 memoir, seventy-eight of his commercials have won major awards.

"Don't be a hero": Michele Babbitt Kane, interview by the author, April 16, 2012.

Williams gladly covered: Richard William, fax to Barbara Babbitt, March 27, 1992, Canemaker Collection.

"I don't know an animator": Tom Sito, introduction to *The Babbitt Notes*, by Art Babbitt (unpublished manuscript, 1973), author's collection.

"Your notes from Dick": Art Babbitt, interview by Canemaker, June 4, 1975.

Babbitt periodically returned: Uli Meyer, interview by the author, May 31, 2012.

Willie Bioff stood trial: "Union Held Lever to Get Film Fund," *New York Times*, October 9, 1941.

Bioff and Browne guilty: "Bioff, Browne Guilty; Facing 30-Year Terms," *New York Times*, November 7, 1941; "Terms Are Given to Bioff, Browne," *New York Times*, November 13, 1941.

The mob had caught up: "Ex-Labor Extortionist Is Slain in Gangster Fashion Outside His Home in Phoenix," *New York Times*, November 5, 1955.

"He was the most displaced": Canemaker, *Bill Tytla*, 24. The quote is by Shamus Culhane.

Epilogue

"It's so nice": Barbara Babbitt, interview by the author.

"If Art had his way": Eric Goldberg, interview by the author, 2012. The line was spoken by Goldberg.

"Art kept a photo": Roy E. Disney, Disney Legend ceremony video recording, Barbara Perry Babbitt Trust.

Appendix

list of the Disney employees on strike: "Studio Strike," accretions 2000, box IB, folder 1-43, Canemaker Collection.

INDEX